Copyright and the Public Interest in China

To Spyros, my lighthouse in London :P

😊

Guan

07 Aug 2014

ELGAR INTELLECTUAL PROPERTY AND GLOBAL DEVELOPMENT

Series Editor: Peter K. Yu, *Kern Family Chair in Intellectual Property Law and Director, Intellectual Property Law Center, Drake University, USA*

Rapid global economic integration and the increasing importance of technology and information goods have created the need for a broader, deeper and more critical understanding of intellectual property laws and policies. This uniquely-designed book series provides an interdisciplinary forum for advancing the debate on the global intellectual property system and related issues that intersect with transnational politics, international governance, and global economic, social, cultural and technological development. The series features the works of established experts and emerging voices in the academy as well as those practising on the front lines. The series' high-quality, informed and accessible volumes include a wide range of materials such as historical narratives, theoretical explanations, substantive discussions, critical evaluations, empirical analyses, comparative studies, and formulations of practical solutions and best practices. The series will appeal to academics, policy makers, judges, practitioners, transnational lawyers and civil society groups as well as students of law, politics, culture, political economy, international relations and development studies.

Titles in the series include:

Copyright and the Public Interest in China

Guan H. Tang

Shanghai University of Finance and Economics, China

ELGAR INTELLECTUAL PROPERTY AND GLOBAL
DEVELOPMENT

Edward Elgar
Cheltenham, UK • Northampton, MA, USA

Published by
Edward Elgar Publishing Limited
The Lypiatts
15 Lansdown Road
Cheltenham
Glos GL50 2JA
UK

Edward Elgar Publishing, Inc.
William Pratt House
9 Dewey Court
Northampton
Massachusetts 01060
USA

A catalogue record for this book
is available from the British Library

Library of Congress Control Number: 2011931006

ISBN 978 0 85793 106 1

Typeset by Servis Filmsetting Ltd, Stockport, Cheshire
Printed and bound by MPG Books Group, UK

This book is dedicated to Deng Mianqing and Tang Xiaming;
two diligent educators I admire,
the first tutors and friends in my life,
my loving parents.

谨将此书献给唐侠鸣先生和邓勉卿女士：
两位我敬佩的勤勉的教育家，
我生命中最初的良师益友，
我深爱的父母双亲！

Contents

Acknowledgements

The views expressed in the book are solely mine and should not be attributed to any other individual, entity or institution. Nonetheless, this book, derived from a PhD thesis, would not have been possible without the generous support of a number of people and institutes. Recognitions are due to Shanghai University of Finance and Economics, the University of Edinburgh, the Arts and Humanities Research Council, Beijing Normal University and Shenzhen University, for having provided funding, material and HR assistance to this project. I am extremely indebted to my PhD supervisor, Hector MacQueen: "A master is the person who passes on knowledge, points out the way to live and solves perplexity."[1] Hector is a genuine master. Words fall short of expressing my gratitude to Gillian Davies; her book on *Copyright and the Public Interest* was the one and only textbook during my study at the University of Edinburgh, her review on my PhD thesis as an external examiner was truly inspiring, and her attitudes towards learning and life have lightened up my spirit. I am particularly grateful to Peter K. Yu for his very constructive comments and criticism, which became my guide, motivation, as well as pressure in the past eight months; I wished to be able to spend more time on this project, and hope I may have other opportunities to work with him in the future. Indeed, I am thankful to Zhang Bigong and Wang Shanmai for their generous assistance during my survey in Shenzhen and Baotou respectively; to Hugh Hansen, Weerawit Weeraworawit, Michael Blakeney, Paul Tauchner, John MacColl and Gustavo Ghidini for their time and expertise; to Sir Hugh Laddie for his sharp advice on developing my capability in Chinese IPRs and beyond, he will never be forgotten. My sincere thanks to Ben Booth, who was kind enough to 'listen' to a stranger and gave me a second chance; to Edward Elgar, who has been unprejudiced and brave, even in the land of the Far East; to John-Paul McDonald, who was always there willing to help; and to David Fairclough, who put everything together with patience as well as efficiency.

---

[1]   i.e. 师者, 传道授业解惑也. See 韩愈, 《师说》(802); Han Yu, The Theory on Masters, 802. Han Yu (768–824) is a celebrated philosopher and also essayist in the Tang dynasty.

Table of cases

Table of legislation

Introduction

> The real measure of a nation's wealth is the stream of goods and services that it creates.[1]

Copyright as a legal concept originated in the United Kingdom (UK) under the 1709 Statute of Anne, which was introduced as an act to promote the encouragement of learning. Thereafter, copyright has developed from a domestic law that regulated the rights of copying in the publishing industry to a generally established global regulation that has extensive influences on almost every modern industry.

In the modern world, copyrighted works are protected both by national laws, in individual countries, and international laws such as the Berne Convention for the Protection of Literary and Artistic Works (Berne Convention). The Berne Convention sets out the international aspects and standard of copyright protection, including the limitations or exceptions to copyright. The exceptions to copyright are justified through the use of the "three-step test", which is the critical measurement for defining all copyright exceptions. It states that firstly, limitations or exceptions to exclusive rights must be confined to certain special cases; secondly, these cases must not conflict with the normal exploitation of a work; and thirdly, these cases must not unreasonably prejudice the legitimate interests of the copyright holder. The three-step test was first set out in the Berne Convention and was then incorporated and enhanced in other international treaties, such as the agreement on Trade-Related Aspects of Intellectual Property Rights (TRIPS) 1994, the WIPO Copyright Treaty (WCT) 1996, the WIPO Performances and Phonograms Treaty (WPPT) 1996 and the EU Copyright Directive 2001.

Recognised lawful uses in situations where an exception to copyright may be claimed are threefold: the direct consent of the authors or right owners; permitted acts such as fair use or fair dealing; and the public interest. The last category is not expressed in the Berne Convention, but is derived from the need to defend and balance the rights of the copyright

---

[1]   E. Butler, *Adam Smith: A Primer* (2007), 38.

owners with broader public interest requirements, primarily in relation to education, research and access to information.[2]

Conceptually, copyright originated and evolved from a desire to expand the public interest and was progressed through legal statute in order to enable the encouragement and promotion of knowledge. The law provides authors and copyright owners with exclusive but limited rights in order to safeguard their rights and needs for the protection of copyrighted works, whilst balancing this against the broader public interest aspiration to encourage the spread of information and knowledge. This is the fundamental and critical balance that copyright aims to uphold, through the specific public interest exemption granted by national copyright laws.

The Berne Convention has provided the overarching common standards of copyright protection, but the development of copyright law in each country may differ owing to the significant effect of individual political, economic, social or cultural circumstances. For instance, whilst the UK, the mother country of modern copyright, enacted the Statute of Anne in 1709 and the United States of America (US) derived its federal copyright law from this model in 1790, it was not until 1990 that modern copyright law came into force in the People's Republic of China (China). Copyright law and its legal structure have developed rapidly in China over the past three decades, being primarily based on the Western model and also being regulated by international standards.

The development and enforcement of copyright in China has been both unique and problematic, being strongly influenced by various factors such as its own history and culture, as well as international pressure. The copyright system in China has been strongly advocated and influenced by the international community including the US and the UK, but also reflects traditional Chinese culture and the values of socialism. In accordance with the Constitution, Chinese copyright has three specific aims. These are to protect the copyright of authors in their literary, artistic and scientific works and their copyright-related rights and interests; to encourage the creation and dissemination of works; and to promote the development and prosperity of science and the socialist culture. The public interest, in the Chinese copyright regime, is not only a fundamental principle emphasised by the law and a recognised legal defence for copyright exemption, but is also a justification in its own right that regulates works free from copyright. Furthermore, it provides the legal basis for administrative copyright enforcement in China, which grants the relevant administrative authority a quasi-judicial power.

---

[2]   See Preamble, Berne Convention.

So as to develop a more dynamic understanding of what the public inter-est means in relation to modern copyright and to facilitate the evolution and development of Chinese law and policy in this respect, this book aims to study and evaluate the topic primarily under the Chinese copyright law, but also making reference and comparison to UK and US law, as appro-priate. The generation and circulation of information and knowledge is a fundamental mission of educational establishments, retaining a wealth of information and data in libraries and archives and in so doing protecting and developing the public interest by making available and building upon this diversity of material and resources. As key institutions in China have greatly benefited from Western concepts and experiences, the application of copyright in these areas and the topical issues arising within them have been selected for discussion in this book, together with the administrative enforcement of Chinese copyright and the development of the Internet in China. Administrative enforcement is sanctioned by Chinese copyright law in the name of the public interest. The development of the Internet is of significance not only to copyright law in China, but also to Chinese society in general and, in this respect, the Chinese approach to Internet regulation has been heavily criticised by the international community.

The book consists of six chapters. It should be noted that most of the chapters include a comparison with the UK and US positions. This is because (1) modern copyright law is absolutely foreign to China, the for-mation of the Chinese copyright system being very much a direct product of the US-China trade agreement; (2) as the copyright system originated in the UK and is well developed in the US, the enforcement of relevant laws is rather effective in both countries, whilst copyright protection together with the legal system in China is still in for the long haul; (3) Chinese stresses 饮水思源, "When drinking water think of its source." Hence the foremost copyright law makers share the experience of studying in the UK and have been influenced by the UK copyright model. Chinese law is therefore in fact akin to the UK provisions in many ways. Above all, it is hoped that such a comparison may facilitate a better understanding of the universal law of copyright despite the typical division of continental and Anglo-American laws, thus allowing an objective evaluation of current Chinese copyright, which most importantly may assist future law-making improvements in particular areas.

Chapter 1 provides an historical background, explaining the diverse Chinese traditions and China's legal culture, as well as the development of the Internet in China, which is of importance to the country's opening up to the rest of the world, its integration into the global economy and a changing notion towards law and the public interest. Chapter 2 offers an introduction to Chinese copyright law and different aspects of the public interest. It also presents relevant knowledge, understanding and an appreciation of this field. With a brief history of the development of copyright and the public interest, the chapter outlines, firstly, how legislation is developing in China; secondly, how the Chinese concepts of copyright together with the public interest and the entire system are affected by international influences; and thirdly, how these laws are enforced in cyberspace. Chapter 3 introduces the Chinese system of copyright enforcement and focuses on administrative copyright enforcement, the quasi-judicial power of the administrative authority, which is granted in the name of the authorship public interest and which results from long-standing cultural and legal practice in China. Particularly, this chapter explores the origin of administrative enforcement in China and its jurisdiction, implementation and coordination with the rule of law, in the light of an up-to-date case analysis. Chapter 4 presents the framework of Chinese education, which is modelled on the Western system and which explores the diverse legal attitudes towards copyright implications within educational institutions on the ground of the public interest. UK and US practices are discussed in order to demonstrate the distinction between the Chinese and Western approaches. Chapter 5 observes the exceptions provided in national copyright law for libraries and library users. It highlights the issue of copying in both actual and virtual environments and looks into how copyright is imbued with the public interest concept and how the legislation balances the interests of the right holders and the users in the context of public libraries. The position in China is contrasted with that in the UK and in the US. The focus of Chapter 6 is the opening of public archives in China and the relevant issues arising in the public's access to and use of archives, which are of particular interest to the Chinese archives sector as well as the public, together with other topical issues such as access to government information and state claims of copyright. Again, the position in China is contrasted with that in the UK and in the US.

The book finishes with conclusions based on the chapters outlined above. It does not summarise all the views and suggestions on the subject matter of the book, but rather focuses on the Chinese system, discussing the prospects for Chinese copyright and its enforcement in the impacted sectors and beyond.

1.   AN EMPIRICAL STUDY IN 2007 AND 2008

In order to examine the adaptation of copyright laws in Chinese educational institutes, including their libraries, and to determine the extent of genuine knowledge about the use of copyright works in these sectors, an empirical study was conducted in 2007 and 2008, when 17 institutes and 55 people were surveyed, including 25 university staff and 30 university students. It was decided to perform the study in Shenzhen and Baotou, owing to their differing and representative characters. Shenzhen exemplifies the fast-growing cities along the east coast, whilst Baotou is representative of numerous prosperous cities in the north and the centre of China. The two cities are different in many ways and it is notable that these differences are reflected in the survey.

2. INTERVIEWS IN SZU

Shenzhen is the oldest Special Economic Zone in South China and is situated close to the border with Hong Kong. It is also the fourth richest city in the country and the GDP in 2007 was over RMB 6000 billion yuan.[3] Adopting semi-structured interviews, the survey was carried out at SZU in order to gain an understanding of up-to-date copyright practices within the university and its library and to understand the awareness and opinions of students and staff relating to the use of copyright works.

The interviews at SZU were conducted with eight staff, including the president of SZU and the head of the university library, and 30 students, between December 2007 and January 2008. Each interview ran for around 60 minutes with the exception of the head of the library, which lasted for over 90 minutes. In the last five to ten minutes of the interview, interviewees were encouraged to make open remarks, and these were duly noted. Two slightly different sets of topics were designed for the university staff and students and for the head of the library respectively, as set out below.

- For the university staff and students the topics for interview included courseware (including its design and photocopying), rights relating to lesson plans and exam questions, recording of lectures, digitisation of works, use of library collections, photocopying and downloading, any concerns regarding photocopying and downloading, copyright notices and knowledge about copyright laws in relation to educational use.
- The topics for interview with the head of the library included the

---

[3] See http://www.sztj.com/pub/sztjpublic/tjfx/tjbg/t20080128_10070.html, retrieved on 22 March 2011.

topics above, but also covered library collections, legal deposits, declaration forms, copyright notice and licensing schemes, services including photocopying and downloading, differences between copying for commercial and non-commercial purposes, charges for photocopying and distribution, interlibrary loans, digitisation and lending and copying of audio, video and other materials.

Overall, the interviews were well received and there appeared to be very positive interaction during the interviews. All interviewees were happy to have these conversations used in any research materials and did not request that their anonymity be protected.

The findings of the interviews are outlined below:

- Of the staff, eight were aware of copyright when designing courseware and acknowledgements were normally given unless "some are too small or minor". However, they did not think it was necessary to obtain permission since it was for an educational rather than a commercial purpose. Of the students, 21 had no opinion on this topic "because I am a student", whilst nine thought it would be better if the lecturers were conscious of copyright requirements.

- A total of 6 staff and 30 students thought that it was not only appropriate but was also more efficient if courseware was photocopied for and distributed to students by the lecturer, which was the most common method at the university. One member of staff pointed out that photocopying for students may be disputed by modern law, but is definitely supported by Chinese custom.

- Seven members of staff thought that the copyright of lesson plans should be owned by the university, unless the lesson plans were not developed for the university curriculum. Of the students, 12 believed that the copyright should be owned by the lecturer, 5 thought it should be owned by the university, 8 said they did not know and 5 said that they did not care.

- Although eight members of staff agreed that exam questions were intellectual and time consuming, six of them believed that exam questions should not be copyrighted for academic benefit and the public interest, whilst two thought it should be further discussed. Of the students, 28 strongly disagreed that the composition of exam questions should have copyright, "otherwise", 17 of them commented, "what would be the differences between our country and the capitalist ones?", whilst two students said they had no opinion on this topic.

- Of the staff members, seven thought that teachers should have copyright over their lectures and 1 was not sure, whilst 10 students thought the lecturer must have the copyright, four thought the university would be the proper owner, 13 did not think there was any copyright over lectures and three did not have an opinion.

- In respect of the recording of the lectures, four members of staff thought that the teacher should own copyright of the talk while copyright of the recording itself should be owned by the person who recorded the lessons unless "they were recorded in secret", whilst another four said they were not sure and were not able to say more because they had never thought about that topic before. The members of staff jokingly advised, "It would not be a problem to me anyway." The opinions of the students were largely the same as for the previous topic, except that 3 out of the 13 above who did not think that there was copyright covering lectures thought this time that "copyright of any recording should be owned by the person who recorded the stuff".
- A total of seven members of staff and 27 students thought digital databases were very helpful for their teaching or study and they were satisfied with the university library's digital collections. In addition, they thought digitisation of works would be necessary to enable distance learning and would also be the future trend for education. They would be comfortable with their works being digitised, but would be "very careful" about the digitisation of others' work. Nine students mentioned that digitisation was more environmentally friendly, whilst one member of staff and two students claimed themselves to be "old fashioned" and did not pay attention to and did not like digital "stuff" at all. The university library had lawful subscriptions to many popular databases and a good collection of digitised works, which allowed campus users to access the material through the Internet, without the need for authorisation for the use of each work. A general text of "we will remove your work immediately if you object" was published on the website.
- Regarding the use of library collections, all interviewees except one member of staff said that they would not spend time checking if materials were pirate copies.
- Five members of staff and five students were copyright-conscious when photocopying and downloading at the university, whilst the rest of the group thought it was unnecessary because "the purpose would not be for making money".
- The main concern for the members of staff when photocopying was the number of copies they made and whether an entire book was being copied, whilst for the students it was the cost.

- Apart from two members of staff, no interviewees knew anything about copyright notices. Of those surveyed, six members of staff and 19 students thought that these notices would help to improve copyright awareness, whilst two members of staff and 11 students felt it would make no difference, but believed that having a notice would be better than having none.
- All the staff and students believed firmly that there must be exceptions for educational uses of copyright works, although only three staff and two students knew even a little about the relevant legal provisions.

3. A QUESTIONNAIRE SURVEY IN BAOTOU, INNER MONGOLIA

Inner Mongolia is one of the autonomous regions in the northern border area of China and Baotou is its largest and most developed city in the Province with 5 universities, 11 colleges and over 660 schools.[4] The GDP in 2007 was RMB 1010 billion yuan,[5] making Baotou the 60th richest of around 3500 cities in China.[6]

The survey in Baotou was conducted from July 2006 on. Initially, short ten-minute duration telephone conversations were held with representatives or persons in charge of five universities, five colleges and six schools, mainly in order to secure the survey. Then, a four-section comprehensive questionnaire, covering topics on both educational and library uses of copyright works, were distributed to all of the 16 institutions interviewed. The distribution and collection of the questionnaires was kindly performed by the Beijing Normal University.

The purpose of these interviews was similar to those conducted at SZU, but this survey sought the relevant information from the institutions rather than individuals and was interested in exploring if any diversity existed because of regional or economic differences. The findings of the survey are outlined below:

- All 16 institutions confirmed that the courseware is designed by individual teachers and as such the school has no control over

---

[4]   See http://www.baotou.gov.cn, retrieved on 7 March 2011.
[5]   See http://www.nmggtt.gov.cn/msshow.asp?id=1051, retrieved on 7 March 2011.
[6]   See http://ccdv.people.com.cn/GB/81438/85932/5861827.html, retrieved on 7 March 2011.

the material, but they encouraged teachers to acknowledge all the references used.

- A total of 13 institutions had no limitation on printing courseware prepared for students, but three would provide copies only if students so requested.
- Of the respondents, 14 thought that copyright for lesson plans should be owned by the institutions, whereas two thought that teaching or other academic activities would not be impacted irrespective of who owns the copyright.
- Of those asked, 13 respondents insisted that the absence of copyright over exam questions would stimulate learning and teaching. However, one thought that exam questions should be seen as copyright work and two thought that a collection of exam questions may be seen as a database and, as such, should be protected by copyright.
- A total of 13 respondents replied that the recording of lectures should be owned by the teacher and the institution, whilst 3 considered that the party who recorded the lecture should be the copyright holder.
- Regarding the digitisation of works, 11 institutions had no experience of this because there was no Internet access in the institution, whilst five admitted that the institution had never obtained any permission, but advised that no dispute had arisen to date.
- Six institutions had no photocopier machine in the library and it was therefore not their method of printing, whilst one institution said there was one but it was broken. The main concern for the institutions when photocopying was the cost.
- No institution posted copyright notices.
- All respondents were generally aware of copyright exceptions for educational institutes and whilst four had a good understanding of the law, eight knew a small amount and four knew very little.
- A total of 11 respondents made very thoughtful and valuable comments in relation to Section 4 of the questionnaire, which highlighted up-to-date knowledge of copyright implications in the Chinese educational sectors. Three comments and their translations are noted below:

版权是对数据劳动的一种保护形式，应予以尊重，但也要有益于知识的传播，发挥其促进社会进步的作用，对获得後风者一方面应给予鼓励，另一方面也应给予必要的约束。

[Copyright is a legal protection to the special labour, which should be respected. However, it must also benefit the spread of knowledge and exert its function of stimulating progress of the society. People who are interested in using copyright works should be encouraged on the one hand, and be properly restricted on the other.]

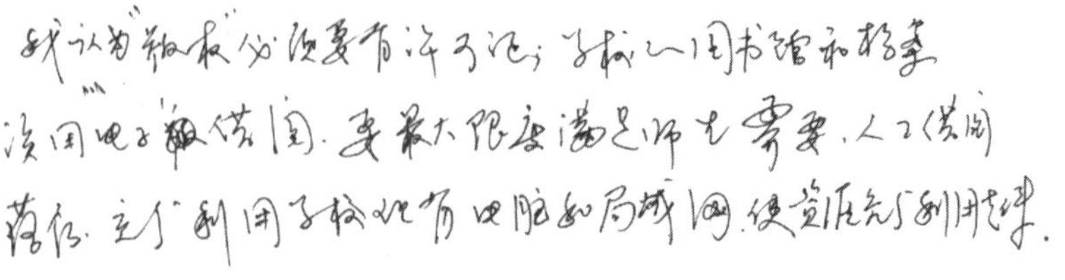
我认为"版权"必须要有许可证；学校的图书馆和档案应该用电子"服务"满足师生需要。人工借阅太落后。充分利用学校电脑和局域网，使资源充分利用起来。

[I think "copyright" must have licences; schools' libraries and archives should provide "electronic" service to satisfy teachers' and students' needs. . . . We . . . should maximise the exploitation of resources.]

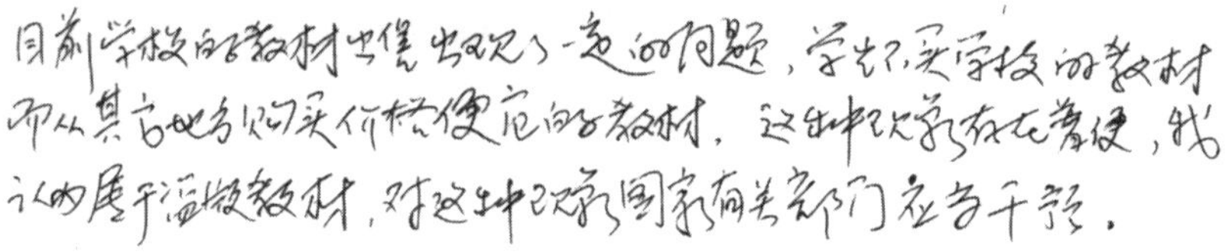
目前学校的教材出售出现了一定的问题，学生们不买学校的教材而从其它地方购买价格便宜的教材，这种现象存在普遍，我认为属于盗版教材，对这种现象国家有关部门应当干预。

[Currently, certain problems have occurred as regards the selling of textbooks in schools. (For instance) the students buy their textbooks somewhere else rather than in the school because of the cheaper price. This phenomenon is now quite common. I think those cheap textbooks are pirated copies and the relevant national organs should interpose themselves into this issue.]

4. SOME COMMENTS

The concept of copyright was not known by the public in China in the 1990s, even though the Chinese copyright law was adopted in 1990. The use of works in the educational sector and government offices reflected the situation at that time, effectively a copyright-free China where the general public had no awareness about the existence of copyright. This situation arose from the collective tradition in China and possibly to a greater extent by the lack of effort by the Chinese government to promote the law. In the late 1990s, copyright law was finally spread throughout the country, primarily to meet the requirements of international treaties and the business sectors and accordingly most of the public saw copyright as a foreign concept and felt that the law was promulgated to protect foreigners' interests. At that time there was a yawning gap between the understanding of copyright in a Chinese educational institute and that to be found in the Western counterpart.

China has changed extensively with regard to copyright in recent years. The Chinese authorities have strengthened not only the advancement of laws and regulations but also their promotion. Most Chinese people are now aware of the phrase "copyright" and some issues arising from this concept. Nonetheless, more endeavours are still required. As demonstrated in the empirical study, the public still do not have clear and correct knowledge of the legitimate provisions of copyright. Obviously, China will prioritise its aims of developing the national economy and reducing the gap between the richer and poorer areas throughout the country in order to benefit the greater population, as echoed in the empirical study. However, it should also be acknowledged that copyright protection is of significance in today's global economy and, as such, an effective copyright system will benefit the country's wealth in the long term, which calls for increasing the public awareness of copyright.

The empirical study demonstrates a perception of strong public welfare and social value concern, together with some newer thoughts or issues in relation to copyright in the education sector. Examples of the comments made in this respect by the surveyed educational institutes are highlighted below:

- While works are seen as "special labour" that justify copyright protection, the social and collective benefits are stressed, which demands an interest-balanced approach within the protection of copyright.
- The collective management and licensing of copyright, currently under development in China, is urged by Chinese educational institutes.
- The Internet has grown rapidly in China and has also made a great impact on the educational sector where users demand convenience, but where copyright clarification is also required. This should be progressed through regulation and guidance provided under Chinese law.
- Piracy is a big problem for both foreign and Chinese copyright owners. Educational institutes are also challenged in this aspect, for instance in relation to their textbooks. Copyright laws should be not only rationally made but also effectively promoted and enforced, as has been requested by both Chinese and foreign copyright owners.

- The demand made by Chinese educational institutes for a crack-down on pirated textbooks reveals that at present the administrative authorities are still the Chinese public's first preference to resolve copyright disputes, which reflects a long history of administrative enforcement in the country. This will be discussed in more detail.

1. The opening up to the world of a once isolated nation

1. INTRODUCTION

With its accession to the World Trade Organization (WTO) in 2001, China officially entered the global economy. As one of the world's fastest-growing economies and the world's second-largest economy by 2010,[1] China's domestic reform, its efforts of opening up to the international community and of moving from a governmental-controlled, planned economy to a market economy within the socialist setting, has focused the world's attention. The entry to the WTO, on the one hand, has stimulated the implementation of the rule of law in China as transparency and accessibility are mandatory; and on the other hand, has created numerous opportunities and challenges for China, a country with a huge population, a poor economic foundation and a long and isolated history, which holds a diverse tradition towards creation and intellectual work, as well as laws in general. Whilst the opportunities exist for an increasingly unlocked and enhanced environment for trade, investment, production, technology and innovation, the challenges arise primarily from transformation of the traditional conception of the public interest, and establishing an effective and of international standard legal and administrative system, stopping acts of copyright infringement across the country.

Meanwhile, China has experienced the rise of the Internet, which started later in the country compared with the West but has caught up rather quickly and become a main channel for people keeping in touch with the world. Although there is clearly a gap between China and the West over the understanding of different aspects of the Chinese Internet, including the limited openness and the imperfectness of copyright enforcement, evidently the popularisation of the Internet in China contributes significantly to the nation's connection with the rest of the world and the advance of the society. It also brings tremendous challenges to China's long-established and diverse legal culture and the notion of the public interest.

---

[1] See report from the National Bureau of Statistics of China; retrieved on 23 March 2011 at http://www.stats.gov.cn/was40/gjtjj_outline.jsp.

Looking back on its traditional background and its rise and fall, China has come a long way to step into the flow of trade globally. Opening up to the international community has shaped China's legal system. As part of its ongoing evolution, China will look to establish a system of effective copyright protection and enforcement throughout the country. Nonetheless, Chinese culture and legal tradition differ from those in the West, and have a dominating influence on the formation of the rule of law, including copyright. In order to facilitate a better comprehension of this process, a brief introduction to the mainstream philosophy on relevant concepts such as law, state interest and individual rights, copying, intellectual creation and economic gain of intellectual works, together with the recent expansion of the Internet and its great impact, will be carried out in this chapter.

2.   THE DIVERSE TRADITIONS AND LEGAL CULTURE

People of all ethnic groups in China have jointly created a distinctive history and culture, which has extensively influenced the progress and enforcement of modern copyright. As one of the four great ancient civilisations that survive to date, the development of China was somewhat detached from other ancient civilisations owing to its geographical location and foreign policy;[2] as were the ancient Chinese laws and the long-established attitude towards the law, of which the latter is one of the characteristics of the Chinese nation as a result of traditional thought, and one that affects the establishment of a unique copyright regime to date.

2.1   Mainstream Philosophy in Ancient China

The golden age of Chinese philosophy is said to be the Zhou Dynasty (1027–221 BC), the longest lasting dynasty in Chinese history and an era of great cultural and intellectual expansion,[3] during which various thoughts

---

   [2]   H.J.S. Sumner Maine, *Ancient Law* (1861); two electronic versions are available at http://socserv2.socsci.mcmaster.ca/~econ/ugcm/3ll3/maine/anclaw/index.html, in English, and in Chinese, http://www.chineseliterature.com.cn/zongjiao/meiyin-gdf/003.htm, retrieved on 11 March 2011.
   [3]   Agriculture became more efficient as iron, the compass and the crossbow were invented in the Zhou Dynasty. The population grew rapidly and parts of the Great Wall were built. During the sixth century BC, General Sunzi completed the *Art of War*, which was the first book on military strategy in the world.

and ideas were developed and discussed freely.[4] The theory that the emperor was 天子, *tianzi*, "the Son of Heaven", was established and later adopted throughout all Imperial China, which set a solid foundation for 人 治, *ren zhi*, "rule of man". The emperor was vested with executive, legislative and judicial power and all the rules created for *tianzi* were binding on all of the subjects, but could be overridden by the emperor. Meanwhile, as the supreme judicial power, the emperor might determine the accusation, dictate the penal sentence or modify the judgments given by any judicial authorities.[5] Furthermore, the origins of traditional Chinese philosophy were developed in the Zhou Dynasty. The distinguished philosophers who made a great impact on Chinese culture and law and who have profoundly influenced people's lifestyles and social consciousness up to the present day include Kongzi (Confucius), founder of Confucianism, and Mengzi (Mencius) and Xunzi, two famous Confucians; Shang Yang and Han Feizi, founders and promoters of legalism; Laozi, founder of Daoism, and Zhuangzi, the most-known Daoist; Mozi (Micius), founder of Mohism; and Zou Yan, the founder of Yin–Yang. Their philosophy is deeply ingrained in Chinese culture and law to date and may be sketched out as follows.

The Confucian doctrines, which in general have been thoroughly interpreted and applied by later rulers as well as the general public, and have profoundly affected the Chinese for over two thousand years, emphasise unity and harmony, correctness of social relationships such as filial piety and loyalty, personal and governmental morality and justice, sincerity and the inborn goodness of the individual. While Kongzi stresses 仁, "the benevolence", Mengzi stresses 义, "the justice" and Xunzi stresses 礼, "the rites", Confucianism neglects the development of a legal system as it believes humans are born with the capacity to be good, thus with a right leader piloting people, the society may certainly be in harmony. Regarding law, Laozi remarks that 法令滋彰，盗贼多有, "the more laws and orders were made, the more thieves and robbers there would be". Moreover, Confucianism was closely applied to the essential virtues of filial piety and obedience to authority, of not presuming to question the opinions or decisions of one's elders or superiors.[6] Under the strong

---

4   Historically, this phenomenon has been called 百家争鸣, bai jia zheng ming, the Contention of a Hundred Schools of Thought.

5   See 崔永东、龙文懋, 中国传统政法文化的现代解读, 《中国人民大学学报》 2002年6期97–103页; Cui Yongdong & Long Wenmao, 'Analysis on Traditional Chinese Legal and Administration Culture', *Journal of Renmin University of China* (2002), **6**, 97–103.

6   The representative literature included The Analects, Five Classics, namely Classic of Changes, Classic of Poetry, Classic of Rites, Classic of History, and Spring and Autumn Annals, The Mencius and The Xunzi.

influence of Confucianism, parties involved in lawsuits were commonly seen as depraved, and disputes between individuals dealing with matters of family, reputation, or land and other property were generally settled through informal mediation, which was conducted by respected leaders or elders who would apply customary rules and concepts of morality to reach agreement between disgruntled individuals.[7] Confucianism is also possessed of optimistic humanism and maintains that an optimistic attitude towards life must be adopted in all situations.[8] For example, people should have faith in their ruler even if severe injustice occurs. In addition, learning by copying from others was greatly encouraged and directed all aspects of life. The master, Kongzi, spent most of his life learning and teaching what the ancients taught, and most of his labour was bestowed on gathering and codifying the philosophy, history and folklore of his predecessors, stating that 述而不作，信而好古, "my function is to transmit rather than to originate; and I treat antiquity with trust and affection".[9] In his school, besides the precepts of the ever-new nature, Kongzi advocated an ethical system of life based on real tradition and copying the great examples of the old world. Confucianism holds that imitation is the greatest form of flattery and emphasises the importance of sharing intellectual products with society; it is considered dishonourable if a scholar makes money by selling his book to others.[10] Such theory has been inherited and practised ever since and opposes the model of contemporary copyright.

Legalism believes the nature of common people is evil, thus strict laws shall be applied and heavy punishments for the enforcement of laws are the only path leading to a society of proper order and value. The essential principle of legalism includes governing by law, with a view that the purpose of law is meant to support the state and the ruler. It holds that all law codes must be clearly written and made public and that all people but the rulers should be equal before the law. It also declares that the rulers are a privileged group and should not be bound by laws written for the masses. Furthermore, legalism stresses the primacy of the state over indi-

---

7 See 邓正来，中国法学向何处去 《中国政法大学学报》 2005, **23**(1), 3–23; Deng Zhenglai, 'Tribune of Political Science and Law', *Journal of China University of Political Science and Law* (2005), **23**(1), 3–23.
8 《论语》述而篇第七, *The Analects* 7.1.
9 Ibid.
"夫遇不遇者，时也；贤不肖者，才也。君子博学深谋而不遇时者，众矣·何独丘哉！且芝兰生于深林，不以无人而不芳。君子修道立德，不为穷困而败节。" Available at http://www.guoxue.com/wk/000243.htm, retrieved on 11 March 2011.
10 See 于丹，《于丹论语心得》 (1996); Yu Dan, *Yu Dan's Understanding of the Analects* (1996).

vidual autonomy and is a philosophy of rule by law that is for the purpose of dominating the country while the interest of the people is disregarded.[11] Legalism was later adopted in several dynasties for complete state control and hence established, amongst the common people, the notion of law enforcement being heavy punishment and the principle of the state's interest being the public interest.

Daoism highlights threefold elements: 道, "the universe"; 无为, "no action", which means that people should avoid explicit intentions, strong wills, or proactive initiatives; and 三宝, "the Three Treasures", that is, compassion, moderation and humility. It cares for the welfare of others and the world of nature and deems that violence should be avoided as much as possible, as well as laws, since the codification of laws would create difficulty and complexity in managing and governing. Besides, Daoism grants women a privileged status and the female identity is expanded to include a much greater ontological concern with inner states and cosmic attainment. It states "no male without female",[12] which was greatly promoted in the Tang and the Song Dynasties and provided women with much more liberty than other dynasties in ancient China. Daoism has become one of the most popular religions since and the aspect of accepting whatever given was also used by Chinese rulers and still possesses strong support amongst some Chinese.

Mohism promotes a universal rule of love and opposes aggression, also a consequence of laws. It advocates morality and a divine force, 天, *tian*, "the heaven", which would know everything, punish the immoral, and praise the moral. It assumes that people are naturally willing to do right things and thus supports a centralised state for absolute peace.

The essentials of the Yin–Yang include that the *Dao* is divided into two opposite but complementary principles: *yin*, "the dark", and *yang*, "the bright". The *yin* and *yang* accomplish changes in the universe through *wu xing*, the five elements, namely *jin*, *mu*, *shui*, *huo*, *tu*, (Metal, Wood, Water, Fire, Earth).[13] All change in the universe can be explained by the workings of *yin* and *yang* and the progress of *wu xing*, which also forms the principles that all rules should be followed; thus, a balance should be maintained in all aspects, whether managing a home or a country.

---

[11]   The literature setting out the philosophy of legalism included the *Book of Lord Shang* and *Han Feizi*.
[12]   And its significant treatises included *dao de jing* and *zhuang zi*.
[13]   The doctrine of *wu xing* tells two cycles of balance, creation and destruction, which are Metal collects Water, Water nourishes Wood, Wood feeds Fire, Fire creates Earth, and Earth bears Metal; and Metal chops Wood, Wood parts Earth, Earth absorbs Water, Water quenches Fire, and Fire melts Metal.

Later, in the Song Dynasty, a new philosophy called Neo-Confucianism was established; it dominated throughout Song China, which then included Japan, Korea and Vietnam, for centuries. Neo-Confucianism defined everything into two universal elements, that is, *li*, "principle", and *qi*, "force of soul, mind and spirit". Zhu Xi, the most influential Neo-Confucian, considered *li* to be *Dao*, the way of heaven, and *Taiji*, Supreme Ultimate or infinity that is in constant movement. Zhu Xi held a complex theory of human nature that contained the possibility of evil as well as that of good, which was owing to variations in *qi* endowments and environments. He believed that *Dao* is expressed in *li* and is surrounded by matter or *qi*, and therefore places emphasis on 存天理, 灭人欲, conserving principles of the heaven and extinguishing human desire. His thoughts also evolved into 三纲五常, *san gang wu chang*, a rigid official creed that stressed the one-sided obligation of obedience and compliance of subject to ruler, child to father, wife to husband, and younger brother to elder brother. Moreover, he selected and edited with commentary the essential classical Confucian texts such as *Sishu*,[14] the Four Books, which became the compulsory reading for the imperial bureaucratic examination from the late Song until the system was abolished at the end of the Qing Dynasty in 1911. Regarding law, Zhu Xi maintained 因事制宜, to adopt appropriate laws for different things, and advocated that the implementation of law should be strict as a principle but with the provision of leniency, 以严为本, 而以宽济之. Knowledge is defined as rediscovery of the way of the ancient sages and a social good, while seeking profit is seen as the characteristic of 小人, "an inferior person".

2.2 Ancient Law

The term "law" in Chinese consists of two words, *fa*, "method", and *lu*, "standard", and means a methodical standard for behaviour in society.[15] China established a large imperial territory in 221 BC, when the Qin Dynasty started. The ruler named himself *Shi huangdi*, "the First Emperor", and inaugurated the tradition of having emperors for rulers. The Qin Dynasty was the first unified, multinational, autocratic and power-centralised state in Chinese history and marked the beginning of

---

14   That is, *Lunyu*, the Analects of Confucius, *Mengzi*, the Book of Mencius, *Daxue*, the Great Learning and *Zhongyong*, the Doctrine of the Mean.
15   Zeng Xianyi & Ma Xiaohong, 'A Dialectic Study of the Structure and Basic Concepts of Traditional Chinese Law and an Analysis of the Relationship Between *li* (ceremony) and *fa* (law)', *Front Law China* (2006), **1**, 34–52.

Imperial China, a period which lasted until the fall of the Qing Dynasty in 1911.[16]

Legalism was fully applied in the Qin Dynasty. *Qin Lu*, the Qin Code, was compiled, which was the first comprehensive code of law in China. Legalists founded the political system based on harsh laws. The country was divided into 34 regions, each of which was ruled by a civilian gover-nor and also a general in charge of the soldiers in the region. All officials were appointed by the emperor and were answerable to him and him only. Centralisation, achieved by ruthless methods, was focused on standardis-ing legal codes and bureaucratic procedures, the forms of writing and coinage, as well as the pattern of thought and scholarship. The length of the wheel axle was also made uniform and expressways standardised to ease transportation throughout the country, which made the centralisa-tion of power possible. Furthermore, to silence criticism of imperial rule, the emperor banished or put to death many dissenting Confucian scholars and confiscated and burned all classic works of the Hundred Schools of Thought, except those of legalism.[17] What the Qin emperor expected was not only a unified country but also a nation with unified thoughts that would secure the implementation of a centralisation of power.

The cruel punishments together with heavy taxes and forced labour caused a great deal of resentment. The last Qin emperor was executed during a rebellion, following which Liu Bang became the first Han emperor. He was more humane than the Qin emperors and abolished many of their savage punishments. He kept some of the legalist policies of his predecessors but also adopted some Confucian policies, which brought Confucianism into the Chinese ruling system. Thereafter, Liu Bang's successors came to favour Confucianism more and more. From 165 BC onwards, the Han emperor decreed that anyone wishing to become an offi-cial must sit an exam, which would test his knowledge of Confucianism. In this way, Confucianism became the official state philosophy and there-after China came to be governed by a bureaucracy trained in Confucian thought. *Han Lu*, the Han Code, was guided by Confucian moral princi-ples and the judicial application displayed the spirit of legalism. Moreover,

---

[16]   See for example 晁福林、施建中主编 《中国古代史》, 北京师范大学出版社 2007年第二版; Chao Fulin & Shi Jianzhong (eds), *History of Ancient China* (2007, 2nd edn). To clarify the different time periods, a brief table has been made to illus-trate the history of China, from the first dynasty Xia to China now (see "Timeline of Chinese history", Appendix).

[17]   That was the famous 焚书坑儒, fen shu keng ru, burning of the books and burial of the scholars, for the purpose of suppressing the freedom of speech, unifying all thoughts and political opinions.

jurisdiction over cases was implemented by local magistrates, the officials whose responsibilities covered all aspects of government within the territories including legal matters. From then on, the Confucian spirit and legalist system constituted the primary content of ancient Chinese law, which was enforced by civil officials.[18]

Chinese civilisation crystallised during the Han Dynasty, which is commonly considered within China to be one of the greatest periods in the history of China. To this day, the ethnic majority still refer to themselves as *Han ren* or *Han zu*, people of the Han, and the Chinese language is also called *Han yu*, language of the Han. The glorious Han reign formally came to an end in AD 220 and China entered an era of division. In AD 580, after almost four centuries of division and political decay, China was again united under one central government, the Sui Dynasty, established with a more advanced *Sui Lu*, the Sui Code. *Sui Lu* turned away from the previous militant culture and reaffirmed civil Confucianism. Furthermore, a bureaucracy examination system was set up for recruiting officers to the government. In spite of its short duration, the Sui laid the foundation of the great Tang empire.

The Tang Dynasty was founded by the Li family and lasted from AD 618 to 907. *Tang Lu*, the Tang Code, reached definitive comprehensiveness, in which 500 sections of ancient laws were compiled into 12 volumes, including 5 forms of corporal punishment and 8 considerations of leniency, while 10 categories of wickedness were exempted from it.[19] As one of the greatest epochs in Chinese history, the Tang Dynasty was an open era and was at the time probably the most advanced civilisation in the world.[20] Confucianism was greatly advocated in the Tang Dynasty. A nationwide governmental system of bureaucracy examination was perfected, which aimed to select the best Confucian literati for the Tang governments.

In AD 907, China split into separate states once again until 960 when it was reunited under the Song Dynasty. *Song Lu*, the Song Code, mainly followed the Tang Code. Moreover, the Song bureaucracy was expanded and the country was ruled by scholar officials. The Song Dynasty was not

---

[18] Zeng Xianyi & Ma Xiaohong, above at n. 15.

[19] Criminals over age 90 and under age 7 received only suspended sentences. For others, sentences could be redeemed by cash payments. Officials were entitled to discounts on sentences on private civil offences, but on public crimes, an additional year was added to the sentence.

[20] The Tang economy and trade boomed, which is well demonstrated by the known "Silk Road". Printing technique was exceedingly improved, Chinese culture thrived and matured further in the Tang. *Tang shi san bai shou*, a collection of 300 Tang poems from the most popular poets, including Li Bai and Du Fu, were widely distributed and studied by the general public in China thus far.

militarily strong and was threatened by surrounding powerful enemies that led to the suspicion and dislike of anything foreign. Confucianism underwent a revival. For the purpose of strengthening Chinese culture, the Song scholars enthusiastically studied and commented on Confucian classics and merged thoughts from other schools such as the nature of the soul and the relation of the individual to the universe.

In 1279, the Mongols, with superior military capabilities, conquered China and started the Yuan Dynasty, which was the first of only two times that China was ruled by an ethnic minority. The value of Confucian officials in government was recognised and Neo-Confucianism was also accepted. Special courts were established to deal with cases involving more than one ethnic group and different laws were implemented. Under this system the Mongols continued to receive certain advantages, which was perfectly described in one of the most popular Yuan dramas *dou e yuan*,[21] "the Injustice to Dou E". However, the legal system left a legacy. One notable aspect was the imposition of a responsibility upon a wrongdoer to provide financial support for his victim in addition to any penalty.

The succeeding dynasty of the Yuan, the Ming Dynasty, was founded by a peasant in 1368. *Ming Lu* followed the Song Code and demonstrated the Confucian spirit and the legalist system. Nonetheless, the Ming emperors saw the outside world as threatening to a peaceful China and thus became increasingly inward looking and isolated from the rest of the world.

In 1636, the leader of Manchu, an ethnic minority living in the north-east of China, claimed to be 真天子, *zhen tian zi*, "the true emperor of China". In 1644, Manchu passed through the Great Wall and quickly defeated the rebels in the north leading to the formation of the Qing Dynasty, which was the second ethnic minority ruling China. Confucianism became an important part of the attempt for the Qing emperors to portray themselves as legitimate rulers of China rather than as alien invaders. The Evidential School was set up to analyse Confucius's authentic texts in the early Qing Dynasty and the Confucian philosophy of social control was enshrined in *Da Qing Lu Li*, the Great Qing Legal Code, which was based on the Ming legal system and was enforced in China for almost 270 years. Moreover, the Qing government was conservative and arrogant, and failed to join the industrial revolution that was spreading across the countries in the West. This led to China falling more and more behind the developing world.

---

[21]   The story was about how the corrupt officials wrongly gave a death sentence to E Dou, a young widow, because she refused to marry a Mongol man, Mule Zhang; and how the ghost of E Dou obtained justice, with Inspector Dou's help, at the end.

Additionally, the treaties signed in 1842 and 1860 following the Opium Wars made China a semi-colonial state and a suffering nation.

2.3   China after the Xinhai Revolution

In 1911, the last Qing emperor was swept away by the Xinhai Revolution that was led by Sun Yixian. Sun put forward 三民主义, "the Three People's Principles", for the newly established Republic of China, namely, nationalism, democracy and socialism, and these were mainly promoted among educated young people. Sun also founded Kuomintang (KMT), which was at that time the only ruling party of the Republic of China and of which Jiang Jieshi became the leader in 1925.

In 1921, the Chinese Communist Party (CCP) was founded in Shanghai as a study society and an informal network. Mao Zedong was first a delegate from the Hunan Communist Group and later became leader of the CCP, which adopted Marxism-Leninism with a rural focus, based on China's social situation at the time. The CCP had strong support among the peasants and soon grew rapidly over the country. Several revolutionary principles were greatly promoted in China, which included the following. Firstly, the working class had to emancipate itself through its own collective action. Freedom could not be given over to the working class; it had to be conquered by the oppressed themselves. Secondly, the working class would have to overthrow the old state and create a new, fully democratic state for itself in order to bring about a socialist transformation of society. And thirdly, revolution would be the only means to achieve the former two and the CCP would be the guide of the revolution. In addition, the CCP set out gender equality as one of its priorities.

In 1927, the Chinese Civil War between the KMT and the CCP started. Overall, it lasted until 1949 with the exception of the period between 1937 and 1945, the eight-year Japanese Invasion, during which the two parties lined up together to fight against the invader. The CCP finally won the Civil War and founded the People's Republic of China in October 1949. Jiang led the majority of KMT in fleeing to Taiwan Island where the Republic of China has been continued to this day.

2.4   New China

新中国, "New China" is the more commonly used term in Chinese for the People's Republic of China, which was founded on 1 October 1949, when Mao declared that "Chinese people have stood up". Since then, China has experienced three stages, which may be summarised as follows.

The first stage was from 1949 to 1966, which was a transitional period.

After a century's disarray, China transitioned from a semi-colonial and semi-feudal state to a socialist country. Socialism was seen as a new society of freedom, in which the working class including workers and peasants became the ruler. Individual benefit was overridden by social value and collective interest (for instance, an author's right to profit from his creations bows to the society's need to access material), which in a way perfectly matched the traditional Chinese culture of sharing and copying. In addition, moral education was seen as an important tool in upholding the socialist nature of the school and society and was consistent with other goals such as ideological and political education. The content consisted of the morality advocated by Confucianism and other Chinese philosophies with a strong input of revolutionary socialism.

Women then were so-called 半边天, *ban bian tian*, "half of the sky", and enjoyed full equal rights in the society. China entered a period of progress in all areas, including the economy, politics and culture, and started to rebuild its legal system, modelled on the continental legal systems mainly from Germany, with support from the Soviet Union. In 1954, the first state Constitution was adopted, which consisted of the Presidency, the National People's Congress (NPC), the State Council, the courts and the procurates, and defined national identities such as the national flag, the emblem and the capital. The President was granted power to convene so-called emergency meetings, known as Supreme National Meetings. The Planned-economy Policy was carried into effect all over the country[22] and all economic as well as political decisions were made on behalf of the public by the central government; the tradition of power centralisation continued in a new wrap.

The second stage, the period from 1966 until 1976, saw the Cultural Revolution decade. The Cultural Revolution was launched by Mao and people in China now call it 十年浩劫, *shi nian hao jie*, "the ten-year disaster", as it greatly damaged the development of the country, especially the economy and the traditional culture. The concept of law was emphatically not seen as providing a new constitutional foundation for the revolutionary state but as a tool for oppression of a class of people.

---

[22]   As a result the population grew rapidly: under the Planned-economy Policy, everything was under governmental control and was rationed to citizens by different levels of authorities. A family of a bigger number also meant more supplies from the government. Besides, Mao continuously advocated *ren duo li liang da*, "more people more power," in the country and each year granted the title of "Honourable Mother" to women who gave birth to ten children or over. 孙伊, 中国女性在家庭中的地位和权利, 《当代中国研究》 2005年第4期; Sun Yi, 'The Position of Chinese Women in Family and Society', *Modern China Research* (2005), 4. See also http://www.chinayj.net/StubArticle.asp?issue=050412&total=91.

Mao declared that *yao ren zhi, bu yao fa zhi*, "China wants the rule of man, not the rule of law". The Constitution was revised in 1975 and reduced the total number of articles to around 30, compared to the hundreds of articles in the previous version. It tied up party and state, and proclaimed that the CCP was the only leading force of the Chinese people. Furthermore, during the ten-year Cultural Revolution, commerce, religions and intellectuals were totally repressed throughout the country. The attitude towards the intellectuals was well presented in a popular Chinese saying at that time:

> Is it necessary for a steel worker to put his name on a steel ingot that he produces? If not, why should a member of the intellectuals enjoy the privilege of putting his name on what he produces? [23]

The third stage, the period from 1978 until the present, is an opening up and rapid development stage. The Reform and Opening-up Policy was adopted at the end of 1978. The national economy has been rescued from the edge of destruction and has come to produce continuous and steady growth; for instance the average growth rate of annual gross domestic product (GDP) was 9.6 per cent from 1979 to 2004 and the total amount increased from RMB 126.49 billion yuan in 1979 to RMB 39.7983 trillion yuan in 2010.[24] The policy marks the country's economic and political reform, as well as its opening up to the rest of the world, particularly to the West. The development of culture, science and technology has been restored. Economic progress and individual gain have been greatly promoted together with socialist spiritual civilisation, social harmony, national solidarity and common prosperity. Moral education has officially turned its emphasis on personal moral quality, as well as individual well-being including psychological health.

2.5   China Joining the World Economy

Since adopting its opening-up policy, China has taken a positive attitude towards and made enormous efforts to join the international community, and its integration into the world economy has come a long way.[25]

---

[23]   See Zheng Chengsi, 'The Future Chinese Copyright System and Its Context', *International Review of Industrial Property and Copyright Law* (1984), **141**(152).

[24]   See http://www.stats.gov.cn/was40/gjtjj_en_detail.jsp?searchword=1979&c hannelid=9528&record=1 and http://www.stats.gov.cn/was40/gjtjj_detail.jsp?sea rchword=%B9%FA%C4%DA%C9%FA%B2%FA%D7%DC%D6%B5&channeli d=75004&record=2, retrieved on 17 March 2011.

[25]   Shen Rengan, *Combat Piracy and Protect Copyright* (1998).

Two notable organisations are of particular significance in this regard, namely, the World Intellectual Property Organization (WIPO) and the WTO.

WIPO was founded in 1970. The predecessor of WIPO was the United International Bureau for the Protection of Intellectual Property (best known by its French acronym BIRPI), which was set up in 1893. WIPO became a specialised agency of the United Nations (UN) system of organisations in 1974, with a mandate to administer intellectual property matters recognised by the member states of the UN. The BIRPI administered only four international treaties in 1898. To date, WIPO has 184 member states and administers 24 treaties, of which the Berne Convention in 1886 is one of the earliest copyright treaties and marks copyright entering into the international arena.[26] China became a WIPO Convention member state in June 1980 and has been continually working on the establishment and development of a domestic copyright system that is in accordance with the international principles of balancing rights and obligations.[27]

The WTO is the other remarkable organisation that has had great impact on Chinese copyright and beyond. Founded in 1995, the WTO is the successor to the General Agreement on Tariff and Trade (GATT), which was established in 1950. It is the only international organisation dealing with the rules of trade between nations and the goal is to help producers of goods and services, exporters and importers conduct their business. The Dispute Settlement Body of the WTO is granted power to arbitrate disputes between member states and to enforce its decisions. Amongst other rules, the WTO obliges transparency and accessibility and demands independent judiciary review, which are essential to the rule of law. Currently, it has 153 member states and the WTO's Agreement on TRIPS has become one of the most influential treaties in the international community.

In 1986, China notified the GATT of its wish to resume its status as a contracting party and has ever since set about establishing the rule of law in the country as its priority.[28] In order to meet the WTO standard, more than 230 laws, over 147 of them concerning all facets of IP, have been enacted and updated since 1979, which are still in effect and are generally

---

[26] See http://www.wipo.int/treaties/en, retrieved on 15 March 2011.

[27] See http://www.wipo.int/about-ip/en/ipworldwide/pdf/cn.pdf, retrieved on 15 March 2011.

[28] See http://www.wto.org/english/news_e/pres01_e/pr243_e.htm, retrieved on 18 March 2011.

consistent with accepted principles of international law.[29] The 1982
Constitution of the People's Republic of China, which was later revised
respectively in 1988, 1993, 1999 and 2004, confirmed the socialist system
and the people's ownership of the state power as well as private property
rights in China.[30] Moreover, the 1999 amendments add the following to
Article 5 as the first paragraph: "China exercises the rule of law, building
a socialist country governed according to law."[31] Whilst the public interest is emphasised,[32] the Constitution protects people's individual rights,
including private property rights,[33] and sets forth that neither individual
nor organisation is privileged to be beyond the Constitution or the law.[34]
China, more than ever, is ready for its integration into the international
community and its emergence into the world economy.

On 17 September 2001, the WTO accepted China as its 143rd member.[35]
"With China's membership," said Mike Moore, the WTO Director-
General, "the WTO will take a major step towards becoming a truly
world organisation." "The near-universal acceptance of its rules-based
system will serve a pivotal role in underpinning global economic cooperation" and has also officially concluded the 15-year-long negotiations and
announced China's entry to the world economy,[36] to which China has
made arduous efforts to accede.

Prior to its accession to the WTO, China enacted and revised over
2000 related laws, regulations and measures in order to satisfy the WTO
member global trading rules, and numerous changes were implemented to
its trade regime.[37] China has to transition out of the government's old role
of directing and controlling markets progressively towards the implementation and enforcement of laws and regulations promoting free markets.
The WTO acceptance also embraces China's commitments to more than

---

[29]   See also R. Taplin, 'Managing Intellectual Property in the Far East – The
Case of China', available at http://scientific.thomsonreuters.com/media/newslet-
terpdfs/2005-04/chinese-ip.pdf, retrieved 18 March 2011.
[30]   Article 1. The previous state constitutions of 1954, 1975 and 1978 were
superseded in turn.
[31]   See Amendment 13.
[32]   For instance, Article 10 states that "the state may, in the public interest,
offer compensation and requisition land for its use in accordance with the law".
[33]   See Article 13.
[34]   See Article 5.
[35]   See http://unpan1.un.org/intradoc/groups/public/documents/APCITY/UN
PAN002120.pdf, retrieved on 15 March 2011.
[36]   See http://www.wto.org/english/news_e/pres01_e/pr243_e.htm, retrieved on
15 March 2011.
[37]   See http://www.chinadaily.com.cn/chinagate/com.html, retrieved on 15
March 2011.

20 existing multilateral WTO agreements, including the TRIPS. China thus has the obligation to adhere to the international standard of copyright protection. China on the one hand had modified its law and regulations before entering the WTO in 2001 and on the other hand is dedicated to strengthening its copyright protection, that is, judicial and administrative enforcement. Indeed, the emergence in the global economy and the integration into the international system present numerous challenges to Chinese copyright.

2.6 Discussion

The current legal system in China has been formed upon two strikingly different bases, the Chinese tradition and the international norm, of which the latter is anchored in the rule of law. The legal system in ancient China was defined through rule under emperors; such feudal and imperial instruments regulated matters that would be considered under criminal law in the modern legal approach; there was no jurisprudential distinction between criminal and civil law, as penal sanctions also applied to acts that would be covered by civil law today. The ancient law, on the one hand, was a political tool to control the people and society, and on the other hand, has never been favoured by the common people owing to the strong influence of Chinese traditions. For centuries, the Chinese public treated lawsuits as bad luck, even evil. Confucianism was the most powerful inspiration to the majority of Chinese, including the judges and magistrates in the traditional legal system before the adoption of the Reform and Opening-up Policy in 1979,[38] whilst legalism's law means rigorous restrictions and severe punishments entrenched in the Chinese legal system, as well as people's understanding.

Looking back on the history of China, each of the Chinese imperial dynasties had its own penal code, based upon that of the outgoing dynasty, and adopted both Confucianism and legalism. With the support of the mainstream of Chinese philosophy, traditional Chinese law evolved in a manner where the ruler and the officials possessed the absolute right to rule the people who in turn had an absolute duty to obey, and hence instituted the rule of man, which was greatly advocated by Neo-Confucianism and respected by the general public. Certainly, the tradition of the rule of man provided a solid base for dictatorship or so-called *yi yan tang*, a practice whereby it is what one person says that counts. Furthermore, the doctrine that set the ruler as the Son of Heaven since the Zhou Dynasty

---

[38] See A.S. Nair & E.R. Stafford, 'Strategic Alliances in China: Negotiating the Barriers', *Long Range Planning* (1998), **31**(8), 139–46.

allowed the ruler to be seen in the role of a quasi-god, which indeed allowed Mao a privileged position beyond all the laws and authorities and thus made the Cultural Revolution possible.

From 1949 until the end of the 1970s, Mao was the major authority in Chinese society. Early socialism as practised under Mao's leadership viewed the law as a tool for oppression of a class of people. Under Mao's indication and promotion, the Chinese intelligentsia, *chou lao jiu*, was repressed not only by the Chinese government but also by the public. For several decades, people in China have been fed, educated and supported by a system that does its best to enforce equality among all its members: no one, including intellectuals, was supposed to profit from their work, together with the Planned-economy, which emphasised the state's needs and control over the people's needs. The legal system throughout the country was almost in ruin.

The adoption of the opening-up policy to the world has not only helped China reduce poverty and realise greater economic achievement, but has also introduced the rule of law to the country and is shaping its legal system towards the international benchmark. Moreover, accession to the WTO has further boosted China's opening-up drive and continuously stimulates the modernisation and standardisation of Chinese laws and regulations, in the global and digital context.

3. THE RISE OF THE INTERNET

The advance of information technology (IT) has led to the mature applications of the Internet, which has dramatically extended the information available to the general public and has changed many people's method of information acquisition, communication and distribution. The Internet, as elsewhere, is in widespread use and has become a force in China's fast-moving society. Moreover, it has become a genuine means for people to access knowledge and stay in contact with the outside world, and has had an intensive ongoing impact upon Chinese law.

3.1   The Internet with Distinctive Characteristics

The Internet, which is vital for making information and knowledge available,[39] was researched in the West in the 1960s, developed in the

---

[39]   H. MacQueen & C. Waelde (2006), 'UK Copyright Law in the Digital Environment', *Electronic Journal of Comparative Law*, **10**(3); retrieved on 15 March 2011 at http://www.ejcl.org/103/art103-10.pdf.

1980s and became well used in the 1990s,[40] whilst in China the Internet was introduced in the 1990s and has developed incredibly swiftly ever since.

3.1.1   The growth of the Chinese Internet

The first Chinese public data network, China Academic Network (CAN), was formed in 1986, assisted by Professor Werner Zorn and the University of Karlsruhe (UoK) in Germany and involving a group of researchers at the Institute of Computing Applications (ICA). A year later, the Institute of High Energy Physics (IHEP) in Beijing connected to the Conseil Européen pour la Recherche Nucléaire (CERN) in Geneva. Meanwhile, the CAN established its first international link when a Siemens 7760/ BS2000 computer at the ICA connected to the UoK via a 300 bits per second packet-switched data network.[41] On 20 September 1987, one of ICA's researchers, Professor Wang Yunfeng, sent out the first ever email from China and the message was entitled, "Across the Great Wall we can reach every corner in the world," which is commonly known in China as "越过长城, 通向世界".[42] In November 1990, initiated by Wang Yunfeng, with Werner Zorn's support and in liaison with Professor Qian Tianbai, China registered the .cn international top level domain at the Defense Data Network Network Information Center (DDN-NIC), the .cn domain name server being hosted at the UoK as China at that point did not have its own direct Internet connection.[43] Qian Tianbai believed that the Internet would be extremely beneficial not only for academics but also for everybody; he claimed that "the Internet would play a great part in Chinese people's daily life in the near future" and was diligent in promoting the Internet throughout the country.[44]

Furthermore, a 64K dedicated circuit to the Stanford Linear Accelerator Center (SLAC) was opened officially on 2 March 1993. Built by the IHEP, the dedicated circuit was linked to the US through an international satellite communication channel rented from AT&T. However, it was only

---

[40]   See http://www.isoc.org, retrieved on 15 March 2011.
[41]   See 李南君, 中国接入互联网的早期工作回顾, Werner Zorn (2006), 'A Review on the Early Works of China Connecting to the Internet'; http://news.xin-huanet.com/newmedia/2006-11/21/content_5358804.htm, retrieved on 15 March 2011.
[42]   See http://www.cnnic.net.cn/html/Dir/2003/10/22/1001.htm, retrieved on 15 March 2011.
[43]   See http://www.cnnic.net.cn/resource/daily/2002-11/15.pdf, retrieved on 15 March 2011.
[44]   See 毛伟, 钱天白与CNNIC - 纪念钱天白先生, Wei Mao, Qian Tianbai and CNNIC – To Commemorate Mr Qian Tianbai (2004), http://www.cnnic.net.cn/html/Dir/2004/02/13/2156.htm, retrieved on 15 March 2011.

allowed to connect to the American energy network, because the US government forbade any socialist countries access to the Internet that contained significant levels of information relating to science and technology and other resources.[45] Nonetheless, it was still China's first dedicated circuit partly accessing the Internet.[46]

On 15 May 1994, the IHEP set up China's first web server and introduced the first set of web pages. Apart from brief introductions on the improvements of high technology in China, a "Tour in China" section was included, which, renamed "Windows of China" later, provided a wider range of information on news, business, culture and trade. On 21 May 1994, Qian Tianbai led the Computer Network Information Center at the Chinese Academy of Sciences (CAS) as it installed China's top domain name servers. Thus, China was recognised as a country within the Internet.[47]

Later in September 1994, a Sino-American Internet agreement was signed between China Telecom and the US Secretary of Commerce. As agreed, China Telecom opened two 64K dedicated circuits, respectively, in Beijing and Shanghai in January 1995 through the US Sprint Co.[48] On 8 August 1995, 水木清华, *shui mu qing hua*, BBS went live online and was the first Internet-based BBS on the Chinese mainland.[49]

The China Internet Network Information Center (CNNIC) is the state network information centre and was founded on 3 June 1997. It was operated by the Ministry of Information Industry (MII) and CAS. In November 1997, CNNIC issued its first Statistic Report on Internet Development in China, which stated that 299,000 computers were connected to the Internet and that Internet users had reached 620,000 by 31 October 1997.[50] Nearly ten years later, according to CNNIC's twentieth Statistic Report, 67.10 million computers were connected to the Internet

---

45   See http://www.edu.cn/introduction_1378/20060323/t20060323_4285.shtml, retrieved on 15 March 2011.
46   See 钱天白, Internet在中国的发展, 《计算机世界》 2006年; see Tianbai Qian, 'Development of the Internet in China', *Computer World* (1996); see http://www.cnnic.cn/resource/daily/199809/6.shtml, retrieved on 15 March 2011.
47   See http://www.cnnic.net.cn/html/Dir/2003/10/22/1003.htm, retrieved on 15 March 2011.
48   See http://www.edu.cn/introduction_1378/20060323/t20060323_4285.shtml, retrieved on 15 March 2011.
49   Ibid. See also shui mu qing hua BBS, http://www.smth.edu.cn/frames.php, retrieved on 15 March 2011.
50   See Statistical Report of the Development of Chinese Internet. Available at http://www.cnnic.net.cn/download/manual/en-reports/1.pdf, retrieved on 15 March 2011.

and the total number of Internet users had reached 162 million by June 2007. Whilst 37.2 per cent of Chinese Internet users surfed online in Internet cafés as many users did not possess their own computers, 31.2 per cent of users accessed the Internet at workplaces and another 12.2 per cent in schools.[51] By the end of 2010, the number of Internet users had risen to 457 million, and China has now become the largest Internet user nation in the world. The Internet has been widely used in educational and library sectors and has started to be used in public archives, which has generated diverse challenges to copyright and will be discussed in subsequent individual chapters.

As noted above, the development of the Internet in China has had a later start than in the West. However, this late start has been followed by an increasingly fast expansion, from initially being recognised as a country with the Internet in 1994 to becoming the largest Internet user nation in the world. The Chinese Internet has followed a unique path. The rapid development and widespread use of the Chinese Internet and the singularities of China as a country have created a unique situation. Indeed, China is producing its own model of Internet expansion – for example, as a developing country with numerous users not possessing their own computers and currently over 50 million people surfing online in public venues – which brings about serious social and legal considerations. Despite the progress in terms of absolute numbers, various problems have originated from this rapid development.

3.1.2 Web 2.0 in China

The transformation of China, including the economy, culture and politics together with the society, has been greatly accelerated by the advance of information and communication technology (ICT), especially Web 2.0, an ICT revolution right after the bursting of the dot-com bubble in 2001, which has turned the World Wide Web from a source of information to a platform on which users can interact and collaborate with one another, exploit the potency of network effects in a social order and take advantage of networks as services architecture.[52] The impact of Web 2.0 on China has been profound and utter; it "has been more evident than anywhere else in the world" and "has facilitated the emergence of China's new

---

[51] See Statistical Survey Report on the Internet Development in China (July 2007), retrieved on 15 March 2011 at http://www.cnnic.net.cn/download/2007/20thCNNICreport-en.pdf.

[52] See Tim O'Reilly, 'What is Web 2.0?' (30 September 2005); retrieved on 25 March 2011 at http://orcilly.com/web2/archive/what-is-web-20.html.

era".[53] The consumer-centred Web 2.0 creates innovative ways for businesses to operate and people to communicate. Such business models have been copied into the Chinese market and quickly localised. For example, being the ultimate copy of Google search, 百度, Baidu holds the absolute lead in terms of market share in China,[54] whilst the YouTube-like video-sharing site 土豆, Tudou, owns 80 million registered users.[55] While investors are enthusiastic over China's economy and its fast-growing Internet sector,[56] people have promptly adopted new forms of expression, socialisation and content production, such as blogging, P2P file sharing, video sharing or tagging, social networking, microblogging and online shopping.

Web 2.0 has also posed contentious challenges to Chinese laws, including copyright and absent privacy. For example, on a social networking site there would be personal information about the users, which may be insecure, and copies of users' favourite cartoon characters, songs and videos, which may infringe copyright. Chinese law has faced these challenges from the moment the Internet became widely used. Seeing online copyright infringement notoriously widespread, the Chinese courts have been making an effort to enforce the law with a premeditated balance of protecting copyright owners and being responsive to new approaches to digital content. While very few cases have been filed against individual infringers, numerous cases have been launched against the Internet Service Providers (ISPs) that enabled individuals to breach copyright. The court decisions on ISPs' liability in distinct copyright infringement cases are somewhat controversial.

As anywhere else in the world, the music industry has been chasing after the main players in the search service industry, which in China are Baidu and Yahoo China (run by Alibaba) for providing links to file-sharing sites and to illegally shared MP3s in many cases. Some of the biggest names in the global recording industry have launched several lawsuits against Baidu and Yahoo for their MP3 search service, yet the decisions of the courts with regard to the defendants' liability are poles apart. In *Universal Music Group v Baidu*,[57] *Sony BMG Entertainment Hong*

---

[53]   See M.Y. Zhang & B.W. Stening, *China 2.0: The Transformation of an Emerging Superpower and the New Opportunities* (2009), 4.

[54]   See http://home.baidu.com/about/about.html, retrieved on 25 March 2011.

[55]   See http://www.tudou.com/about/about.php, retrieved on 25 March 2011.

[56]   See 'Web 2.0 Madness Grips China', *China Daily* (8 June 2007); retrieved on 25 March 2011 at http://www.chinadaily.com.cn/bizchina/2007-06/08/content_890368.htm.

[57]   See   北京市第一中级人民法院民事判决书(2005)一中民初字第8474号, Beijing First Intermediate People's Court Judgment Number (2005) 8474.

Kong Ltd v Baidu,[58] *Warner Music Hong Kong Ltd v Baidu*,[59] *EMI Group Hong Kong Ltd v Baidu*,[60] and *Go East Entertainment Ltd v Baidu*,[61] the Beijing First Intermediate People's Court found that Baidu was not hosting the MP3s itself but merely providing search results and thus was not liable for copyright infringement. Such decision was later upheld by the higher court in the second hearing. Whilst in similar cases *Universal Music Group v Alibaba (Yahoo China)*,[62] *Sony BMG Entertainment Hong Kong Ltd v Alibaba (Yahoo China)*,[63] *Warner Music Hong Kong Ltd v Alibaba (Yahoo China)*,[64] *EMI Group Hong Kong Ltd v Alibaba (Yahoo China)*,[65] and *Go East Entertainment Ltd v Alibaba (Yahoo China)*,[66] the Beijing Second Intermediate People's Court supported fully the plaintiffs' appeals. The court decreed that Yahoo was guilty of copyright infringement by providing deep-links, direct hyperlinks to illegally shared MP3s, and must remove such links from its search results. Encouraged by the latter decisions, Universal, Sony BMG, Warner, EMI, Go East and other IFPI members once again brought Baidu to the Beijing First Intermediate People's Court respectively in February 2008, accusing Baidu of supporting copyright violation. Court decisions were made in January 2010, and again the judgments were in favour of the defendant. The court asserted that, by providing a search service including deep-links to MP3s, Baidu did not violate copyright law; in addition, it pointed out that the plaintiff failed to identify any of the sites that were allegedly hosting illegal MP3s.[67]

---

58   See   北京市第一中级人民法院民事判决书(2005)一中民初字第10170号, Beijing First Intermediate People's Court Judgment Number (2005) 10170.

59   See   北京市第一中级人民法院民事判决书(2005)一中民初字第8995号, Beijing First Intermediate People's Court Judgment Number (2005) 8995.

60   See   北京市第一中级人民法院民事判决书(2005)一中民初字第8488号, Beijing First Intermediate People's Court Judgment Number (2005) 8488.

61   See   北京市第一中级人民法院民事判决书(2005)一中民初字第7978号, Beijing First Intermediate People's Court Judgment Number (2005) 7978.

62   See   北京市第二中级人民法院民事判决书(2007)二中民初字第02622号, Beijing Second Intermediate People's Court Judgment Number (2007) 02622.

63   See   北京市第二中级人民法院民事判决书(2007)二中民初字第02628号, Beijing Second Intermediate People's Court Judgment Number (2007) 02628.

64   See   北京市第二中级人民法院民事判决书(2007)二中民初字第02625号, Beijing Second Intermediate People's Court Judgment Number (2007) 02625.

65   See   北京市第二中级人民法院民事判决书(2007)二中民初字第02621号, Beijing Second Intermediate People's Court Judgment Number (2007) 02621.

66   See   北京市第二中级人民法院民事判决书(2007)二中民初字第02627号, Beijing Second Intermediate People's Court Judgment Number (2007) 02627.

67   See for example http://news.xinhuanet.com/newmedia/2010-01/26/content _12875495.htm, and http://news.sohu.com/20071222/n254235775.shtml, retrieved on 1 March 2011.

The contradictory rulings above may be divided into two phases, prior to July 2006 and then after, as China's Regulations on the Protection of the Right to Network Dissemination of Information came into force on 1 July 2006. Amongst other provisions, the 2006 Regulations provide a safe harbour for ISPs by adopting a Notice and Remove approach for assessing ISPs' liability,[68] upon which the Beijing Second Intermediate People's Court relied to give the plaintiffs the judgments in 2007 and also held that establishing an adequate Notice and Remove policy may insulate an ISP from liability. As for the Beijing First Intermediate People's Court, the 2006 decisions stated that Baidu was free of guilt owing to the litigation being brought to court in 2005, prior to the enforcement of the 2006 Regulations; though what would be the legal basis for its decisions made in 2010? Was it possible that Baidu attested the adequacy of its Notice and Remove policy in the court? What did the court mean when it mentioned that the plaintiff failed to identify the illegal MP3s hosting sites? How would that affect the rulings? It is difficult to speculate on the factual intention and rationale of the court without success in obtaining the original verdicts.

For the purpose of guiding the courts' implementation of the 2006 Regulations, the Supreme People's Court issued the revised Interpretation of the Supreme People's Court on Several Issues Concerning the Application of Law in the Trial of Cases Involving Copyright Disputes over Computer Network in November 2006.[69] It states that "when an ISP is aware of the Internet users' act of infringement on any other people's copyright through the network, or has been warned by the copyright owner with good evidences, but fails to take such measures as removing the infringement contents so as to eliminate the consequences of the infringement, the people's court shall impose contributory infringement liabilities on the ISP and the users".[70] Which suggests that in the search service industry, a copyright owner no longer need give a search engine the written notification as stated in Article 14 of the regulations in order to have the deep-links to illegal sites removed; the search engine is obliged to remove such links once it "is aware". This may be comparable to the "red flag" infringement test under the Digital Millennium Copyright Act, which shows the common law tradition has not yet really been effectively used

---

[68]   See Articles 14–17.
[69]   See http://www.chinacourt.org/flwk/show1.php?file_id=114658, retrieved on 1 March 2011.
[70]   See Article 4. The Interpretation was published in November 2000, and first amended in December 2003.

in the US courts.[71] Pioneering scholar, Qian Wang, has written a series of papers discussing ISPs' liability with a strong support of implementing the "red flag" standard.[72] Nonetheless, how and who to decide whether an ISP "is aware" of the infringement acts/sites? The Supreme Court interpretation fails to provide clear and precise guidance, which ought to be provided under future regulations especially for a country with no tradition of the rule of law. Moreover, the Notice and Remove approach introduced in the 2006 Regulations may be easier to put into practice for all parties including the courts and should be perfected through years of exercise.

3.1.3 The overture of Open Access and Creative Commons

Advocating the idea of "free availability" of copyright works on the Internet, the Open Access (OA) movement began in the late 1990s. The issue of the Budapest Open Access Initiative in 2001 marked that the international recognition and measure of OA "permits any users to read, download, copy, distribute, print, search, or link to the full texts of these articles, crawl them for indexing, pass them as data to software, or use

---

[71] See Section 512(c)(1)(A)(ii), which requires ISPs to remove content where they are "aware of facts or circumstances from which infringing activity is apparent". The test to determine a "red flag" infringement is to see "whether infringing activity would been apparent to a reasonable person operating under the same or similar circumstances". While the plaintiff's "red flag" plea in *Perfect 10 Inc v CCBill LLC* was dismissed, *IO Group Inc v Veoh Network Inc* confirmed that it must be proven that ISPs have concrete or actual knowledge of the infringement to use a "red flag" clause.

[72] See for example王迁、《信息网络传播权保护条例》 中"避风港"规则的效力,《法学》 2010年 06期128-140页, Qian Wang (2010), 'The Effect of the Safe Harbour Provision under the Regulations on the Protection of the Right to Network Dissemination of Information', *Legal Science*, **6**, 128–40; 王迁, 搜索引擎提供"快照"服务的著作权侵权问题再研究《东方法学》 2010年 03期126-139页, Qian Wang (2010), 'Studies on Copyright Infringement in Search Engine's Snapshot Service', *Oriental Law*, **3**, 126 39; 王迁, 视频分享网站著作权侵权问题再研究《法商研究》 2010年 01期85-94页, Qian Wang (2010), 'Further Studies on Video Sharing Websites' Copyright Infringement', *Studies in Law and Business*, **1**, 85–94; 王迁, 网络环境中版权直接侵权的认定《东方法学》 2009年 02期12-21页, Qian Wang (2009), 'Direct Copyright Infringement in the Network Environment', *Oriental Law*, **2**, 12–21; 王迁, 三论"信息定位服务"提供者"间接侵权"行为的认定《知识产权》 2009年 02期3-12页, Qian Wang (2009), 'Third Discussion on Indirect Infringement of the Information Allocation Service Providers', *Intellectual Property*, **2**, 3–12; 王迁, 视频分享网站著作权侵权问题研究《法商研究》 2008年 04期42-53页, Qian Wang (2008), 'Studies on Video Sharing Websites' Copyright Infringement', *Studies in Law and Business*, **4**, 42–53; 王迁, 论"信息定位服务"提供者"间接侵权"行为的认定《知识产权》 2006年 01期11-18页, Qian Wang (2006), 'Discussion on Indirect Infringement of the Information Allocation Service Providers', *Intellectual Property*, **1**, 11–18.

them for any other lawful purpose".[73] Founded in the US in 2001 by Cyberlaw and IP experts James Boyle, Michael Carroll, Lawrence Lessig and Eric Saltzman, MIT computer science professor Hal Abelson, and public domain web publisher Eric Eldred, Creative Commons (CC) promotes "some rights reserved" or even "no rights reserved" in copyright works, and believes that people may "get fulfilment from contributing to and participating in an intellectual commons".[74]

OA and CC are termed, in China, as 开放存取 and 知识共享, of which the literal translations are "open save and withdraw" and "knowledge sharing". OA and CC were formally introduced to China in 2004 and 2006 respectively, when Yongxiang Lu, representing CAS, and Yiyu Chen, representing the National Natural Science Foundation, signed the Berlin Declaration on Open Access to Knowledge in the Sciences and Humanities (Berlin Declaration); and the China Mainland version of the CC licences was launched in Beijing.[75] Supported by the Ford Foundation, CC China has been holding a range of promotional events, such as CC Salons, CC Birthday Parties, CC Seminars, and annual CC Photograph Contests.[76] As the foremost promoter of the OA movement in China, CAS has organised and hosted various activities, notably a conference on "Strategies and Policies for Open Access to Scientific Information" in 2005 and the "Berlin 8 Open Access Conference" in 2010 to "promote effective and sustainable open access in today's and future digital research, education, and cultural environments".[77] To date, nine OA journals from China have been acknowledged and included in the Digital Open Access Journal.

Adopting the system of licensing based upon the rule of law, the free sharing aspect of both OA and CC harmonises the traditional Chinese culture and the socialist principle as discussed earlier in the chapter. However, it seems that OA and CC are not appreciated and flourishing in China as they could have been. The reasons behind this must be compound but may be perceived as twofold, lacking the recognition of the public and the recommendation of the government. Most of the general public is not aware of the concepts of OA and CC. Among those who may know the phrases, many misinterpret OA and CC as "free of copyright"; for scholars who have a proper understanding, OA and CC may likely be still out of their consideration since only contributions to SSCI journals

---

[73]   Para 3, the Budapest Open Access Initiative 2002.
[74]   See http://creativecommons.org, retrieved on 25 March 2011.
[75]   See   http://cn.creativecommons.org/en/abouten/development-of-ccchina, retrieved on 25 March 2011.
[76]   See http://cn.creativecommons.org/en, retrieved on 25 March 2011.
[77]   See http://www.berlin8.org, retrieved on 25 March 2011.

would bring them merit, for academic and other promotions. Movements of OA and CC have been taking a bottom-up approach, which in this traditionally power-centralised nation would never work as effectively as a top-down approach. Seeing the OA and CC's effort in making resources freely availability to the public, why has the socialist Chinese government not promptly endorsed them as such? The interpretation may be simple; the spread of OA and CC would very possibly deteriorate the power of the government, which is against the tradition of power centralisation and certainly unfavourable for now. In addition, the conclusion brought out by Professor Xuechao Song, a CAS law scholar, may somewhat reflect the concern of the government.[78]

> Currently, the most urgent (issue) is not how to "share" but how to "protect", how to follow the trend of the development of international protection of IP, how to meet the requirement of digitization of information products for the legal system of copyright, and how to perfect the Chinese IP. If anyone wanted to share his/her work with the public, he/she may certainly do as a renowned professor did, attaching the following to the article, "author's statement: welcome all media's republication, free of charge", but no need to use this so-called "CC" license that may cause negative effect.[79]

The view expressed above is interesting yet unconvincing. Apparently it also shows vital misunderstandings of both copyright law and licensing of OA and CC, as, whilst the former provides protection for copyright owners alongside a concept of sharing with the public that is secured by the law for the balance of interests and rights, the latter offers an alternative and flexible approach to licensing schemes, which stands within the current copyright framework and which greatly contributes to the worldwide dissemination of scholarly content and to the universal progress of knowledge.

3.2 Divergent Views on the Chinese Internet

The Chinese Internet has been observed thoroughly both at home and abroad, with contradictory views every so often. When talking about

---

78 See 宋学超, "CC"应当缓行-参加"简体中文版知识共享协议发布会"后的思考, 《法律适用》 2006年第10期85-94页, Xuechao Song, 'Hold Your Horses CC – Thoughts After Attending the CC China Launch Conference', *Journal of Law Application* (2006), **10**, 85–94.

79 Ibid., 94. 当前最为迫切的, 不是怎样去"共享", 而是如何去"保护", 是尽快适应知识产权国际保护的发展趋势和信息产品数据化对版权法律制度的要求, 进一步完善我国的知识产权法律制度。如果有人愿意与大家分享自己的创作, 完全可以像一位著名教授那样, 在文章上载明"作者版权声明: 欢迎一切媒体免费转载", 而不一定非要用目前的这种可能引起负面作用的"CC"协议。

the Chinese Internet as viewed from the West, two institutions should be mentioned, the OpenNet Initiative (ONI) and Reporters Sans Frontières (RSF). The ONI is a collaboration among Toronto, Harvard, Cambridge and Oxford, four leading international universities, that intends to "investigate, expose and analyse Internet filtering and surveillance practices in a credible and non-partisan fashion".[80] The ONI maintains the following categorisation schemes: pervasive, substantial, nominal, indirect detentions and watchlist, to indicate a country's Internet filtering level. China is in the pervasive category because "China blocks access to numerous websites at the Internet backbone level for content related to human rights, opposition political movements, Taiwanese and Tibetan independence, and the Falun Gong movement. Some international news sources, such as the BBC, are also blocked."[81] The RSF is a Paris-based international non-governmental organisation that advocates "freedom of the press". Currently, it has national branches in all five continents and has consultant status at the United Nations. In October 2007, Robert Ménard, the RSF's Secretary-General, issued an open letter asking the head of China Telecom to restore its service. He believes that China Telecom has partially blocked Internet access in Guangdong Province and Shanghai from the end of August 2007 because of online comments or posts that were regarded as "illegal" by the government.[82] RSF holds an Internet enemy list. China is on the Enemies of the Internet 2006 as its Internet model is "based on censorship and surveillance,"[83] and the Enemies of the Internet 2010 for China "keeping a tight control over the Web's political and social content, whilst Chinese filtering systems are becoming increasingly sophisticated," and also "demonstrating a deep intolerance for critical opinions".[84]

Furthermore, running a simple search for "Internet" and "China" on Google produced about 393,000,000 results and out of the first 100, over 40 per cent related to censorship and the Chinese authorities' control of information over the Internet.[85] When Professor Lilian Edwards, in her editorial for *SCRIPTed*, remarked on the decision to block access to all

---

[80]   See 'About ONI', http://opennet.net/about, retrieved on 15 March 2011.

[81]   See http://map.opennet.net//index2.html, retrieved on 15 March 2011.

[82]   See 'Open letter asking head of China Telecom to keep promise to restore Internet services' (26 October 2007), http://www.rsf.org/article.php3?id_article=24126, retrieved on 28 March 2011.

[83]   See http://www.rsf.org/article.php3?id_article=19603, retrieved on 28 March 2011.

[84]   See http://en.rsf.org/web-2-0-versus-control-2-0-18-03-2010,36697, retrieved on 28 March 2011.

[85]   See http://www.google.co.uk/search?q=Internet+China&hl=en&start=0&sa=N, retrieved on 28 March 2011.

websites containing illegal images of child abuse in the UK, she strongly raised the question: "Today child porn; tomorrow, China?"[86] The Chinese Internet has become a pronominal term for "bad guy", censoring everything in the Western view.

The Internet was advocated as an independent world in the West and governments were asked to "leave it alone" because it did not lie within any borders.[87] Certainly, no government could leave the Internet alone since it is a part of the real world. In the UK, for instance, a series of laws have been enacted since 1978, including rules on child abuse images, criminally obscene content, incitement to racial hatred content and the liability of Internet Service Providers (ISPs).[88] In addition, the Internet Watch Foundation and the Computer Crime Unit have been established to deal with Internet and computer-related crimes.[89] Still, laws and regulation are challenged. According to the House of Lords Science and Technology Committee's report in August 2007, the Internet "has increasingly become the playground for criminals" and a lawless "wild west".[90] IT-related crimes make it completely necessary to regulate the Internet in all countries, including copyright, privacy and censorship. To date, China has not clearly outlined the scope of its censorship and, by often making it excessive, has been much criticised by the West. However, it could also be argued – are the views of institutions such as RSF and ONI unprejudiced and free from economic or political influences? Despite acknowledging that it is essential to denounce and combat disproportionate censorship and other laws, it should be remembered that China still lacks the rule of law culture forged in the West over hundreds of years. China still is, and has the status of, a developing country and this should be borne in mind when making any comment.

Indeed, the Internet has generated nationwide discussions in China since it eventually publicly spread in the late 1990s. Most Chinese users including scholars believe that the Internet is transforming China,[91]

---

[86] See L. Edwards, 'From Child Porn to China, in One Cleanfeed', *SCRIPTed* (2006), **3**(3); http://www.law.ed.ac.uk/ahrc/script-ed/vol3-3/editorial.doc, retrieved on 15 March 2011.

[87] See   http://w2.eff.org/Censorship/Internet_censorship_bills/barlow_0296. declaration, retrieved on 17 March 2011.

[88] See http://www.iwf.org.uk/police/page.22.htm, retrieved on 17 March 2011.

[89] See the Computer Crime Unit at http://www.met.police.uk/computercrime, retrieved on 17 March 2011.

[90] See   http://www.parliament.uk/parliamentary_committees/lords_press_ notices/pn100807st.cfm, retrieved on 17 March 2011.

[91] See for example 陈立辉, 互联网与社会组织模式重塑:一场正在进行的深刻社会变迁, 《社会学研究》,1998年6 期 11-28页; Chen Lihui, 'The Internet and

and see the Internet as a technological revolution as well as a boost to a more open, prosperous and democratic future China.[92] As Qian Tianbai foresaw, the Internet has made a great impact on Chinese people's everyday lives. They now learn online, shop online, game online, make friends online, chat online and even get married online.[93] They challenge authorities, comment on governments' policies and actions, and set up forums to discuss topics of interest, including the Dalai Lama[94] and "Tibetan independence".[95] According to a survey on Internet usage and impact done by the Chinese Academy of Social Science (CASS), people believe that the Internet will have a positive impact on political transparency and expanding discourse.[96] The survey highlights that 65.9 per cent of users' primary purpose of surfing online is reading news, 62.8 per cent of users believe that people will acquire better knowledge of politics by going online and 60.4 per cent believe that higher level officials will better understand common people's views. Respectively, 54.2 per cent and 45.1 per cent believe the Internet provides more opportunities for criticising the government and expressing political views.[97] In addition, people are concerned about how to make the Internet a safer place for youngsters and, in maintaining moral standards, how to develop the Internet healthily and how to perfect Chinese legislation regarding the Internet.[98] The majority

---

the Reform of the Social Organisational Model: An Ongoing Deep Social Transformation', *Social Science Research* (1998), **6**, 11–28.

92   See for example 许英, 互联网·公共领域与生活政治--刍议数位民主, «人文杂志»2002年 3期 141-146页; Xu Ying, 'The Internet, Public Domain and Living Politics – Discussion on the Number Digit Democracy', *The Journal of Humanities* (2002), **3**, 141–6.

93   "网婚", "Internet Marriage", which is not accepted nor protected by Chinese laws. For some definitions of it, see http://zhidao.baidu.com/question/27599061. html?fr=idrm; for a site that hosts Internet weddings, see http://love.club.sohu. com/search_wedding.php. Both retrieved on 17 March 2011.

94   See 达赖喇嘛放弃西藏独立, 'Dalai Lama gives up Tibetan independence', available at http://www3.beidabiz.com/bbs/viewthread.php?tid=4567, retrieved on 17 March 2011.

95   See 大家对西藏独立问题怎么看? 'Dear All, what do you think about the Independence of Tibet?' Available at http://www.thegreatwall.com.cn/phpbbs/ index.php?id=80341&forumid=4, retrieved on 17 March 2011.

96   Available at http://www.wwm.cn/Research/guo_liang_2005_toc.htm, CASS Survey on Internet Usage and Impact; retrieved on 17 March 2011.

97   Ibid.

98   See for example 孙金青, 互联网健康发展才是正道 «中国电信业»2010年 07期34-36页; Jinqing Sun, 'Developing a Healthy Internet: The Only Right Way to Go', *China Telecommunications Trade* (2010), **7**, 34–6. 禾火, 抵制低俗推动互联网健康发展 «互联网天地»2009 年 3期 (2009) 3, 5; Huo He, 'Boycott Vulgarity and Promote the Healthy Development of the Internet', *China Internet* (2009), **3**, 5. 高

of Chinese think that certain Internet content should be controlled, including 84.7 per cent who support the ban on pornography, and 72.6 per cent who uphold the ban on violence.[99]

Indeed, Chinese people are positive about the impact of the Internet in areas such as political transparency and freedom of expression. The Internet has become a powerful tool in today's life. Censorship is not wholly seen as the oppression of democracy; certain censorship is understood as an effective means to control unwanted contents and to maintain a healthy cyberspace. There is apparently a clear gap between the view of the West and that of the East. This could be explained in terms of culture, primarily Confucianism; while the West see what is left to be done and tend to be negative, the Chinese view the progress already achieved and therefore are more optimistic.

3.3 A Guarded Openness

Whilst the Internet in China is strongly criticised by the West for its censorship, Chinese legislators have striven to ensure a "harmonious and healthy" cyberspace through governmental control[100] and claim that the Internet in China is a "guarded openness".[101]

In February 1994, the State Council issued the Regulations for the Safety Protection of Computer Information Systems, which confirmed that the Ministry of State Security (MSS) would supervise all information systems in China. In addition to that, the Public Security Bureau (PSS) was put in charge of civilian network security, which was codified in the Regulations on Computer Information Network and Internet Security, Protection and Management approved by the State Council on 11 December 1997 and promulgated by the Ministry of Public Security on 30

志明和张德淼, 论社会和谐视野下的互联网发展与治理, 《中南财经政法大学研究生学报》, 2009年 05期 9-15页, Zhiming Gao & Demiao Zhang, 'The Development and Governance of Internet in the Context of Social Harmony', *Journal of the Postgraduate of Zhongnan University of Economics and Law* (2009), **5**, 9–15. 王瑛, 让孩子在网络生活中健康成长, 《中小学信息技术教育》 2007卷6期11-13; Wang Ying, 'Children's Health on the Internet', *School IT Education* (2007), **6**, 11–13. 何宝宏, 从技术的角度看互联网治理 《电信网技术》2005年 10期1-3页; Baohong He, 'Governance of the Internet: From the Technical Prospect', *Telecommunications Network Technology* (2005), **10**, 1–3.

99   See http://www.wwm.cn/Research/guo_liang_2005_toc.htm, CASS Survey on Internet Usage and Impact; retrieved on 17 March 2011.

100   See http://www.mii.gov.cn/art/2006/05/22/art_21_13930.html, retrieved on 17 March 2011.

101   See http://www.ucsusa.org/global_security/china/chinese-perspectives-on-transparency-and-security.html, retrieved on 17 March 2011.

December (Regulations 1997). The PSS and the MSS are the most important bodies that are responsible for, respectively, internal and external security, both offline and online.

The Regulations 1997 clarifies that no unit – "unit" is *dan wei* in Chinese, and means "establishment" – or individual may use the Internet to violate the freedom and privacy of network users.[102] It also states that "no unit or individual may use the Internet to harm national security, disclose state secrets, harm the interests of the State, of society or of a group, the legal rights of citizens, or to take part in criminal activities".[103] It defines nine types of prohibited information, which are

- inciting to resist or breaking the Constitution or laws or the implementation of administrative regulations;
- inciting to overthrow the government or the socialist system;
- inciting division of the country, harming national unification;
- inciting hatred or discrimination among nationalities or harming the unity of the nationalities;
- making falsehoods or distorting the truth, spreading rumours, destroying the order of society;
- promoting feudal superstitions, sexually suggestive material, gambling, violence, murder;
- terrorism or inciting others to criminal activity;
- openly insulting other people or distorting the truth to slander people;
- injuring the reputation of state organs.

In line with the Law on the Protection of State Secrets and other related regulations, to facilitate the strengthening of the management of secrets in the computer systems on the Internet and to ensure the safety of state secrets, the State Secrets Protection Regulations for Computer Information Systems on the Internet came into effect in January 2000. They hold that no unit or individual shall release, discuss or disseminate state secrets on BBS, chat rooms or network news groups, and that the principle of managing state secrets shall be "whoever places materials on the Internet takes the responsibility".[104] In addition, national backbone networks, Internet access providers and users are obligated to be supervised and checked by departments in charge of protecting secrets, and to report a leak or possible leak.[105]

---

[102]   See Article 7.
[103]   See Article 4.
[104]   Articles 8 and 10.
[105]   See Article 16.

In September 2000, the Telecommunications Regulations were promulgated by the State Council and, in Chapter V, they regulate telecommunications security and affirm that no organisation or individual may use telecommunications networks to make, duplicate, issue, or disseminate information containing the following:[106]

- material that opposes the basic principles established by the constitution;
- material that jeopardises national security, reveals state secrets, subverts state power, or undermines national unity;
- material that harms the prosperity and interests of the state;
- material that arouses ethnic animosities, ethnic discrimination, or undermines ethnic solidarity;
- material that undermines state religious policies, or promotes cults and feudal superstitions;
- material that spreads rumours, disturbs social order, or undermines social stability;
- material that spreads obscenities, pornography, gambling, violence, murder, terror, or instigates crime;
- material that insults or slanders others or violates the legal rights and interests of others;
- material that has other contents prohibited by laws or administrative regulations.

Furthermore, "for the purpose of regulating Internet information services (IIS) and promoting the healthy and orderly development of such services", the Measures for Managing Internet Information Services came into effect in October 2000.[107] They demand that all IIS providers must guarantee that their information is legal.[108] For those providing services related to information, the publishing business and e-announcements, they shall record the content of the information, the time that the information is released, and the address or the domain name of the website, and keep the information for 60 days.[109]

Later, the Decisions of the NPC Standing Committee on Safeguarding Internet Safety were promulgated in December 2000. They deal with subverting state power, stealing state secrets and organising or contacting evil cults through the Internet.

---

[106]   See Article 57.
[107]   See Article 1.
[108]   See Article 13.
[109]   See Article 14.

In addition, China formed its team of cyber police in September 1998 and they patrol the network everyday.[110] In September 2007, Beijing sent two virtual police officers (VPOs), *Anan* and *Ningning*, "to safeguard the virtual world".[111] In fact, a pair of VPOs, *Jingjing* and *Chacha*, have also been introduced to Internet users in Shenzhen by the Internet Supervision Department of the Shenzhen Public Security Bureau since January 2006. People can click on the cartoon police officers' icon and ask questions about information safety or report Internet crimes.[112] The newly revealed VPO images are computer-generated.[113] They pop up on Beijing's gateway websites every 30 minutes and have patrolled all websites and forums in Beijing from December 2007 onwards. To report any suspicions, a double-click is all that is required and it is promised that real police officers will respond to the report within 30 minutes.[114] It is said that virtual police intend primarily to combat nine types of Internet crime – online pornography, violence, terrorism, Internet-related frauds, stealing, gambling, money laundering, superstition, and selling guns and other prohibited objects.[115]

Whilst most users believe that VPOs would protect cyberspace and fight Internet crime,[116] some worry about VPOs becoming a "political show" rather than policing the Internet;[117] some find VPOs "cute" and have even tried hard to meet them;[118] some fear that they can no longer watch porn online at home as the IP address would be recorded;[119] and, very interestingly, detailed techniques and methods for preventing VPOs'

---

[110]   See http://www.people.com.cn/GB/it/51/20030209/919987.html, retrieved on 17 March 2011.

[111]   See   http://www.chinadaily.com.cn/china/2007-08/29/content_6066310. htm, retrieved on 17 March 2011.

[112]   See   http://english.peopledaily.com.cn/200601/10/eng20060110_234314. html, retrieved on 17 March 2011.

[113]   See http://www.bj.cyberpolice.cn/index.htm, retrieved on 17 March 2011.

[114]   See   http://www.chinadaily.com.cn/china/2007-08/29/content_6066310. htm, retrieved on 17 March 2011.

[115]   China has been extremely tough with online pornography and violence; the provisions are tied together with terrorism in both civil and criminal laws. Available at the Internet Society of China website http://www.isc.org.cn/ ShowArticle.php?id=8005, retrieved on 17 March 2011.

[116]   See   http://bbs.soxj.com/dispbbs.asp?boardID=53&ID=63606&page=1, retrieved 28 March 2011.

[117]   See http://it.sohu.com/20060516/n243251957.shtml, retrieved on 17 March 2011.

[118]   See http://club.163.com/viewArticleByWWW.m?boardId=v-tdkj&article Id=v-tdkj_114f9d74b242a40_0&boardOffset=0, retrieved on 17 March 2011.

[119]   See http://topic.csdn.net/t/20041002/15/3424047.html, retrieved on 17 March 2011.

"watch" were posted to a hacker's BBS in April 2007, almost half a year prior to the official launch of VPOs.[120]

While it seems obvious that a level of censorship is acceptable and even recommended, it is difficult to draw the line between what is tolerable and what is not. This is the dilemma with the Regulations of 1997 and 2000. While the objective of the law is logical and clear, the application of it has to be very well monitored. Could freedom of expression conflict with national security? Could injury to the reputation of state organs mean just democratic political opposition?

What should be concerning is the extent of censorship and the barriers this creates for the natural development of a free society and an open government. China has surely not evolved enough from its traditional approach of censorship and needs to revise some aspects. However, in a framework of already rapid social change, it would not be beneficial to force the challenge faster than it could go.

4. DISCUSSION

The Internet had a late start in China but has had incredibly rapid growth thereafter. For example, from 620 000 in 1997 to 162 million users in 2007, the number of Chinese Internet users has multiplied over 2600 times in 10 years. Furthermore, amongst 457 million Internet users, more than 50 million users surf online in Internet cafés. These unique phenomena are creating numerous challenges for Chinese society and the developing legal system, including copyright, privacy and censorship in relation to the Internet. The gap between China and the West certainly exists with regard to these three aspects of law but the approaches to understanding the situation and solving the evident problems that this rapid development poses to China and its legal system are varied. Western views on the Chinese Internet have not been too positive, some even seeing it as a synonym of "governmental censorship", which is detested by a number of democratic Westerners since it is against the ideal of an independent cyberspace. However, unfettered freedom in respect of the use of the Internet does not promote a healthy development of the Internet, whilst laws and regulations imply the intervention of the government to accomplish an end beneficial to the public. Contrary to that, people in China seem to maintain a rather optimistic attitude, which continues the Chinese traditions, towards the

---

[120] Retrieved on 17 March 2011 at http://bbs.hacker.cn/redirect.php?fid=217&tid=25972&goto=nextoldset.

Internet. Most Chinese Internet users pay great attention to the progress that has been achieved over the country and also what happens around the world. They believe that the Internet is helping China to improve its political transparency, discourse and democracy. Moreover, they demand a controlled cyberspace, especially for the youngsters, and support legal restrictions and censorship on certain content. It is known that advice and help from international parties are vital for China's development. For instance, in the case of the Internet, without the UK and Professor Werner Zorn's liberal efforts, the arrival of the Internet in China might have been even further delayed. Obviously, China needs to take Western criticisms and comments seriously and take action to improve, whilst international watchdogs ought to keep the views objective and most importantly keep the intention constructive.

With regard to censorship on the Internet, the Chinese majority support certain censorship on the Internet for a healthy cyberspace. Different cultures, traditions and values may bring about different viewpoints and approaches on the legislation, which should be respected. However, the law should be made clear and so should Chinese censorship, which should clarify the following. What is the information that may injure the reputation of state organs? And what are the other contents, specifically, that are prohibited by laws or administrative regulations? Moreover, censorship is a double-edged sword. It may be used by the government to censor what people do not want, but it may also be used to censor what people do want. The technology behind censorship may allow them to watch for lawbreakers online, and may also allow them to watch for each and every one of the users online. Censorship should be carefully exercised by the authorities, as in all laws a balance must be maintained. This balance, however, is of particular complexity for the Chinese authorities, because of the history and because of the legal tradition stressing the power of the state. China has opened itself to the world since the 1980s and is opening up day by day, as shown in dealing with the 5.12 quake. The Chinese authorities should understand that in no way do people want to go back to the closed, obscure and repressive old days. A harmonious but more open, transparent and democratic China is the Chinese people's will, as well as the future for China.

China, the nation, was significantly ahead in philosophy, science and technology in early times. However, its feudal bureaucratic system and xenophobic policy held back its further progress from the Middle Ages on and has resulted in China falling far behind the West in modern science and technology. Furthermore, chronic warfare made Chinese people long for social harmonisation and national consolidation, as was emphasised by major Chinese philosophies including Confucianism, legalism and

Daoism, with their strong emphasis on society and culture, which was also adopted by Chinese socialism.

Although the notion that "in Chinese civilization it has been an elegant offense to steal a book" may reflect a major misunderstanding of the Chinese culture in the West[121] – "to steal a book is an elegant offense" was in fact a quotation by Kong Yiji, who was a fiction figure of a dark comedy created by Mr Zhou Shuren in the winter of 1918 to scorn the conservative group and to urge social innovation and revolution[122] – the sharing and copying of intellectual works have been regarded as necessary and honourable in traditional Chinese culture. Such values for the collective good may be odd to the West yet are still understandable, being similar to certain contemporary ideas such as OA and CC; although both OA and CC are developed within the modern copyright regime and embrace the system of licensing that is based upon the rule of law.

Indeed, cultural values are of determining influence in the way law is viewed within a society; Chinese people's view of law was very different when compared with that in Western countries. For thousands of years, China was isolated in its implementation of the rule of man. This can be seen in the review of its history, from legalism's governing by law with heavy punishments to Confucianism's stress on harmony and despising laws, Daoism's avoiding explicit intentions, strong wills and proactive initiatives, Mohism's waiting for the heaven's judgement, Yin–Yang's seeking for harmony among the universal elements and Neo-Confucianism's one-sided obligations of obedience. These have offered the rule of man a concrete and powerful foundation.

Furthermore, power centralisation has been adopted since the Qin Dynasty and no institution existed to apply law against the state in Imperial China. In addition, the long-lasting Imperial system granted the administration rights to enforce the law. The traditional Chinese legal system was a mechanism for retaining imperial control over the populace and the ancient Chinese law was mainly conceived as penal law that focused on state concerns and dealt with private matters only incidentally. It was operated vertically and used as a supplementary means for maintaining a hierarchical social relationship that continued for centuries. The dominant Chinese philosophy supported the rule of man and centralisation. Historically, joint credit and collective benefits were

---

[121] See W.P. Alford, *To Steal a Book Is an Elegant Offense: Intellectual Property Law in Chinese Civilization* (1995), 123.

[122] Zhou Shuren was one of the founders of the Chinese League of Left-Wing Writers and is one of the most renowned contemporary writers in China; his pen name is Lu Xun.

emphasised, which has had a profound impact on laws in China to date. Therefore, the development of civil law came late into China.

China wishes to maintain a harmony and balance in its society as well as in its legal system. Following international treaties and standards, the Chinese government has adopted the Western approach of rule of law instead of traditional rule of man. The essence of the rule of law is an autonomous legal order, which means that it regulates government power, defends the rights of individuals with equality, and provides procedural and formal justice. In contradiction of the rule of man, the rule of law stresses that no one, including the government and party, is above the law. In a positive step Article 5 of the Chinese Constitution has been written to include the rule of law, which demonstrates that China is willing to twist its system towards the rule of law, for which efforts will be needed in all areas and at all levels.

Today, China has opened itself up to the world and has joined the international economy. The Chinese government is learning from history to avoid putting the nation in another great danger like the Cultural Revolution and intends to promote the rule of law, slowly yet steadily. Moreover, as the biggest Internet country in the world, the Internet will constantly play a vital role in China's progress of openness and transparency. Regardless of different understandings and attitudes towards the Chinese Internet between China and the West, the Internet has become the significant practical means for the Chinese public to learn, to network and to advocate their desires, as well as their rights. Optimistically, the Internet would grow to be an influential force over China's transition, of aspects including the economy, culture, law and politics.

To be brief, China traditionally lacked a rule of law culture in which the law was held in high esteem. In strict contrast, law used to be seen as a "troublemaker" and lawsuits were treated as wickedness; thus people were never in favour of tribunals. Moreover, the legal system in Imperial China, from 221 BC to AD 1911, embraced the essence of the rule of man throughout and was an imperial tool of control never registering the interest of the general public. Ancient Chinese law was an authoritative top-down operation, a system that intended to control not only the country but also the thoughts of individuals. Historically, private interest and rights in China were safeguarded only under the condition of satisfying the state's concern first, which was in accordance not only with the highlights of the traditional culture but also with the socialist principles. These have influenced Chinese laws to date and provided a fairly diverse basis for the establishment and promotion of modern copyright, a law that is of great importance in the global market economy.

2. Authorship, access and the public interest*

> Information is the lifeblood of a knowledge-based economy, and intellectual property laws and policies play a central role in transforming this intangible asset into economic, social and cultural wealth.[1]

1. INTRODUCTION

The essence of copyright law is the power of securing private property rights. Gillian Davies identifies the four interrelated principles that were part of the original efforts in the UK to develop copyright. The first of these is the idea of natural law as it applies to the author. In this concept, the work is viewed as an extension of the author, an expression of personality. The second is the broadly held view that the author deserves just reward for creative labour. The third is that without some law in place that protects the creation of individuals there would be no stimulus to creativity. This is based on the assumption that writers, painters, musicians and innovators would cease producing in the absence of a law guarding their works from piracy. The final principle is one of social requirement. This ideal argues that it is a social requirement in the public interest that authors and other owners of rights should be encouraged to publish their works so as to permit the widest possible dissemination of works to the public at large. It should also be recognised that these principles allow for the passing of authorial rights to other owners.[2]

Copyright protection embodying these principles is currently available in most countries. Copyright owners are generally given the exclusive

---

* This chapter was adapted from Guanhong Tang (2004), 'A Comparative Study of Copyright and the public Interest in the United Kingdom and China', *SCRIPTed*, **1**(2), 272. The work is licensed through *SCRIPTed*'s Open Licence and available at http://www.law.ed.ac.uk/ahrc/script-ed/issue2/china.asp, retrieved on 18 March 2011.

[1] See P.K. Yu (ed.), Intellectual Property and Information Wealth: Issue and Practice in the Digital Age (2007), Preface, vii.

[2] G. Davies, *Copyright and the Public Interest* (2002), 14–17.

right, and the right to authorise others, to reproduce and create derivative works, to distribute copies or phonorecords of the work to the public, and to publicly perform and display the copyright work.[3] These rights, however, are not unlimited in scope. The law also deals with such matters as the freedom of information, educational interests and the spreading and availability of knowledge. It thus grants individuals the right to use copyrighted work without the owners' consent in these and similar circumstances.

Copyright systems therefore have a twofold purpose: "to accord exploitation rights to those engaged in literary and artistic production and to answer to the general public interest in the widest possible availability of copyright material". They intend to balance the exclusive rights of authors, publishers and copyright owners with the users' rights and the need for the free flow of information.[4] Such balance, endorsed by national laws, forms the public interest doctrine as understood in this book.

The public interest in copyright law is multidimensional. For instance, the exclusive author rights granted by the law are considered to be in the public interest because they promote creativity and learning and provide a framework for investment by the creative industries. As such they may be termed the *authorship public interest*. In addition, with the intention of safeguarding public rights of access, it is required that certain limitations and exceptions are permitted to these rights, which are defined as the *access public interest*. Further, in some systems, certain works may be excluded from copyright protection should they be immoral, scandalous and injurious, such as pornography[5] or works published in breach of a life-long obligation of secrecy;[6] this is said to result from *public policy* rather than public interest. This book will not address these last issues much, but concentrate instead on the authorship and access public interests.

Accordingly, the public interest has more than one aspect: it ratifies to authors the exclusive private property rights for their copyrighted works on the one hand and grants users access to the works through limitations and exception to copyright on the other. These elements have been affirmed and endorsed by international copyright law, which also aims to

---

[3] W. Cornish & D. Llewelyn, *Intellectual Property: Patents, Copyright, Trade Marks and Allied Rights* (2007).

[4] See G. Davies, *Copyright and the Public Interest* (2002), 7.

[5] In *Glyn v Weston Feature Film Company* [1916] 1 Ch 261, the court refused to award a copyright infringement injunction because the plaintiff's sexually explicit novel that was adapted into a film by the defendant was "grossly immoral in its essence, in its treatment, and in its tendency".

[6] See *Attorney General v Guardian Newspapers Ltd* (No 2) [1990] 1 AC 109.

balance the benefit of the global community with the domestic welfare of individual states. However, the diversity of social dimensions may lead to different understandings and practices of copyright and the public interest in different countries. In the UK, for example, the access public interest, the interest or the right of the public to access or use information including copyright-protected works, "is based upon a general principle of common law" and "it is a defence outside and independent of statutes",[7] which although recognised by the courts has yet to succeed. The UK courts have held that it will be rare for a defence based on the access public interest to succeed in situations where the fair dealing defences provided by copyright legislation had been found to be inapplicable.[8] whereas in the US the access public interest rests particularly in the fair use provisions, which offer a general doctrine in establishing whether a use of work(s) is fair.

China, on the other hand, in the name of the public interest, excluded copyright from its modern legal system until the late 1980s but has awarded copyright – the private property rights – since 1990 and also provides for public, non-criminal enforcement of these rights. As part of the world community, China must fulfil its obligations in protecting copyright under international treaties including the Berne Convention and TRIPS. As such, China has developed a copyright system that meets international standards but also fits within its socialist system. Since the adoption of its first modern copyright law, it recognises a threefold balance: between the interests of the authors and copyright owners and of the public users; between the interests of the international communities and of China; and between the interests of private property and of the state possessions. Certainly, the adaptation and development of copyright in contemporary China – a socialist country that not long ago embraced the rule of law – have greatly challenged its traditional philosophy, its socialist ideology and its early modern legal system, in relation to intellectual works and beyond; such tensions are significant.

This chapter aims to examine Chinese copyright law and the public interest and to outline how Chinese copyright legislation was formed under international pressure, its consistency with international treaties such as the Berne Convention and TRIPS, the movements in the concept of copyright together with the public interest and the implementation of the law on the Internet, and its diversity in comparison with selected leading countries, the UK and the US.

---

[7]   See H. MacQueen, 'Appropriate for the Digital Age? Copyright and the Internet', in C. Waelde & L. Edwards (eds), *Law and the Internet* (2009), 183–225.

[8]   H. MacQueen, C. Waelde & G. Laurie, *Contemporary Intellectual Property: Law and Policy* (2010), 187.

2. THE INTERNATIONAL FRAMEWORK

Works subject to copyright are mainly protected under law by two separate structures: international law such as the Berne Convention, TRIPS
and WCT, and national law.[9] Whilst national laws may differ widely
between individual countries owing to the influence of diverse political,
economic, social and cultural backgrounds, international instruments
set up a minimum standard of copyright protection for all participating
nations to prevent violation of legitimate rights.

Initiated in 1886 and last updated in 1971, the Berne Convention
governs the international aspects of copyright protection in 164 signatory
countries. The main aim of the Berne Convention is to help nationals of
its member states obtain international protection of their right to control,
and receive payment for, the use of their creative works. Further to ensure
the authorship public interest, the convention establishes that copyright
does not have to be asserted or declared, as it is automatically in force at
creation. In countries adhering to the Berne Convention, therefore, an
author need not register or apply for a copyright for his or her works and
the term of the protection should be at least the author's life plus 50 years
for most works.[10] Adopted in 1996, the WIPO Copyright Treaty (WCT), a
special agreement under Article 20 of the Berne Convention for the protection of literary and artistic works, extends not only the scope of copyright
protection to computer programs and compilations of data or other material (databases),[11] but also the term of protection for phonographic works
to life plus 50 years instead of previously 25.[12] It confirms for authors
the rights of distribution, rental and communication to the public.[13] The
right of communication enables copyright owners to control the communication of their works to the public and includes broadcasting and
transmission on the Internet; it is vital for WIPO member states enforcing
copyright in cyberspace.

The Berne Convention also recognises the access public interest and

---

   9   A common standard may be adopted by some united countries, for instance
the European Union (EU). In order to harmonise the laws within the member
states of the EU, certain European Directives have been passed, including the
"Directive 2001/29/EC of the European Parliament and of the Council of 22 May
2001 on the harmonisation of certain aspects of copyright and related rights in the
information society", which is commonly known as the InfoSoc Directive, as well
as the EU Copyright Directive.
   10   See Article 7.
   11   Articles 4 and 5.
   12   See Article 9.
   13   Articles 6–8.

contains various exceptions that permit signatory countries to set limitations on the scope of copyright protection. For example, Article 10(1) grants a mandatory and uncompensated exception to copyright owners' exclusive rights, permitting quotation for copyrighted works in accordance with "fair practice". Article 10(2) allows signatory countries to create the uncompensated exceptions and limitations, subject to certain conditions, for use of copyrighted works for illustration in publications, broadcasts and sound recordings for teaching purposes, and a special compulsory licence regime for the reproduction and translation of texts by developing countries, subject to strict conditions.[14]

The Berne Convention further acknowledges the need to maintain a balance between the different dimensions of the public interest, the rights of authors and the larger public, particularly education, research and access to information, and enables member states to permit the reproduction of works under their national copyright laws in respect of "certain special cases, provided that such reproduction does not conflict with a normal exploitation of the work and does not unreasonably prejudice the legitimate interests of the author",[15] that is, the Berne three-step test clause. Specifically, the three steps are firstly, that limitations or exceptions to copyright must be confined to certain special cases; secondly, that these cases must not conflict with the normal exploitation of a work; and thirdly, that these cases must not unreasonably prejudice the legitimate interests of the right holder.

The lawful uses of copyright works as recognised by international law may be summarised as threefold. (1) *With legitimate permission of the authors*, that is, copyright works can be reproduced, "in any manner or form", "with the authors' authorisation".[16] (2) *Exceptions to copyright*, that is, "certain free uses of works",[17] which constitute reproduction of works in limited circumstances for purposes such as press summaries, teaching, press broadcasting or public communication, and reporting current events.[18] They do not require the permission of the copyright owner or the payment of royalties and as such are most often used as defences to an action for copyright infringement. Nevertheless they do

---

[14] See Appendix.

[15] See Article 9(2).

[16] See Article 9(1).

[17] "Permitted acts" is the statute term in the UK and is more commonly known as "fair dealing", which provides an exhaustive list; whilst in the US "fair use" provides general criteria to determine whether the use is fair instead of a list of acts of fair dealing.

[18] Articles 9 and 10.

require mention of the source, such as the title of the work and the author. And (3) *the public interest*, to which the Berne Convention makes no express reference but which is reflected in and recognised by the WCT, which states that there is a need to "maintain a balance between the rights of authors and the larger public interest, particularly education, research and access to information".[19] The concept of public interest here justifies actions both on the side of upholding rights and limiting the rights, which may be interpreted as twofold: copyright originated and developed within concepts of the public interest where one of its fundamental purposes is to serve the public interest by encouraging learning and the advancement of knowledge through a system of exclusive, but limited, rights for authors and copyright owners;[20] and the public interest may in some circumstances provide a legitimate defence to copyright infringement, whereby use of the work without the copyright owner's authorisation is deemed justified. The exceptions specifically mentioned in the Berne Convention fall within this aspect of the public interest. Nevertheless, all exceptions to copyright must be within the three-step test, which was first applied to the exclusive right of reproduction by the Berne Convention in 1967,[21] and has been transplanted and extended into TRIPS in 1994, which is the agreement that must be adhered to by all members of the WTO, subject to some transitional provisions for developing countries.

In order to be accepted by the WTO, national copyright law must comply with TRIPS, which is in compliance with and goes beyond the provisions of the Berne Convention except for those on moral rights. It includes the protection of computer programs and databases;[22] introduces the right of rental for computer programs, cinematographic works and phonograms; and protects performers, phonogram producers and broadcasters. Meanwhile, the exceptions to copyright are available to signatories of the TRIPs Agreement, which incorporates the Berne Convention. The access public interest is recognised; most importantly, repeating the three-step test of the Berne Convention, Article 13 TRIPS requires members to confine limitations or exceptions to exclusive rights to certain special cases that do not conflict with a normal exploitation of the work and do not unreasonably prejudice the legitimate interests of the right holder.

The three-step test may prove to be extremely important if any nation

---

19   See para 5, Preamble, the WCT; retrieved on 10 February 2011 at http://www.wipo.int/treaties/en/ip/wct/trtdocs_wo033.html#preamble.
20   G. Davies, *Copyright and the Public Interest* (2002).
21   See Article 9(2).
22   E. Derclaye, *The Legal Protection of Databases: A Comparative Analysis* (2008).

attempts to extend the exceptions to copyright, because, unless the WTO decides that its modifications comply with the test, it is likely to face trade sanctions. For instance, although China strove to build up an understanding of the correct application of the test, the limitations and exceptions in its first copyright law were criticised as being too broad and so likely to damage copyright owners' exploitation of works and thus required revision to accede to the WTO.

As copyright has become an extremely important international issue, especially since the late twentieth century, TRIPS has become one of the most powerful IP treaties, although some scholars argue whether its enforcement should remain in the WTO. Picciotto considers that, with any "multilateral framework" for intellectual property rights, it is essential to see whether it enables the full scope of the protection of intellectual property right to be defined by public interest criteria. He appeals to "rescue the TRIPS and the WTO from the damaging effects of their capture by private interests", and argues for the possibility of an international public welfare standard. He further urges that developing countries should "adopt a common stand to resist bilateral pressures and insist that the TRIPS be treated as maximum and not a minimum".[23] His assertion has been supported and extended to the digital environment.[24]

Nonetheless, as a developing country and a member of the world community, China has benefited greatly from international pressure with regard to building up a modern copyright system that upholds both the authorship and access public interests. It has sought an approach to fit copyright into its socialist system, allowing private property rights to be protected whilst firmly maintaining the collective benefit.

3. COPYRIGHT – ITS ORIGIN AND DEVELOPMENT

This section intends to brief on how modern copyright law formed and developed, and how this Western copyright system has responded to the requirements of international treaties and struck a balance between the different dimensions of the public interest, together with the context for development of a limited "public interest defence" outside the express provisions of the copyright legislation.

---

[23] See S. Picciotto, 'Defending the Public Interest in TRIPS and the WTO', *EIPR* (2003), 229.
[24] See for example Hong Xue, 'Copyright Exceptions for Online Distance Education', *IPQ* (2008), 213–229.

3.1   Copyright and the Public Interest in the UK and the US

The concepts of copyright and the body of laws regulating them originate in the fifteenth-century invention of the printing press. In 1476 the printing press was introduced in England. The printing press revolutionised information storage, retrieval and usage, and duplications of text and images became easier and more accurate. Starting in 1529, laws were passed requiring manuscripts to be licensed by the Crown before publication. An important consideration, at least for the Crown, was the numerous dissident tracts made available through the printing press. To be brief, copyright was a controlling mechanism for the government. This was true not only in the UK, but also in other European countries and (later) the US.[25]

The 1688 revolution in England provided an opening for the emergence of a debate on the link between liberty and property.[26] Whilst not complete, this new discourse helped build the foundations for thinking about the author as a proprietor in the early eighteenth century. Making the link between notions of rights in tangible property and intangible property was a critical aspect of the emerging discourse over proprietary authorship.

Prior to the Statute of Anne, printed matter was controlled through the Licensing Act, which allowed authorities to prohibit publication of anything "dangerous". The Licensing Act, repealed in 1694, mandated that all books be licensed before publication by registering them with the Stationers' Company, a body established by the Crown to censor printed material, which therefore had a virtual monopoly over all printed matter.[27] Registration occurred when the book was entered into the register, recording who owned the "copy-right". The "copy-right" was the Stationers' Company's right to copy and publish rather than the author's right to prevent copying.

The Statute of Anne, "an Act for the Encouragement of Learning, by vesting the Copies of Printed Books in the Authors or purchasers of such Copies, during the Times therein mentioned", was enacted in 1709 and came into effect on 10 April 1710. Among other things, the Statute of Anne established the copyright term as 14 years, with a possible renewal for another 14 available to the author. It made statutory copyright protection available to anyone, not just the stationers, although registration at Stationers' Hall was still necessary to obtain the right. Additionally,

---

25   J.C. Ginsburg, 'A Tale of Two Copyrights: Literary Property in Revolutionary France and America', *Tulane Law Review* (1990), **64**(5), 991–1031.

26   M. Woodmansee & P. Jaszi, *The Construction of Authorship: Textual Appropriation in Law and Literature* (1993).

27   M. Rose, *Authors and Owners: The Invention of Copyright* (1993).

copyright for material already published was extended for 21 more years and thereafter the book would enter the public domain. This last provision specifically addressed the concerns of the London booksellers and their already existing copyrights.

The Statute of Anne replaced the previous system and succeeded in conferring all rights in a book to authors for a limited amount of time instead of some rights for an unlimited amount of time.[28] This demonstrated the public interest underlying the system, both upholding and limiting such monopoly rights. The Statute of Anne is "the starting point for a modern history of copyright law" and "the role of the public interest" within.[29]

In 1774, the Statute of Anne finally reached the House of Lords when *Donaldson v Beckett* came before the court, on an appeal from an injunction against publishing a book, whose statutory term of copyright had expired.[30] *Donaldson v Beckett* conceptually approved that authors had rights invested in their works and also limited these rights to statutory ones; it also confined copyright to what was in the statute, and so ensured that materials fell into the public domain after the term expired. *Donaldson v Beckett* thus upheld both rights of authorship in works and of access to works.

Owing to the advent of new technology around the turn of the twentieth century, musicians and publishers called for a revision of the law, which resulted in the Copyright Act 1911. The 1911 Act implemented the Berne Convention, and affirmed the automatic rights of copyright and abolished the requirement to register works. It also granted foreign authors the same rights and privileges to copyright works as domestic authors.[31] It brought provisions on copyright into one Act for the first time by revising and repealing almost all the earlier Acts. Among other changes, it extended the term of copyright to author's life plus 50 years, confirmed the exclusive right of translating and oral delivery in respect of nondramatic works, including lectures, and abolished the requirement to register copyright with Stationers' Hall. Most notably, the 1911 Act granted unpublished works statutory copyright protection and codified the "fair dealing" doctrine, which ratified the dual aspects of the public interest: authorship and access. On account of the speed at which technology con-

---

[28] See M. Rose, 'The Author as Proprietor: *Donaldson v Becket* and the Genealogy of Modern Authorship', *Representations* (1988) 23, 51–85.

[29] See I. Alexander, *Copyright Law and the Public Interest in the Nineteenth Century* (2010), 17.

[30] *Donaldson and another v Becket and another* (1774) 4 Burr. 2408.

[31] See L. Bently & B. Sherman, 'Great Britain and the Signing of the Berne Convention in 1886', *Journal of the Copyright Society of the USA* (2001), **48**, 311.

tinued to develop, two further laws were passed: the Copyright Act 1956, which took into account further amendments to the Berne Convention and extended copyright protection to films and broadcasts. In turn, this was replaced by the Copyright, Designs and Patents Act 1988 (CDPA), which is the current copyright law. The CDPA provided another major overhaul and updating of copyright law. Moral rights were introduced into UK law and computer programs were protected as a literary work. The arrival and rapid development of the Internet have challenged the CDPA, the aim of which is "clearly to establish as strong a regime of protection as possible for authors, providing a situation where publication on the Internet can realise its full economic potential".[32] In brief, the CDPA affords protection to copyright works with broader scope and longer duration, but also a set of possible defences, as fair dealing. Reflecting the access public interest, as did the 1956 Act, fair dealing permits individuals to make a single copy of an (un-clarified) "reasonable proportion" of literary, dramatic, musical and artistic works for "research and private study",[33] and offers specific provisions for use in the sectors of education, libraries and archives.[34] In order to improve copyright protection in cyberspace and to implement the European Copyright Directive 2001/29/EC that itself implemented the WCT, the Copyright and Related Rights Regulations came into force on 31 October 2003.[35] Taking account of the development of the Internet, the 2003 Regulations introduce a number of changes to the CDPA. Amongst these a new exclusive right has been granted within the scope of certain statutory limitations, for instance, the right to communicate a work to the public by Internet transmission, which includes communication by means of broadcast and on-demand electronic transmission; a new exception has been authorised to permit temporary copies; also, fair dealing for research is now limited to apply only for non-commercial purposes, while criticism or review has been limited to published works.[36]

The US copyright law was first derived from English copyright law (Statute of Anne) and common law in 1790; to date US copyright is the most influential system in the international community. Unlike many other laws in this country, the framers of the US Constitution made statutory copyright law purely federal (that is, not a matter for the individual

---

[32]   See above at n. 7, 183.
[33]   See section 29, CDPA.
[34]   Sections 32–36, and sections 37–44.
[35]   H. MacQueen, C. Waelde & G. Laurie, *Contemporary Intellectual Property: Law and Policy* (2010).
[36]   See Part 2, the Copyright and Related Rights Regulations 2003.

states): "the Congress shall have power … to promote the progress of science and useful arts … by securing for limited times to authors and inventors the exclusive rights to their respective writings and discoveries". All the US copyright power therefore derives from the constitutional clause, where both the authorship and access public interest have been upheld. Copyright in the US has been constructed to seek balance; it protects the authors only to the extent necessary to advance the public interest in the progress of knowledge. Differing from the fair dealing defence, US copyright law employs a general fair use doctrine, which also reflects the access public interest. Section 107 states that fair use for purposes such as (that is, not limited to) teaching, scholarship, or research, is not an infringement of copyright.[37] Furthermore, it provides clear guidance in determining whether the use made of a work in any particular case is a fair use. The four factors that must be considered are:

- the purpose and character of the use, including whether such use is of a commercial nature or is for non-profit educational purposes;
- the nature of the copyrighted work;
- the amount and substantiality of the portion used in relation to the copyrighted work as a whole; and
- the effect of the use upon the potential market for or value of the copyrighted work.

Fair use doctrine also applies to unpublished works; the fact that a work is unpublished shall not itself bar a finding of fair use if such a finding is made upon consideration of all the above factors.

3.2 The Public Interest in the Courts

The public interest defence is a "common law" tradition and provides a shield against an injunction or damages. Sitting outside the statutory regime in the UK, it would justify use of copyright works without authorisation in certain circumstances, although its application in the regime is complicated.[38]

The UK courts recognise that, if the allegedly infringing act is in the access public interest, this can give a valid defence despite the fact that the CDPA did not give the court any general power to enable such act. The courts note that if the work is not published or confidential, the defence

---

[37] See Section 107, Limitations on exclusive rights: Fair use.
[38] See R. Burrell & A. Coleman, *Copyright Exceptions: The Digital Impact* (2005), 80–81.

is unlikely to succeed, and it also depends on the status of the work from which a substantial part is copied. Such defence would be based on the court's inherent jurisdiction to refuse an action for infringement of copyright where the enforcement of copyright would offend against the policy of the law. This inherent power has been preserved by section 171(3) of the CDPA: "nothing . . . affects any rule of law preventing or restricting the enforcement of copyright, on grounds of public interest or otherwise". In theory, the access public interest would allow the courts in rare cases to refuse to enforce copyright for the balance of interests.

On 30 August 1997, the day before their deaths, Princess Diana and her friend Dodi Fayed visited Villa Windsor, Mr Mohammed Al Fayed's property in Paris. Mr Al Fayed was Dodi's father. That visit, including times, was recorded on videotape by security cameras. Murrell, an employee of the security company, gave a copy of printed stills that showed the time of the couple's arrival and departure to *The Sun* in return for payment. *The Sun* published the stills on 2 September 1998, disputing Mr Al Fayed's assertion made two days earlier in the *Daily Mirror* that Princess Diana and Dodi were making marriage arrangements, and that the couple had been at Villa Windsor for at least two hours with an interior designer. The stills showed that Mr Al Fayed had given false information about the length of the couple's visit to the villa. The security company that owned the videotape commenced proceedings for infringement of copyright and sought summary judgment. *The Sun* claimed that the use of the stills was fair dealing for the purpose of reporting current events under s.30(2) of the CPDA and was in the public interest, meaning the access public interest in our terminology. This was because the use exposed the falsity of Mr Fayed's claims in a matter of public concern.

These were the facts and the legal arguments in the famous case, *Hyde Park v Yelland*.[39] Jacob J in the first instance upheld both defences and the security company appealed. Jacob J's judgment was then overturned in the Court of Appeal, where the leading judgment was given by Aldous LJ.

In reply to the defences, the Court of Appeal accepted that the use of the stills related to "current events", although the publication of the stills occurred over a year after the August 1997 Villa Windsor visit. The claims made by Mr Al Fayed in the *Daily Mirror* had given the August visit fresh impetus, and the resulting media coverage made the use of the stills "current". The Court of Appeal stated that for the purpose of deciding whether the fair dealing defence was allowed it was appropriate to take into account the motives of the alleged infringement, the extent and

---

[39]   *Hyde Park Residence Ltd v David Yelland* [1999] RPC 655–672.

purpose of the use and whether that extent was necessary for the purpose of reporting the events in question. The court had to judge the fairness by the objective standard of whether a fair-minded and honest person would have dealt with the copyright work in the manner in which *The Sun* did. In this case the court's view was that it would not. A fair-minded and honest person would not pay for dishonestly taken stills and publish them when their only relevance was that the couple had stayed at the villa for only 28 minutes.

In *Hyde Park*, both Aldous LJ and Jacob J cited the impressive judgment given by Ungoed-Thomas J in *Beloff v Pressdram Ltd*,[40] which affirmed that the public interest defence may be available to an action for infringement of copyright. The claimant was a political correspondent with *The Observer*. Without the claimant's consent, a journal called *Private Eye* reproduced the secret memorandum about a conversation between the claimant and a senior politician. *Private Eye* defended its action on the ground that the disclosure of the memorandum was in the public interest. Although the defence of public interest did not apply in the case (because the publication of the memorandum did not disclose any iniquity or misdeed), Ungoed-Thomas J stated that "public interest is a defence outside and independent of statutes, is not limited to copyright cases and is based on a general principle of common law".[41]

The court stated that there was no defence of public interest to an action for infringement of copyright in this case. However, the courts did have an inherent jurisdiction not to allow their process to be used in certain circumstances. That jurisdiction could be exercised in the case of an action in which copyright was sought to be enforced just as it could be exercised in the case of enforcement of a contract that offended against the policy of the law, for example, because the contract was immoral. The difficulty was to define the circumstances under which that was appropriate. Since copyright is assignable the circumstances have to derive from the work in question, not from ownership of the copyright. Further, the court would be entitled to refuse to enforce copyright if the work was, for example, immoral, scandalous, contrary to family life, injurious to public life, public health and safety or the administration of justice, which falls into the public policy. In this case, the stills may have been of interest to the public, but there was no need in the public interest to publish them when the information could have been made available by *The Sun* without infringement of copyright.

---

[40] *Beloff v Pressdram Ltd* [1973] All ER 241–273.
[41] See para h, 259.

This was further developed in a later case, *Ashdown v Telegraph Group Ltd.*[42] The claimant in this case was a Member of Parliament and the former leader of the Liberal Democrat Party. In October 1999, he made a minute of a meeting he attended with the Prime Minister, a copy of which was disclosed to the defendant newspaper. The defendant subsequently published a number of articles incorporating substantial sections of the minute. In December 1999 the claimant commenced proceedings against the defendant for breach of confidence and infringement of copyright. On the claimant's application for summary judgment of the copyright claim, the defendant contended that it had good defences to the claim under section 30 and section 171 of the CDPA. The defendant also contended that, by article 10 of the European Convention on Human Rights ("freedom of expression"), in every action for infringement of copyright the court was required to consider all the individual facts to ascertain whether the restriction on the right of freedom of expression was necessary in a democratic society, notwithstanding that the facts did not bring the case within any of the statutory exceptions or defences. The defence was rejected both at first instance by the Vice-Chancellor and then by the Court of Appeal.

The Vice-Chancellor acknowledged in his judgment that it was arguable that the publication was in the public interest and he rejected a submission that an arguable public interest defence to the copyright claim could be fashioned from Article 10, or from section 171(3) of the CDPA construed in the light of Article 10.[43] The court accepted, however, that copyright could act as an illegitimate restriction on freedom of expression in certain circumstances and held that in such circumstances a general public interest defence would be available, for which section 171(3) provided the foundation. The court was obedient to the principle laid down by the Court of Appeal in *Hyde Park*, that the public policy concern applies where works (i) are immoral, scandalous or contrary to family life, (ii) are injurious to public life, public health and safety or the administration of justice, or (iii) incite or encourage others to act in a way referred to in (ii).

The Court of Appeal disagreed with the Vice-Chancellor on some of the points and also disagreed with the approach of Aldous LJ in the *Hyde Park* case on the question of public interest as a defence to a copyright claim. The Court of Appeal considered whether the newspaper could claim the defences of fair dealing or public interest pursuant to the CPDA. Fair dealing was held to be not applicable, since it was unnecessary for so

---

42   *Paddy Ashdown MP PC v Telegraph Group Ltd* [2002] Ch 149.
43   See para 35.

much of the minute to have been reproduced verbatim. The publication was also held to be not in the public interest, when only the most colourful extracts from the minute had been reproduced for the purposes of increasing the newspaper's profits. In the end, the Court of Appeal concluded that there may be circumstances where the public interest requires the verbatim publication of copyright material. However, these are rare.

This has been further confirmed by a later case. On 17 March 2006, the Prince of Wales was granted a summary judgment against Associated Newspaper Limited for infringement of copyright in relation to the publication of a series of articles based upon an unpublished journal written by the plaintiff.[44] Blackburne J rejected the defence of "fair dealing for the purposes of reporting current events"[45] as the articles published by the defendant were not confined to dealing with current events, and the overall theme of the articles, and the use of extracts from the journal therein, appeared to be solely for the purpose of reporting on the revelation of the contents of the journal as an event in itself. The defence of "fair dealing for the purposes of criticism or review"[46] also failed on the basis that it requires that the copyright work has already been lawfully made available to the public, which in this case it had not. Further, the court turned down the public interest defence provided by section 171(3) CDPA for lack of any clear public interest considerations. The judge stated that, to succeed, specific clear public interest considerations would be required over and above those set out in the fair dealing defences. In this case, the defendant failed to establish that either the fair dealing or public interest defences could apply.

Also, the balance between Article 8 of the European Convention on Human Rights 1950, ("right to respect for private life"), and the Article 10 right to freedom of expression was examined.[47] Blackburne J referred to a dictum of Eady J that "even where there is a genuine public interest, alongside a commercial interest in the media in publishing articles or photographs, sometimes such interests would have to yield to the individual citizen's right to the effective protection of private life".[48]

Such statements also represent the courts' interpretations of different

---

[44] See para 5.35, *HRH The Prince of Wales v Associated Newspapers Ltd* [2006] EWHC 522 (Ch); [2006] EWCA Civ 1776.

[45] See s.30(2) CDPA 1988.

[46] See s.30(1).

[47] See also P. Mitchell & S. Bourn, 'HRH The Prince of Wales v Associated Newspapers Limited: Copyright versus the Public Interest', *Ent. L.R.* (2006), **17**(7), 210–13.

[48] See para 120; and also para 57, *McKennitt v Ash* [2005] EWHC 3003 (QB); [2006] EMLR 178.

dimensions of the public interest in copyright and are divergent from the Chinese courts' understanding in general, as will be seen later in a number of cases. In addition to the fair dealing doctrine, the UK courts recognise a common law defence of public interest, the access public interest, which is incorporated into, yet not defined in, copyright law.

3.3   Discussion

Copyright as a legal concept was introduced in the Statute of Anne and has been embodied in international law to safeguard the exclusive property rights of copyright holders. But these rights are by no means unlimited; the Berne three-step test sets certain limitations and exceptions to the exclusive rights, which are a vital part of an effective copyright system and may differ extensively in national laws as individual countries may be in dissimilar developmental stages or founded on various legal traditions.

The UK fair dealing exception is an enumerated set of possible defences against any copyright-infringing acts, which can be applied to acts falling within one of the permitted use categories only, and meets particularly the Berne three-step test. While the access public interest is generally satisfied by the fair dealing doctrine, the UK case law has very limited additional concepts of public interest as a limitation on copyright and of public policy as an exclusion of certain kinds of work from copyright.

Certainly, the specific UK approach to copyright exceptions is not the only possible way of complying with the Berne three-step test. Copyright law in the US adopts a general fair use clause, which is an open exception to copyright intended to achieve a socially optimal level of protection to encourage and approve authorship, while leaving the public with sufficient information vital for the progress of society. The rights of the copyright owners may thus be restricted to facilitate education, research and dissemination of knowledge for social, economic and cultural progress, which underlines the access public interest. The US fair use clause provides a more flexible approach than fair dealing in the UK copyright; whilst it does not phrase that limitations on exclusive copyrights must be limited in certain cases only, satisfying its four factors would conform to the Berne three-step test.

4.   LEGISLATIVE DEVELOPMENTS IN CHINA

China has joined the global community since its reform and opening up and has become a signatory for major international instruments. Although China, historically, possessed the rule of man and deemed sharing intellectual works with masses honourable, as a socialist country that places the common good ahead of the individual interest, it has nevertheless adopted the rule of law in its constitutions and awarded individual rights, including copyright, albeit creating diverse tensions by so doing.

4.1 Copyright in Ancient Times

Copyright as the name of a printing control regime emerged in China with the invention of printing; compared with the European invention of printing in the fifteenth century, the technique had existed in China centuries earlier.[49] In 1907, Aural Stein discovered in Mogaoku (Dunhuang, China) a copy of a Chinese version of the Diamond Sutra, which was printed in the ninth year of the reign of the Xiantong Emperor Yizong of the Tang Dynasty (AD 868).[50] That was for many years recognised as the first book in the world ever printed from wooden blocks, until another Chinese version of a different Buddhist sutra, which was printed in Tianbao, in the reign of Emperor Xuanzong of the Tang Dynasty (AD 704–751), was found in South Korea in 1966. As Zheng has pointed out, because Chinese is composed of characters rather than a phonetic alphabet, the mere ability to print from engraved plates led to the publication of books on a comparatively large scale.[51]

Copyright as a means of printing control existed in ancient China about a hundred years after the invention of printing by movable type (AD 1042), by Bi Sheng of the Song Dynasty. According to *Shi Yi* by Luo Bi of the Song Dynasty, the Imperial Court, in order to protect the Imperial College edition of the Nine Chinese Classics, issued orders forbidding their engraving and printing by unauthorised persons. Those who wanted to engage in the engraving and printing of these books had to apply to the Imperial College for approval. That was in substance a measure taken for the protection of the exclusive right of the Imperial College to print and publish its own edition of the Nine Chinese Classics.

Another example in the Song Dynasty, a book entitled *Biographical Sketch of the Capital of the Northern Song*, was printed with the following stamp of declaration.

Printed by the Cheng Family of Mei Shan. The right has been registered with the competent authority. No reprinting without authorisation is allowed.

---

[49] UNESCO, *The ABC of Copyright* (1981), Ch. 1.
[50] 张秀民, 中国印刷史 (2006); Zhang Xiumin, *The History of Printing in China* (2006).
[51] 郑成思 《版权法》 (1997); Zheng Chengsi, *Copyright Law* (1997).

This is similar to modern copyright notices, and such forms of notice for the purpose of "rights to print" protection lasted from the Song Dynasty until the Qing Dynasty in the early twentieth century.[52]

4.2   Copyright 1903–1979

In 1903, the Qing government signed the "Renewed Sino-American Treaty of Trade and Navigation" with the US, and for the first time the word *zhuzuoquan*, "copyright", was introduced to China. In 1910, the first Chinese copyright law – the Authors' Rights in the Great Qing Empire – was promulgated, modelled on the Japanese law. This law introduced copyright for authors and a number of punishments for unapproved uses of their works.[53] Thereafter, two more copyright laws were published. The first was the 1915 Law on Authors' Rights, which was published by the government of the Northern Warlords of China and based on the 1910 Law; and the second was a 1928 Law on Authors' Rights, published by the Kuomingtang government.

When New China was proclaimed by the victorious revolutionaries in 1949, a new legal system started to be established but then ceased from the beginning of the Cultural Revolution, which was also a disaster for all creative activities throughout the nation. Copyright legislation made no progress except for three "contracts" drafted by the People's Publishing House (PPH): the PPH Standard Contract for the Submission of a Manuscript, the PPH Standard Contract for Publication of a Work, and the PPH Measures Governing Remuneration. It should be noted that the former two "contracts" were in no way parallel to the modern concept of contract but were more similar to declarations of political correctness and means of censorship; they were abolished together with the third, the tariff of remuneration, during the Cultural Revolution.

4.3   Modern Copyright Laws

Following the Reform and Opening-up Policy, the re-establishment of a modern legal system in mainland China has been fairly effective, but problematical. The remuneration system, that is, the practice of paying a contribution fee to authors, was revived, as were many other "cultural" institutions. In April 1979, China put forward the project of drafting a

---

[52]   Zheng Chengsi & M. Pendleton, *Chinese Intellectual Property & Technology Transfer Law* (1987).

[53]   张秀民, 中国印刷史 (2006); Zhang Xiumin, *The History of Printing in China* (2006).

copyright law, directly prompted by a 1979 trade agreement with the US; the agreement committed China to reciprocate copyright protection for US works under Chinese law in accordance with international copyright treaties.[54]

Nonetheless, whether China needed a copyright law was uncertain. Some then saw copyright as a law of capitalism, privileges for foreigners; to adopt copyright would damage the Chinese public's interest. Some held that China was too poor to have a copyright law; and some questioned whether the aims of copyright law would defy China's socialist ideals and policy.[55] It took Chinese lawmakers over a decade to work out an appropriate approach combining the principles of the Berne Convention with the Chinese circumstances and eventually to finalise the rules. On 7 September 1990, the 15th Session of the Standing Committee of the National People's Congress approved the Copyright Law of the People's Republic of China (1990 CCL), and on 1 June 1991 the law and its Implementing Regulations came into force.

4.3.1 The 1990 CCL

The 1990 CCL was enacted, "in accordance with the Constitution, for the purposes of protecting the copyright of authors in their literary, artistic and scientific works and the rights related to copyright, of encouraging the creation and dissemination of works which would contribute to the construction of socialist spiritual and material civilization, and of promoting the development and flourishing of socialist culture and sciences".[56] The Constitution, adopted on 4 December 1982, states that citizens

> have the freedom to engage in scientific research, literary and artistic creation and other cultural pursuits. The state encourages and assists creative endeavours conducive to the interests of the people made by citizens engaged in education, science, technology, literature, art and other cultural work.[57]

Moreover, the Constitution safeguards citizens' rights to lawful income, savings and other private property.[58]

---

[54] See P.B. Potter, *The Chinese Legal System: Globalization and Local Legal Culture* (2001). Note that the US became a signatory to the Berne Convention in November 1988, see P. Goldstein, *International Intellectual Property Law: Cases and Materials* (2001). In 1979, the US was a member of the Universal Copyright Convention (UCC).

[55] See 沈仁干, 《版权论》2001年出版 257-277页; Shen Rengan, *Discussions On Copyright* (2001) 257–77.

[56] See Article 1.

[57] See Article 47.

[58] Articles 13, 20 and 47.

In line with the Berne Convention, the 1990 CCL confirmed that copyright was an automatic exclusive right arising on creation of a work. The term of protection granted in general was the lifetime of the author plus 50 years post mortem auctoris; when the copyright was owned by an entity and also with regard to copyright in cinematographic, television, videographic or photographic works, the term of protection was 50 years after first publication of the work.[59] The law defined the works protected as "literature, art, natural science, social science, engineering technology and the like" and was applied to both published and unpublished works.[60] This all reflects the authorship public interest.

Copyright in a work belonged to its author[61] except where otherwise stated in Articles 11 to 19, although copyright might be owned by authors, or other citizens, legal entities and entities.[62] Both personality rights and property rights were authorised, that is, the right of publication, authorship, alteration, integrity and the right of exploitation and the right to remuneration.[63] Also certain neighbouring rights were granted, that is, the rights of publication of books, newspapers and periodicals, performance, sound and video recording, and broadcasting by a radio or television station.[64]

Phrased similarly to the Berne three-step test, Article 22 asserted that in certain circumstances "a work may be exploited without permission from, and without payment of remuneration to, the copyright owner, provided that the name of the author and the title of the work shall be mentioned and the other rights enjoyed by the copyright owner by virtue of this Law shall not be prejudiced". The following acts were permitted under this heading:[65]

- use of a published work for the purposes of the user's own private study, research or self-entertainment;
- appropriate quotation from a published work in one's own work for the purposes of introduction to, or comments on, a work, or demonstration of a point;

---

59   See Article 21.
60   See Article 2.
61   See Article 11.
62   See Article 9.
63   Articles 10(1)–(5).
64   Articles 29–44.
65   Applicable also to "the rights of publishers, performers, producers of sound recordings and video recordings, radio stations and television stations". See Article 22.

- use of a published work in newspapers, periodicals, radio programmes, television programmes or newsreels for the purpose of reporting current events;
- reprinting by newspapers or periodicals, or rebroadcasting by radio stations or television stations, of editorials or commentators' articles published by other newspapers, periodicals, radio stations or television stations;
- publication in newspapers or periodicals, or broadcasting by radio stations or television stations, of a speech delivered at a public gathering, except where the author has declared that publication or broadcasting is not permitted;
- translation, or reproduction in a small quantity of copies, of a published work for use by teachers or scientific researchers, in classroom teaching or scientific research, provided that the translation or reproduction shall not be published or distributed;
- use of a published work by a state organ for the purpose of fulfilling its official duties;
- reproduction of a work in its collections by a library, archive, memorial hall, museum, art gallery or similar institution, for the purposes of the display, or preservation of a copy, of the work;
- free-of-charge live performance of a published work;
- copying, drawing, photographing or video recording of an artistic work located or on display in an outdoor public place;
- translation of a published work from the Han language into minority nationality languages for publication and distribution within the country; and
- transliteration of a published work into Braille and publication of the work so transliterated.

However, not all the above permitted acts were within the Berne three-step test: some of them were too broad and imprecise. For instance, the exceptions for the media would certainly conflict with the normal exploitation of copyright works, and would prejudice the legitimate interests of the authors or copyright holders. So were the provisions for use by state organs. These exceptions revealed the influence of the imperial tradition and the planned economy policy: the entire media, so-called 政府喉舌, "governments' throats and tongues", functioned for and were controlled by governments at all levels and were thus privileged.

The 1990 CCL also explicitly maintained that copyright owners, in exercising their copyright, must not prejudice the public interest, while "works the publication or distribution of which is prohibited by law" were not protected.[66] This reflected a strong public policy concept in Chinese copyright law, although no further clarifications were given with regard to "works prohibited by law". This might cover works of immorality, for example, pornography, and works of controversial political dissent.

Infringement of copyright and the consequent legal liabilities were set forth in two categories: acts that bear "civil liability for such remedies as ceasing the infringing act, eliminating the effects of the act, making a public apology or paying compensation for damages"; and acts that not only bear such civil liability, but also might "be subjected by a copyright administration department to such administrative penalties as confiscation of unlawful income from the act or imposition of a fine".[67] We will return later to the significance of this for the concept of public interest in Chinese copyright law. Here it suffices to note that copyright enforcement was made a public as well as a private matter.

The 1990 CCL also did not conform to international law in a number of ways: (1) computer databases were not protected; (2) no protection was afforded to unpublished works of foreign copyright owners; (3) although copyright was authorised as an automatic right, to file a complaint with an administrative authority or pursue litigation in a court regarding copyright infringement over computer software was possible only if the software had been registered with the software registration office; and (4) the state's power was over-stressed in the 1990 CCL. It situated the people's court as only the second option for prosecuting breach of copyright or copyright contracts, stating that a dispute over copyright should be settled by mediation first.[68]

4.3.2   Movements in the 1990s

The 1990 CCL nonetheless was one of the great efforts taken by China to integrate into the world economy and also showed its adaptation and implementation of the international copyright treaty.[69] China has since been actively building up and refining its domestic copyright system, and fulfilling its international obligations in protecting copyright. China signed the Berne Convention in October 1992, the TRIPS in 2001 and the WCT and the WPPT in June 2007.[70]

Copyright is of a territorial nature; prior to 1 June 1991 there was no

---

66   See Article 4.
67   Articles 45 and 46.
68   Articles 48 and 49.
69   Shen Rengan, *Combat Piracy and Protect Copyright* (1998).
70   See http://www.wipo.int/about-ip/en/ipworldwide/pdf/cn.pdf, retrieved on 13 March 2011.

copyright protection for works and no use of foreign works by Chinese persons constituted copyright infringement in China.[71] The situation fundamentally changed when China started to build up its modern copyright law system and acceded to international copyright conventions to begin the protection of copyright from other member countries. Reproducing and distributing the works of others (including foreigners) may amount to infringement. There have been three different stages in the evolution of copyright protection in China. Between 1979 and 1989, the first stage focused on whether there should be a system of intellectual property, and whether copyright should be protected.[72] Thereafter, until the mid-1990s, the second stage related to the existence of a "positive" position in the implementation of the first copyright law owing to the small number of copyright owners and the large percentage of imported technologies. However, the public in general considered copyright legislation as a rule benefiting foreign ventures. Finally, in recent years, people are beginning to be in a more "active" position since they are aware of the fact that the protection of copyright is not only required by international standards but also by individual authors and the creative industries inside the country; a third stage has now been reached.

The Chinese government has increasingly recognised the significance of copyright in contemporary society. Following the establishment of the State Intellectual Property Office (SIPO) in the State Council, the National Copyright Administration of the People's Republic of China (NCAC) was set up in 1985. Moreover, the Copyright Protection Centre was established in Beijing in September 1998,[73] and an official website was set up to advocate the protection of IP rights and provide information on various court decisions.[74] Meanwhile, to promote public awareness of intellectual property rights issues, China observed 26 April as the "World Intellectual Property Day" and held annual activities and training sessions to mark the occasion for building up an improved environment for use of copyright works and an enhanced copyright protection system.

Incontestably, compared with many other industrial countries, China had a rather late start in establishing the modern copyright system. Although a great deal of work has been done in the last decade or so and results have been achieved, attracting worldwide attention, the sense of

---

[71] J.C. Lazar, *Protecting Ideas and Ideals: Copyright Law in the People's Republic of China* (1996).

[72] See J.T. Simone, 'Silk Market Fakes: Light at the End of the Tunnel?' *China Business Review* (2006), **33**(1), 15–45.

[73] See http://www.chinadaily.com, retrieved on 9 March 2011.

[74] See for example http://www.sipo.gov.cn, retrieved on 9 March 2011.

copyright in society as a whole is still somewhat hazy, as illustrated by the survey discussed in the introduction. Copyright owners still lack sufficient awareness and capability to take up the weapon of the law to protect their own rights and interests. Despite the implementation of the Copyright Law, acts of infringement still occur from time to time. In certain localities, such aggravated infringing activities as piracy of others' books, audiovisual products, and computer software are still quite rampant.

As one of the biggest copyright holders of China's imported works, the US became the first country to object to the limits of Chinese copyright protection.[75] US industry associations have been the catalyst for most campaigns; their lobbying of Congress has led to IPR protection gaining an important place on the agenda of all trade negotiations in China. The US Trade Act 1974, Section 301, includes IPR infringements as an unfair trade practice in trading partner countries. Industry complaints are investigated, and a Watch List and a Priority Watch List of the worst offending countries are published annually.[76] Following a Section 301 procedure, a Memorandum of Understanding was signed between the US and China in January 1992. China pledged to strengthen its copyright laws, and improvements included the agreement to accede to the Berne Convention and to treat computer software as protected literary works.

While the scope of Chinese copyright law was narrower than the US would prefer, the enforcement of the law was also a major issue. US frustration with Chinese enforcement led the US Trade Representative (USTR) to place China on the Priority Foreign Country List again in 1994,[77] because its practices in IP, which included copyright protection, were deemed to have the greatest adverse impact on US products.[78] After six months of investigation, the US threatened China with trade sanctions unless serious measures to combat piracy of US products were undertaken. An agreement was signed on 26 February 1995, in which China bowed to the US demands.[79]

Foreign governments, chiefly the US government, believed that stronger protection of their copyrights in China, and the subsequent decrease in copyright infringement, would serve the needs of their companies trying

---

[75] See http://www.bjreview.com.cn/quotes/txt/2007-07/24/content_69996.htm, retrieved on 13 March 2011.

[76] Deng & Townsend et al., *A Guide to Intellectual Property Rights in Southeast Asia and China* (1996).

[77] See above at n. 71.

[78] K. Ho, *A Study into the Problem of Software Piracy in Hong Kong and China* (1995).

[79] See http://query.nytimes.com/gst/fullpage.html?res=990CE4DE153EF934 A15751C0A963958260, retrieved on 12 March 2011.

to break into the Chinese market. China certainly recognised the need to meet some international demands and responded by developing a comprehensive copyright law system to enforce it. As pointed out by Lazar, while the modern Chinese copyright system meets China's needs, it does not completely satisfy those of others, namely, US business concerns. Nevertheless, the copyright system in China should be recognised by the US and other governments as a legitimate legal system that reflects the cultural and social background of China while at the same time meeting the basic need of foreign businesses.[80]

Responding to the Memorandum of Understanding with the US, China promulgated the Regulations on Computer Information Network and Internet Security, Protection and Management in 1997, and also the Revised Provisional Regulations Governing the Management of Chinese Computer Information Networks Connected to International Networks, which is formulated to reinforce "the management of computer information networks connected to international networks and safeguard the healthy development of the international computer information exchange".[81] Moreover, in the same year China adopted an amendment to the Criminal Law devoting a special section to crimes related to IP infringement.[82] It stipulates that violators who gain huge profits through piracy should be sentenced to prison for no more than seven years.[83] The major demands of foreign governments were thus met.

4.3.3 The 2001 CCL

To enable accession to the WTO, a revision of the 1990 CCL was approved by the 24th Session of the Standing Committee of the 9th NPC in October 2001 (2001 CCL).[84] The main amendments include:

- extension of the scope of objects that are protected by copyright;[85]
- a more defined classification for 17 types of right granted to copyright owners;[86]

---

[80] See above at n. 71.
[81] Article 1.
[82] M. Schlesinger, 'Intellectual Property Law in China: Part I – Complying with TRIPs Requirements', *East Asian Executive Reports* (1997).
[83] 唐德华主编《著作权法新释新解》2003; Tang Dehua (ed.), *The Amendments of Copyright Law* (2003).
[84] See also http://english.peopledaily.com.cn/200111/08/eng20011108_84101. html.
[85] Articles 2, 3 and 5.
[86] Articles 9 and 10.

- narrowing of the permitted acts;[87]
- provision to regulate contracts for copyright assignment;[88] and
- specification of the legal obligations and enforcement measures that embrace criminal prosecution of certain infringing acts.[89]

In compliance with the Berne Convention and TRIPS, the 2001 CCL continues to provide for the maintenance of protection for the author's lifetime plus 50 years after death. In order to clarify the concept, the statutory Chinese term for copyright is confirmed to be both *zhuzuoquan*, right(s) arising from or in relation to work(s), and *banquan*, right(s) arising from or in relation to publication(s). A work, which is named *zuo pin* in Chinese, is defined as "a fruit of intellectual creation, in literature, arts and sciences, which is original and capable of being reproduced in a tangible medium".[90] Nine types of work are listed for the subsistence of copyright:

- written works;
- oral works;
- musical, dramatic, *quyi*, choreographic and acrobatic works;
- works of fine art and architecture;
- photographic works;
- cinematographic works and works created by virtue of an analogous method of film production;
- drawings of engineering designs, and product designs; maps, sketches and other graphic works and model works;
- computer software; and
- other works as provided for in laws and administrative regulations including folklore.[91]

Amongst these, *quyi* work requires elaboration. According to the Regulations for the Implementation of the Copyright Law 2002, *quyi* works are the traditional Chinese theatrical talking and singing, including *xiang sheng* (cross talk), *kuai shu* (clapper talk), *da gu* (ballad singing with drum accompaniment) and *ping shu* (storytelling based on classical

---

87   Articles 22 and 23.
88   See Article 25, which provides that such contracts must contain the following basic clauses: (1) title of the work; (2) category and geographic area of the assigned right; (3) assignment price; (4) date and manner of payment of the assignment price; (5) liabilities for breach of the contract; and (6) any other matters that the contracting parties consider necessary.
89   Articles 46–55.
90   郑成思 《版权法》 (1997); Zheng Chengsi, *Copyright Law* (1997).
91   See Article 6.

novels), which are all used for performance involving mainly recitation or singing, or both.

Essentially, therefore, the 2001 CCL extends the scope of the law to involve more subjects, such as architectural designs and literary and artistic works published on the Internet,[92] and granted public communication right as set out in the WCT. The 2001 CCL leaves out some important categories, including broadcasts, sound recordings and typographical arrangements, which the law provides for elsewhere. Moreover, (1) government documents, (2) reports of current events and (3) calendar, mathematical and general tables, and formulae, are three types of work excluded as non-copyright. But it is quite hard to find a consensus view as to the nature, scope and justifications for these exclusions, especially (1) and (2).

Copyright vests in the authors of works, unless the law provides otherwise. The 2001 CCL presumes the author to be the individual or unit whose name is stated on a work, unless proved to the contrary, including "service works", works created in the course of employment. This provision diverges from the previous "all belongs to the state" approach and intends to safeguard private property rights in the regime.

Rights arising from creative works are of two kinds, economic (property) rights and moral (personal) rights, the latter including the right of attribution and the right to the integrity of the work. The Anglo-American copyright tradition emphasises the economic role of copyright,[93] while authors' right is the concept of Continental copyright protection, rooted in the traditions of the French Revolution and ideas about the rights of man.[94] The historical contrast between the two traditions is reflected in current laws; as, in general, the commercial value of copyright is stressed more in the Anglo-American tradition, while its cultural value is stressed in the Continental counterpart.[95] Reflecting its own unique culture, Chinese copyright weighs both elements. Whilst the economic rights secure rights to use copyright works and receive benefits therefrom, moral rights are concerned with protecting the personality and reputation of authors and are particularly important to authors to control the use of copyright works. Since the treatment of an author's works may easily affect the author's honour and reputation, which has been always emphasised in Chinese culture, right of reputation claims tend to pervade

---

[92] See Zheng Chengsi, 'Looking into the Revision of the Trade Mark and Copyright Laws from the Perspective of China's Accession to WTO', *EIPR* (2002), **24**, 313.

[93] See above at n. 7.

[94] See above at n. 27.

[95] See above at n. 7.

Chinese copyright disputes, and sometimes even override the monetary claims.

To balance the interests of authors and of users, the 2001 CCL imposes two restrictions on the exercise of copyright, namely Article 22, "limitation on rights", and Article 24, "statutory licence". The former consists of 12 acts as follows:

- use of a published work for the purposes of the user's own private study, research or self-entertainment;
- appropriate quotation from a published work in one's own work for the purposes of introduction to, or comments on author's work, or demonstration of a point;
- reuse or citation, for any unavoidable reason, of a published work in newspapers, periodicals, radio or television programmes or any other media for the purpose of reporting current events;
- reprinting by newspapers or periodicals, or rebroadcasting by radio stations, television stations, or any other media, of articles on current issues relating to politics, economics or religion published by other newspapers, periodicals, or broadcast by other radio stations, television stations or any other media except where the author has declared that the reprinting and rebroadcasting is not permitted;
- publication in newspapers or periodicals, or broadcasting by radio stations, television stations or any other media, of a speech delivered at a public gathering, except where the author has declared that the publication or broadcasting is not permitted;
- translation, or reproduction in a small quantity of copies, of a published work for use by teachers or scientific researchers, in classroom teaching or scientific research, provided that the translation or reproduction shall not be published or distributed;
- use of a published work, within proper scope, by a state organ for the purpose of fulfilling its official duties;
- reproduction of a work in its collections by a library, archive, memorial hall, museum, art gallery or any similar institution, for the purposes of the display, or preservation of a copy, of the work;
- free-of-charge live performance of a published work, where performance neither collects any fees from the members of the public nor pays remuneration to the performers;
- copying, drawing, photographing or video recording of an artistic work located or on display in an outdoor public place;
- translation of a published work of a Chinese citizen, legal entity or any other organization from the Han language into any minority

nationality language for publication and distribution within the country; and

● transliteration of a published work into Braille and publication of the work so transliterated.

In order to be consistent with TRIPS, the 2001 CCL made a number of changes regarding limitations on rights. For example, the reuse or citation of a published work for the purpose of reporting current events was tightened.[96] The use of published works by governmental departments is confined to "within proper scope" and "for the purpose of fulfilling its official duties".[97] Even so, not all the limitations on rights may meet the Berne three-step test: for example, the defence of "use of copyright works for the purpose of self-entertainment", without a clear legitimate definition otherwise. Advocating *socialist spiritual civilisation*, the 2001 CCL confirms that, in the case of free performances of a published work, no prior authorisation and no compensation are required to be made to the author, with a twofold clarification of the term "free": the performance is free to members of the public and the audience and no remuneration is paid to the performers.[98] In addition, with regard to translations from the Han language into any minority nationality language, works can be used without the copyright owner's permission if the copyright is owned by a Chinese citizen, Chinese legal entity or any other Chinese organisation.[99] In other words, the 2001 CCL has identified a category of translation that requires the consent of copyright owners only when the copyright is owned by foreigners, and thus has provided better protection for copyright owners from foreign countries, which is also not in line with international law.

The statutory licence rules in Article 24 provide that, where the copyright owner has not declared that the work concerned is forbidden to be exploited by others, a newspaper or periodical may reprint or print an abstract of the work that was published in another newspaper or periodical, and work so published may also be exploited for public performance or for the production of a sound recording, video recording, radio programme or television programme; but subject to the payment of remuneration.

Whilst the 1990 CCL offered no provisions for collective management of copyright, the 2001 CCL set forth such, stipulating that:[100]

---

[96] See Article 22(3).
[97] See Article 22(7).
[98] See Article 22(9).
[99] See Article 22(11).
[100] See Article 8.

The copyright owners and copyright-related right holders may authorise an organisation for collective administration of copyright to exercise the copyright or any copyright-related right. After authorisation, the organisation for collective administration of copyright may, in its own name, claim the right for the copyright owners and copyright-related right holders, and participate, as an interested party, in litigation or arbitration relating to the copyright or copyright-related right.

The 2001 CCL also makes specific modification on the subject of legal liabilities and enforcement measures. For the first time, contract law and criminal law are introduced into copyright. Where a person fails to fulfil the contractual obligations or executes them in a manner that is not in conformity with the agreed conditions of the contract, the person will bear civil liability in accordance with the relevant provisions of the Contract Law[101] and other relevant laws and regulations. In circumstances where the act constitutes a crime, the criminal liability shall be prosecuted consistently with the criminal law.[102]

Following the 2001 CCL, the Regulations on the Implementation of the Copyright Law and the Regulations on the Protection of Computer Software were both revised in 2002 in which the restriction of copyright disputes over software is eliminated; foreign right holders now may lodge complaints with any copyright administrative authorities. The amended measures allow for the preservation of property and evidence before legal proceedings are instituted, and prescribe tougher penalties for copyright infringement. It has raised the evidential burden under the civil procedure concerning copyright litigation on publishers or producers allegedly reproducing works without acquiring the relevant rights. In addition, copyright and related rights are upheld by Chinese Civil Law[103] and copyright infringers may be subject to criminal penalties.[104]

4.3.4 The 2010 CCL

Chinese copyright law was revised, for the second time, in the 13th meeting of the Standing Committee of the 11th National People's Congress on 26 February 2010 and came into force on 1 April 2010 (hereafter referred

---

[101]   Which was adopted at the Second Session of the Ninth National People's Congress on 15 March 1999.

[102]   See Article 47. The amended Criminal Law of the People's Republic of China 1997 provides measures for copyright infringement crime; prior to it, there were no such provisions and copyright infringements were prosecuted only for civil or administrative liabilities.

[103]   See Article 94.

[104]   See Article 217, Criminal Law of the People's Republic of China 1997.

to as the "2010 CCL"). Two changes were made, namely, the revision of Article 4 and the addition of Article 26.[105] While Article 4 of the 2001 CCL claimed that:

> Works the publication or distribution of which is prohibited by law shall not be protected by this Law. Copyright owners, in exercising their copyright, shall not violate the Constitution or laws or prejudice the public interests.

Article 4 of the 2010 CCL reads:

> Copyright holders shall not violate the Constitution or laws or jeopardize public interests when exercising their copyright. The State shall supervise and administrate the publication and dissemination of works in accordance with the law.

The revision of Article 4 may be seen as a reaction to the WTO decision in March 2009, which was in response to a complaint from the US in 2007 against China's IP protection and enforcement, including its exclusion of copyright for works offending the state, and held that the lack of protection for works prohibited from publication or distribution was not in line with the Berne Convention or TRIPS. The effects of revised Article 4 could be significant as it may provide protection for previously prohibited works. Nonetheless, such provisions might also be of no consequence in practice. It will be worth observing how this amendment will be interpreted by the courts and administrative authorities and whether any clarification is to be offered in the future.

4.4 The Chinese Experiments in Cyberspace

Copyright has been often misunderstood as "publishing" or "rights to publish" in China.[106] Historically, publishing and copyright had a close link. Publishers of books were quick to realise that sustaining a viable publishing business was dependent upon a right to prevent others copying. When the Statute of Anne was promulgated, the law was not merely a book publisher's registration law; what it protected was the copying of printed work. The copyright situation is closely linked to the development of copying technology – the easier to copy, the harder to protect copyright

---

[105] Article 26 states that "Where a copyright is pledged, both the pledger and pledgee shall undergo the formalities for registration with the copyright administration department under the State Council."

[106] See above at n. 90.

– and this is especially true in the information age.[107] Some scholars regard technical devices as a solution to private copying.[108] Along with the rapid growth of the Internet, enormous changes have occurred as regards means of publishing and copying and more, which greatly challenged the late instituted Chinese copyright law, especially its implementation in cyberspace.

The first Chinese cyberlaw was promulgated by the State Council on 1 February 1996, and was entitled "Provisional Regulations of the People's Republic of China Governing the Management of Computer Information Networks Hooked Up With International Networks" (Provisional Regulations). It was soon revised on 20 May 1997. The Provisional Regulations legalised connections between the Chinese domestic network and the international Internet. Thereafter, various cyberlaws have been enforced, on the one hand, to support the rapid development of ICT over the country and, on the other hand, to catch up with the international treaties' requirements.

The 1990 CCL did not take the Internet into account since it was not then introduced in China. And for a few years, Chinese people regarded the Internet as a great place for "free stuff" such as music, films, games, software and books, and did not think that copyright law would also apply to cyberspace.[109]

4.4.1   *Chen Weihua*, the almost forgotten pioneer case re authorship

The 1990 CCL was eventually challenged to deal with Internet issues in May 1999, when Chen Weihua, an Internet user, appealed to Beijing Haidian District People's Court against Computer Business Information (CBI), a publisher. Chen Weihua claimed that CBI had infringed his copyright and asked for a public apology, a remuneration of RMB 231 yuan for the article together with punitive damages of RMB 50 000 yuan for the infringement. The plaintiff, whose name online was Wu Fang, wrote a paper, 'A Playful Discussion on MAYA' (MAYA), talking about 3D animation designs, and uploaded it on his own homepage, '3D Sesame Street' in May 1998. Without Chen Weihua's consent, CBI published MAYA in its newspaper in October the same year. In November, the plaintiff emailed the defendant, declaring himself to be the author of the article. In

---

107   W. Hayhurst, 'Copyright and the Copying Machine', *Canadian Business Law Review* (1984), **9**(2), 129.

108   See above at n. 20.

109   See for example 陈丽英, 免费Internet: "中西套餐", 《互联网世界》 1999年 4期86页; Chen Liying, 'Free Internet: "The Chinese and the Western Set Menu"', *Chinese Internet Times* (1999), **4**, 86.

December, the plaintiff faxed the defendant, alleging copyright infringement. The defendant received both the email and the fax, but rejected the plaintiff's request for a written apology and a remuneration of RMB 231 yuan.

In court, CBI argued that the 1990 CCL did not take the Internet into account; and that the paper was recommended by a reader and was sent in via an email not referring to any copyright restriction. CBI had replied to the reader asking for more information about the author but had got no response. Therefore, the defendant said that CBI had no intention to breach Chen Weihua's copyright and should not make any apologies.

In April 1999, judgment was given for the plaintiff. First, the court explained expansively, on the one hand, the definition of *zuo pin*, "works", and held that MAYA was a work protected by copyright even though there were no specific legislative provisions about works published on the Internet. The plaintiff proved that the work was written by him in May 1998, that he was copyright owner of the work, and that he uploaded the work to his homepage, which meant the work was published. The court stated that MAYA was confirmed as a work owing to its being fixed in a digital format stored in the hard drive of a computer. It was uploaded to the Internet via a www server and was kept stable to permit public access or reproduction through any host. This fixed the work in a tangible medium that could be kept stable to allow the public to reproduce or access it. The court concluded that CBI's unauthorised publication of Mr Chen's work in the newspaper was a commercial act that infringed the plaintiff's rights to use the work and to be remunerated, and hence infringed the plaintiff's copyright. Nonetheless, the plaintiff's claim of RMB 50 000 yuan punitive damages was rejected, for he failed to provide evidence to support his claim of loss.

Based on Article 11 ("ownership of copyright") and Article 46(2) ("reproducing and distributing a work for commercial purposes without the consent of the copyright owner"), the court ordered CBI, first, to cease the infringement immediately; secondly, to apologise to Chen Weihua and publish the apology in its newspaper; thirdly, to remunerate Chen Weihua RMB 924 yuan; and finally, to pay Chen Weihua the litigation fee RMB 2017 yuan.[110] Neither the defendant nor the plaintiff appealed the ruling.

The *Chen Weihua* case raised questions about copyright protection in an Internet environment to the Chinese law. Evidently, the 1990 CCL offered no specific provision for enforcing copyright on the Internet and was

---

[110] See 北京市海淀区人民法院民事判决书 (1999) 海知初字第18号, Beijing Haidian District People's Court Judgment Number (1999), 18.

lagging behind the development of IT. The case showed, on the one hand, that the courts had appreciated the authorship public interest and took a sensible and flexible approach to enforce copyright in cyberspace despite the absence of statute law, and, on the other hand, that a revision of the 1990 CCL to meet the rapid growth of the Internet was urgently required.

4.4.2 Authorship and access

In June 1999, another lawsuit was filed in the same court. This time, six renowned Chinese writers – Wang Meng, Zhang Chenzhi, Zhang Kangkang, Bi Shumin, Zhang Jie and Liu Zhengyun (the Six Writers) – sued Shiji Internet Communication Technology Ltd (Shiji) for its copyright infringement online. The defendant was a leading company in the IT industry based in Beijing and it owned a website http://www.bol. com.cn, Beijing Online. A great number of literary works were collected on Beijing Online, and registered users were allowed to download them for free. Works of the named six famous Chinese writers were included. The Six Writers demanded judgment for infringement of copyright and remuneration and punitive compensation for both economic and spiritual damage.

Shiji defended on the basis that the 1990 CCL had not extended to the Internet and no regulations provided that permission must be obtained for distributing published works online, or set benchmarks for remunerating copyright owners in such circumstances. In addition, all works were collected from other Internet sites for archival purposes, open to the public for free, and provided full information about the authors. Shiji had no intention to infringe the Six Writers' copyright and did not damage the Six Writers' economic and spiritual interests.

In September 1999, judgment was given in favour of the Six Writers. The court explained in detail that, although the 1990 CCL was not up to date with the newly developed technology of the Internet, it could be understood that the digitisation of a work was only a change of format, not a new work. Authors certainly had copyright over their digital works and the entitlement to decide whether their works could be distributed and in what format. Thus, the first part of the appeal was allowed, but the other claim was dismissed. The court stated that the judgment took into account, not only the copyright owners' and company's benefits, but also the general public's interest in accessing works, which was of great importance to socialist China.

Based on 1990 CCL Article 10 and Article 45(6), (8), the court ruled Shiji must: firstly, cease use of the Six Writers' works immediately; secondly, publish an apology for its infringement on Beijing Online's homepage; and finally, remunerate the plaintiffs according to the number of words of their works and pay the litigation costs.[111] In October, Shiji appealed to Beijing First Intermediate People's Court with the same defences, and the first instance judgment was upheld in December 1999.

Owing to the involvement of celebrities, this court case gained great attention over the country. Central China Television (CCTV) broadcast the entire trial live on 18 September 1999. Numerous members of the general public attended the hearings, and also carried out intensive discussions online; for many of them it was the first time they had heard the word copyright.[112] The case was greatly analysed by lawmakers, law practitioners, academics and ISPs,[113] mainly urging the law to provide specific clauses for enforcing copyright on the Internet. Other voices could be heard: some said that the court was influenced by US practice, and cautioned against its adoption in China;[114] and some believed that the court had exceeded its jurisdiction by expanding the scope of the Copyright Law without legitimate authorisation.[115]

It should be noted that the *Six Writers* case not only firmly confirmed copyright protection in cyberspace but also proclaimed the access public interest in Chinese copyright law, as the judge pointed out that it is also important to ensure that works can be accessed cheaply by the masses, even though the defendant did not raise such argument to the court.

4.4.3   Authorship and access on trial after the 2001 CCL

Article 47(1) of the 2001 CCL stipulates that infringing acts on the Internet can bring about prosecution, which is also a response to the cases

---

[111]   See 北京市海淀区人民法院民事判决书 (1999) 海知初字第57号, Beijing Haidian District People's Court Judgment Number (1999), 57.

[112]   See http://news.sina.com.cn/china/1999-9-19/15748.html, retrieved on 9 January 2011.

[113]   See 张广良, 王蒙,张抗抗,张承志,张杰,毕淑敏,刘震云等六位作家诉世纪互联通信技术有限公司 《科技与法律》 2000年第1期84–89页; Zhang Guangliang, 'Six Writers v Shiji Internet Communication Technology Ltd', *Law and Technology* (2000), **1**, 84–89. 温旭, 简评王蒙等六作家诉北京某网站著作权侵权 《科技与法律》 2000年第1期93–94页; Wen Xu, 'Comments on Six Writers v Beijing On Line', *Law and Technology* (2000), **1**, 93–94. 张平, 网络环境下著作权法的作用:王蒙等六作家诉世纪互联一案的思考 《科技与法律》 2000年第1期90–92页; Zhang Ping, 'Copyright on the Internet: Review Six Writers v Shiji Ltd', *Law and Technology* (2000), **1**, 90–92.

[114]   See http://news.sina.com.cn/comment/1999-12-14/41971.html, retrieved on 9 March 2011.

[115]   See http://news.sina.com.cn/comment/1999-10-21/24207.html, retrieved on 9 March 2011.

mentioned above.[116] The new rules were soon tested in Beijing Haidian District People's Court. In April 2002, the plaintiff, Chen Xingliang, a law professor from Peking University, found that the China Digital Library Ltd (Digital Library) had collected his three academic books on its website, www.d-library.com.cn, without his authorisation. By paying a very small sum as a subscription, users could become members of the Digital Library and then browse or download its collections for free.[117] Users could download the full copies online. Based on Article 37 of the 2001 CCL, Professor Chen appealed against the Digital Library's infringement of the copyright and applied for compensation of RMB 400 000 yuan.

In court, the Digital Library defended the claim on the basis that, as a non-commercial organisation leading the exploitation and advance of digital libraries in China, it was aware of copyright issues and attempted to establish an improved system of online copyright authorisation. Moreover, as a non-profit-making digital library, its uses of Professor Chen's books were justified by a defence of the access public interest.

After confirming Professor Chen's copyright in the three books, the court explained that Article 10(12) of the 2001 CCL should be understood to provide that the author had exclusive rights to communicate his work to the public, by wire or wireless means. According to Article 47(1), the Digital Library had breached Professor Chen's copyright.[118]

The court also accepted that the Digital Library's uses of works had met a public demand and had a fair objective. But the digitisation of works without copyright owners' permission was unlawful reproduction, and providing digital copies on the Internet to members had violated the copyright owner's right of remuneration and made future unlawful copying possible.

In June 2002, the court held that: (1) the defence of access public interest failed and the appeal was permitted, since it was breach of the plaintiff's copyright to upload books in digital format without authorisation; (2) the Digital Library must cease the infringement without delay; (3) the Digital Library must pay Professor Chen compensation of RMB 80 000 yuan.

The court in *Chen Xingliang v China Digital Library* stated that it is a breach of copyright to disseminate others' works on the Internet without

---

116 See http://english.peopledaily.com.cn/200111/08/eng20011108_84101.html, retrieved on 9 March 2011.
117 The membership policy is broadly adopted in Chinese libraries, including the public libraries, and non-member users are not allowed to borrow books etc.
118 Note that public communication right is awarded in Chinese law since 2006.

the authors' permission or without taking any action to tamper with the right of information administration. It also led to a discussion on the public interest defence. The major arguments say that, in line with the library privilege, the law should also offer digital libraries exceptions to stimulate their development, in the name of the access public interest. The opposing viewpoints deem the compensation should have been much higher, as it is crucial to force digital libraries in the country to take a strict approach towards copyright from the beginning, in the name of the authorship public interest.[119]

In this case, books were digitised and distributed online in the virtual library. Current laws in all countries state that book publication, circulation and usage involve intellectual property rights, and this applies to electronic books. The 2001 CCL regards storing works in digital form in the electronic media as "copying". Offering digitised works for others to skim, read, copy and print through networking also means public communication. People who download, copy or print others' works without the authors' permission violate copyright laws and are liable. Electronic media should get permission from copyright owners, and measures such as charging browsers and using codes and digital watermarks should be taken to prevent illegal downloading.

Nonetheless, questions arise: may digital libraries enjoy the exceptions for libraries; how will users read electronic books more cheaply than going to libraries; how can authors be compensated; how can digital libraries find a balance between the two groups' interests? If technical devices are the only methods to prevent unlawful copying, then collective contract may be an approach towards better online copyright protection.

In brief, the three cases discussed above have illustrated the enforcement of Chinese copyright on the Internet and the progress of the law. Regarding copyright on the Internet in China, three periods may be summarised: first, from the middle 1990s to the late 1990s, a copyright-free Internet period, with the 1990 CCL not challenged in this regard until 1999; second, from the late 1990s to 2001, a questioning period, when the debates were focused on whether there should be a system of copyright in cyberspace and whether digitising a work created a new work; and third, from 2001 on, a period of exploiting and perfecting the law, when discussions have gone further including privileges for digital libraries, the access public interest defence, enforcement and so on.

---

119   See for example 谭玲玲, 首例数字化图书馆侵权案给我们的启示 «法治论丛» 2002年第6期76–79页; Lingling Tan, 'The Enlightenment of the First Digital Library Case in China', *Law Journal of Shanghai Administrative Cadre Institute of Politics & Law* (2002), 6, 76–79.

Rulings against the award of damages in the above cases also reflect the courts' use of the access public interest, even if the defence as such was not granted in the judgment. As a developing country, online reading in China has been playing a very positive role in raising the education levels of its population. For the general public of the massive poor areas, it is much more possible to read in an Internet café with very basic facilities: it is far cheaper and more convenient than to buy or to travel hundreds of miles to a big town with a library. Influenced by tradition and socio-economic conditions, Chinese courts are obviously taking a rather different approach from courts in the UK with regard to the access public interest in copyright: those who enable access should not have to pay full damages for the infringement of copyright involved. This also reaffirms the relevant opinion given by participants of the survey.

4.4.4   Other relevant rules

In recent years, more infringing acts via the Internet have been taken into serious consideration in China.[120] On 30 April 2005 the Measures on Administrative Protection Rules of Internet Copyright (the Measures) were jointly released by the National Copyright Administration of China (NCAC) and the Ministry of Information Industry (MII). In addition, the WCT and the WPPT were enforced in China on 9 June 2007.[121] They require Chinese law to protect copyright in literary and artistic works and the rights and interests of performers and producers of phonograms on the Internet effectively.

The 2005 Measures include 19 articles for the purpose of enhancing the protection of copyright on the Internet: from unauthorised dissemination on the one hand, to improving administrative enforcement on the other.[122] They apply to both services – including uploading, storing, linking or searching online literary, audio, or video products in accordance with the instructions of the Internet content providers, without editing, revising and selecting the stored or transmitted content[123] – and the administrative protection of the rights of performers, audio and video producers, and

---

120   See Article 47(1).
121   See   http://english.ipr.gov.cn/ipr/en/info/Article.jsp?a_no=45335&col_no=118&dir=200701 and http://english.ipr.gov.cn/ipr/en/info/Article.jsp?a_no=45342&col_no=118&dir=200701.
122   See 国家版权局就"打击网络侵权盗版专项行动"答记者问; NCAC News Conference: Crack Down Actions on the Internet Copyright Infringement, retrieved on 18 January 2011 at www.gapp.gov.cn/GalaxyPortal/inner/zsww/zongsu3.jsp?articleid=9922&boardpid=715&boardid1=11501010111515.
123   See Article 2.

other copyright-related rights holders to spread their performances on audio and video products via the Internet.[124]

In addition, the Measures give practical guidance on how to implement the regulations. For instance, when a copyright owner finds that an ISP has violated his/her copyright, a notice should be sent to the ISP,[125] including the following items:

- copyright certificate for the alleged infringing content;
- specific identification proof, address and contact information;
- location of the infringing content on the information network;
- related evidence of copyright infringement; and
- declaration of authenticity for the notification.[126]

The Regulations on Protection of the Right of Communication through Information Network (Communication Right Regulations) were issued by Prime Minister Wen Jiabao on 18 May 2006 and enacted on 1 July 2006, which is in accordance with the WCT. The Communication Right Regulations clarify Article 10(12) of the 2001 CCL as "the right of communication to the public" and are specific. The term "right of communication through information network" is defined as the right to make available works, performances, or sound and video recordings to the public by wire or wireless means so that the public may choose a place and time to access those works, performances, or sound and video recordings.[127] The regulations aim to promote such right, strike online copyright infringement and seek a balance between the right owners' interest and the public interest in cyberspace.[128] No one should, without legitimate authorisation, intentionally remove, amend or provide electronic rights management information of works, performances, or sound and video recordings available to the public.[129] Copyright owners are granted legitimate rights to control their works' communication on the Internet and ISPs are obliged to correct any infringing acts, together with exceptions including uses for the following purposes: classroom teaching and research, non-commercial exploitation for blind people, lawful administrative or judicial action and the test of system or network.[130]

---

[124] See Article 17.
[125] See Article 7.
[126] See Article 8.
[127] See Article 26.
[128] See Article 1.
[129] See Article 5.
[130] See Article 12(1)–(4).

It is, however, stipulated that, for non-commercial purpose, libraries, archives, memorial halls, museums and art galleries may digitise their legitimate collections and provide users with access to their collections in digital format on condition that such works are kept within their premises.[131] Exceptional uses of works including wording, music, single art and photography pieces for course plans in compulsory education or state educational programming are authorised by the Regulations.[132] Furthermore, the Communication Right Regulations contain a lengthy Article 9, which offers lawful exemptions to uses of copyrighted works intended to alleviate poverty over the country, provided that such uses should have no direct or indirect economic gain.

Another eight exceptions for the use of copyrighted works on the Internet are granted:[133]

- introducing, analysing and commenting upon a published work;
- news reporting;
- school teaching or scientific research;
- acts of a state organ for the purpose of fulfilling its official duties;
- translation of a published work of a Chinese citizen, legal entity or any other organisation from the Han language into any minority nationality language for publication and distribution within the country;
- changing published wording-works into the format that blind people could appreciate for non-commercial purpose;
- providing the public with published articles regarding current events in fields of political and economic issues; and
- providing public speeches to the public.

The protective measures include:

- protecting the network communication right generally by requiring the users to obtain permission from and pay right holders for this, except where otherwise provided for in laws and administrative regulations;
- protecting the technological measures employed by right holders to guard the works, including the prohibition of the circumventing acts, devices and service;
- prohibiting the removal or alteration of the electronic rights

---

[131]   See Article 7.
[132]   See Article 8.
[133]   See Article 6.

management information if the defendant knew or should have known the electronic rights management has been removed or altered; and

- establishing the summary procedure of "notice to delete".

The last measure, notice to delete, establishes a brief procedure for settling disputes over copyright infringement on the Internet. When copyright infringement acts occur, the right owners may contact the ISPs, requesting the unauthorised works to be removed or hyperlinks to be disconnected; the ISPs should thus seize the infringing acts immediately or convey the notification to parties responsible for providing such works or hyper-links.[134] This controversial procedure will be analysed in line with the Berne three-step test in subsequent chapters.

Any person who commits an act of infringement prohibited by the Communication Right Regulations shall bear civil liability to such remedies as ceasing the infringing act, eliminating the effects of the act, making an apology or paying damages. Where public interests are prejudiced, the copyright administration may order the person to cease the act of infringement, confiscate the unlawful gains and impose a fine of up to RMB 100 000 yuan. If the circumstances are serious, the copyright administration may also confiscate the equipment used for providing the network service. Where the acts constitute crime, the infringers shall be prosecuted for their criminal liabilities.[135]

Nonetheless, as admitted by the Legislative Affairs Commission, the Network Regulation 2006 leaves some issues with very general provisions and does not refer to some other issues at all owing to inexperience and the complexity of copyright protection in the network environment.[136]

Breach of copyright on the Internet has been continually increasing over the country. In 2007 half of the cases related to copyright infringement were Internet-based.[137] It is urged that the Chinese lawmakers ought to make the regulations not only more specific, but also more rational and clear, in order to meet the rapid development of the Internet as well as to balance the interest of copyright owners, ISPs and the mass of Internet users.

---

[134] Articles 14 and 15.

[135] Articles 19–25.

[136] See http://www.gov.cn/zwhd/2006-05/29/content_294127.htm, retrieved on 14 March 2011.

[137] See http://news.sohu.com/20080421/n256429133.shtml, retrieved on 14 March 2011.

5. DISCUSSION

Copyright law protects private property rights and has been standardised internationally, although with diversity based upon political and economic policies in individual countries. Generally speaking, the public interest in terms of copyright embraces diverse dimensions, namely, authorship, access and public policy. From the capitalist point of view, property should be owned by individuals and can be operated for profit; the authorship public interest has been widely recognised. The doctrine of the access public interest is for the purpose of balancing the exclusive property rights of the copyright owners with the social benefit in the free dissemination of information. Authors or owners of works are thus granted exclusive rights subject to limitations and exceptions, for a certain period of time. The access public interest would involve only a very limited limitation of property in rare circumstances and the owner remains free to exploit the work commercially. Moreover, according to the comparative evidence discussed in this chapter, the access public interest in the UK has been employed only by the media sector and has never succeeded in actual fact nor been used by the library or other sectors. The fair use doctrine in the US provides a set of guidelines pursuant to which researchers, educators, scholars and others may use copyrighted works without seeking permission or paying royalties, and presents a defence against accusations of copyright violation for people who reasonably believed that their use of a copyrighted work was fair use. But once a use is challenged, the user will have the burden of proving that such use qualified as fair use. Nonetheless, the UK courts accept that the access public interest may in exceptional circumstances give rise to a limited right of using copyrighted works without the copyright owner's authorisation, although such defence must not override copyright in general.

Obviously, it has not been easy for China to find an appropriate place in its socialist system for modern copyright and the concept of securing private property rights in general. The Chinese government was anxious that upholding such rights would threaten its socialism ideology and challenge its long-standing command of central control. Nonetheless, the imperfect Chinese copyright law was introduced late in 1990, stating that its purposes were for protecting the copyright of authors in their literary, artistic and scientific works and rights related to copyright, while encouraging the creation and dissemination of works that would contribute to the construction of socialist spiritual and material civilisation, and promote the development and flourishing of socialist culture and sciences.[138] These

---

[138]   See Article 1.

purposes reflect two principles: protection of the legitimate rights of authors and disseminators of works so as to encourage them to undertake such endeavours and thereby promote the creation and wide dissemination of excellent works; and coordination of the beneficial relationships among authors, disseminators and the general public so as to encourage the public to take an active part in social and cultural activities with a view to enhancing the scientific and cultural quality of the whole nation and promoting the development and prosperity of culture and sciences and the construction of spiritual and material civilisation in its socialist setting.

Chinese copyright is strongly influenced by a traditional and socialist culture, which mainly includes, on the one hand, Confucianism, emphasising the values of harmony, sharing works with society and learning by copying; and, on the other hand, Chinese socialism, stressing social value and public welfare where individuals are obliged to share their creations and developments with their community. Chinese copyright thus has its particular characteristics compared with other countries such as the UK. First of all, China has struggled to make both the idea and the system of private property rights harmonious with its socialist regime. Secondly, the notion of law that Chinese people have is undergoing variation and alteration. And thirdly, people in China have a very deep-rooted and different notion of the public interest owing to the influences of Chinese culture. The concept has an additional dimension, that is, the socialism public interest, which emphasises public welfare and social value. As the Chinese proverb puts it 人民的利益高于一切, "the people's interest is the highest esteem". This dimension of the public interest is much more stressed in China; it is in general beyond any other private rights, including copyright, and appears very often in Chinese judgments, which might be used as one of the means of governmental control. It may be interpreted as public policy and censorship, of which the concept and regulation are diverse compared to the industrial countries.

Indeed, the judicial system in China has been facing a dilemma. On the one hand, it has to satisfy the demands of other developed countries such as the US and is obliged to keep in line with international treaties that originated from the well-developed system in industrial countries such as the UK; this therefore commands defending the authorship public interest and implementing Chinese copyright law in general. On the other hand, the access public interest is nevertheless emphasised much more than in other countries for the purpose of retaining and developing *socialist spiritual civilisation*. In addition, public welfare and social value have been historically stressed in Chinese culture, and have been recognised not only within the copyright system, but also extensively in Chinese society. As a ramification of private property rights, copyright law, especially its enforcement, is intensely challenged by the traditions of the country.

Bearing in mind the long tradition of sharing intellectual works with the community and the current ideology of placing the common good ahead of individual interest, Chinese lawmakers have made great efforts to install and to enforce copyright. Copyright law was formerly excluded from the New China's legal system because it was always seen as a capitalist rule safeguarding an individual's private property, in contradiction to the country's socialist principles and system. Even after it was adopted in 1990, the law remained foreign to most Chinese, including the courts, for more than a few years. In the *Chen Weihua* case, the court had to look for some rather awkward justifications to confirm the protection for a work in the digital environment, which would have been much more readily granted in any other developed system. The decision in the *Chen Weihua* case, however, demonstrated the Chinese courts' comprehension of the authorship public interest, which was confirmed and better explained later in the *Six Writers* case and in *Chen Xingliang v China Digital Library*.

In contrast with UK cases, however, courts in China have shown a strong access public interest orientation in copyright enforcement, which has resulted from Chinese traditional and socialist philosophy and has led to no or low punitive compensations, as seen in the discussed cases. While upholding both the authorship and access public interests, Chinese copyright laws have established that it is a breach of copyright to disseminate others' works on the Internet without lawful authorisation, and have also granted digital libraries a summary procedure of "notice to delete", which will be examined in the light of the three-step test in Chapter 5.

However, how to obtain the author's authorisation efficiently or to exercise the access public interest for using literary works, pictures, music and video products on the Internet without the author's consent, and what copyright measures should be taken so as to ensure a protective mechanism for a sustainable and healthy development of the online information industry, have become not-so-new tests for the not-so-old Chinese copyright law, the 2010 CCL.

To keep copyright up with the rapid development of technology is a challenge for all nations. The unique Chinese Internet phenomenon has also put the developing copyright system to a rigorous test. Seeing that 50 per cent of the infringement cases were Internet-related in 2007, a more effective copyright protection system in general as well as in cyberspace is urged, which requires China to learn more from experiences in the developed countries and also to study better its own circumstances based upon the rule of law.

The following questions ought to be answered by and clearly written in the Chinese copyright law in the near future. What is the public interest in the context of Chinese copyright? How can China exercise the defence of the access public interest? Last but not least, who should bear the burden of proving that copies of the works have been lawfully authorised – the copyright owners or the suspected infringers?

It should be pointed out that it is worthwhile to study carefully the representative cases while researching Chinese copyright, even if China is not a case law country. The Constitution provides the legal basis and statute laws offer abstract rules that judges must apply to cases. Court and administrative cases in general play an extraordinarily important role in Chinese lawmaking, enforcement and promotion. This also reflects the deep-rooted influence of the traditional Chinese culture.

With its own characteristics, China has established a copyright system in its regime, within which the access public interest is highlighted on the one hand, and the authorship public interest has been imposed and taken further on the other. It also provides for public, non-criminal enforcement – copyright administrative enforcement – in the name of the public interest. This will be explored in the next chapter.

3. Administrative copyright enforcement – the authorship public interest*

1. INTRODUCTION

Since adopting 改革开放政策, "the Reform and Opening-up Policy" in 1979, China has been forming its government based on 中国特色的社会主义, "socialism with Chinese characteristics": socialism is the basic principles of practice and Chinese characteristics are what these principles embody in the country.[1] A multi-ownership-oriented basic market economic system (with public ownership dominant) has thus been established and sustained together with a unique legal system. To date, "a Constitution-centred socialist legal system with Chinese characteristics has basically taken shape".[2]

The implementations of these "Chinese characteristics" in the legal system are varied and sometimes might seem peculiar and contradictory. For instance, whilst the Constitution affirms that all state power belongs to the people and authorises the NPC and the local People's Congress at all levels, being the organs through which the people exercise state power,[3] it states that Chinese people of all nationalities come under the leadership of the CCP.[4] This also reinforces the idea that China is currently

---

* This chapter was adapted from Guan H. Tang, 'Is Administrative Enforcement the Answer? Copyright Protection in the Digital Era', *Computer Law and Security Review* (2010), **26**(4), 406–17.

[1] See 中国社会科学院网站刊载贺瑞教授 《从列宁晚年的构想到有中国特色的社会主义社会》 一文; Rui He, 'From Linen's Late Years' Blueprint to Socialism with Chinese Characteristics', Chinese Academy Social Science online publication; retrieved at http://myy.cass.cn/file/1999050111627.html.

[2] See White Paper published on China's rule of law, retrieved on 11 March 2011 at http://www.chinadaily.com.cn/china/2008-02/28/content_6494029_3.htm.

[3] See Article 2.

[4] With advice from the Chinese People's Political Consultative Conference (CPPCC) that consists of CCP members, members from other parties and non-party members. See Preamble of the Constitution.

an authoritarian one-party state, although Article 5 of the Constitution embraces the rule of law and states that the CCP must be subject to the rule of law, the authority of the state and the Constitution, which is the fundamental law of the state and has supreme legal authority as clarified in its Preamble.

Recalling its history, China has nonetheless taken a positive step toward, and is committed, more than ever, to implementing a system of the rule of law throughout the nation. Gradually learning the practice of the rule of law, the country has made rapid progress in legislation: numerous laws and regulations have been made and enforced, including copyright, a regime that secures private property rights in the course of a legitimate concern of balancing the rights of individual authors and of general users. It has been around two decades since the first copyright law initially came into effect in China, ahead of a more complete system for copyright protection being established. Certainly, modern Chinese copyright law also carries Chinese characteristics; it is coloured by the country's distinctive history, culture, economic and political policies of the state, as well as containing substantial elements inherited from ancient Chinese law.

A significant manifestation of these Chinese characteristics is the implementation of a dual-track system for copyright enforcement. In addition to judicial protection, Chinese copyright law offers a legal basis for administrative enforcement and defines certain responsibilities including civil liabilities, criminal liabilities and exposure to administrative sanctions. Currently, whilst interest in court action grows steadily within the country, the Chinese administrative remedies still offer copyright proprietors the most popular enforcement for protection, which has obvious advantages over judicial enforcement, such as simpler process, shorter time and cheaper cost. Compared with other legal systems in most Western countries, Chinese law is unique in providing this administrative enforcement in relation to copyright protection. The quasi-judicial power of the administrative authorities is justified by Article 47 of the copyright law, "the public interest clause", the interpretation of which has most likely been misunderstood as being socialist public interest that emphasises public welfare and social value instead of the author's public interest, owing to long-standing cultural and legal practice.

This chapter will introduce copyright enforcement in the Chinese legal framework, and will explore copyright administrative enforcement, primarily its implementation and jurisdiction, by means of an up-to-date case analysis.

2. THE DUAL-TRACK SYSTEM

The 2010 CCL adopts a dual-track system for copyright protection, that is, judicial enforcement and administrative enforcement. Below, we will start with a brief introduction to China's overall legal structure to see how the dual-track system fits in.

2.1   Modern Legal Structure and Judicial Copyright Protection

Broadly speaking, the Chinese judicial system comprises institutions of three parts, namely, the people's court system, the people's procuratorate system and the public security system. The People's Court system is paralleled by a hierarchy of prosecuting organs called the People's Procuratorates, of which the Supreme People's Procuratorate (SPP) is the apex.[5] The People's Courts exercise judicial power on behalf of the states, while the People's Procurators are state organs for legal supervision.[6] The People's Procuratorates at all levels perform legal supervision and safeguard the enforcement of laws,[7] and their main functions are fourfold:

- to intercede in cases of endangering state and public security, damaging economic order and infringing citizens' personal and democratic rights, as well as other important criminal cases;
- to examine cases scheduled for investigation by the public security agencies, and decide on whether a suspect should be arrested or not, and whether a case should be prosecuted or exempt from prosecution;
- to institute and to support public prosecution in criminal cases; and
- to supervise the activities carried out by public security agencies, people's courts, prisons, houses of detention and institutions of 劳改, "reform through labour".[8]

---

[5] See Article 129.

[6] Articles 123 and 129, Constitution of the People's Republic of China.

[7] See Article 1, the Organic Law of the People's Procurators.

[8] See Article 5. And the SPP is primarily responsible for: leading the procuratorial work of regional and special procuratorates at all levels; accepting and hearing cases of corruption, bribery, tort to citizens' democratic rights and misconduct in office, and placing them on file for investigation and prosecution; performing legal supervision of the judicial process of courts and investigation of criminal cases; deciding arrest and prosecution concerning severe criminal cases; performing legal supervision of the trying of criminal cases; lodging protests against effective but wrong judgments and rulings made by various courts to the Supreme People's Court according to law; exercising legal supervision of activities conducted in

The Organic Law of the People's Courts explicates the nature, functions, organisation and activities of the courts and stipulates that the Chinese court system consists of the Supreme People's Court (SPC), local People's Courts at various levels and military courts, and other special People's Courts.[9] According to the Constitution, the SPC is the highest judicial organ and is responsible to the NPC and its Standing Committee; all levels of local courts are responsible to the organs of state power that instituted them and are subject to the supervision of the SPC, while lower level courts are subject to the supervision of the higher level courts.[10] The local People's Courts include:

- Higher Level People's Courts, which are established at the provincial and autonomous regional level;
- Intermediate Level People's Courts, which are established at levels of prefectures including autonomous prefectures, provincial capitals including cities under direct control of the provincial or autonomous region government, relatively big cities, and within the municipalities directly under the central government; and
- Basic Level People's Courts, which are established at county or autonomous county levels and also in urban districts.

On 20 April 2010, the SPC published its first White Paper, in both Chinese and English, entitled 'Intellectual Property Protection by Chinese Courts in 2009', which provided an official review of IP enforcement; Chinese IP courts received and concluded 166408 civil cases and 6387 administrative cases from 1985 to 2009, and 14509 criminal cases from 1997 to 2009. The White Paper stated that "the current comprehensive judicial intellectual property protection regime embodies the ideals of socialism with Chinese characteristics, embraces the country's development needs, observes Chinas duties under international conventions" and that "it is an essential part of China's judicial architecture".[11] It summarised that Chinese courts had accomplished the following in the last 30 years:

---

prisons and reform through labour institutions; providing legal explanations of the application of laws in practical procuratorial works; formulating regulations and by-laws concerning procuratorial works; leading and administrating public procurators according to law; organising and guiding the education and training of officials with the procuratorial departments; sponsoring negotiations with foreign procuratorial departments; and developing judicial assistance. See http://www.spp.gov.cn/site2006/2006-02-23/00016-324.html, retrieved on 15 September 2008.

9   See Article 2, the Organic Law of the People's Courts.
10   See Article 127.
11   See Intellectual Property Protection by Chinese Courts in 2009, 25.

- expanded their functions and powers in IP protection;
- enlarged the scope of judicial protection for IP;
- increased the level of judicial protection for IP;
- enhanced the effectiveness of judicial protection for IP;
- improved the judicial system in IP protection; and
- bettered the capacity in providing judicial protection for IP.

It also pointed out that "copyright cases represent the largest caseload since 2002".[12]

At present, China practises a two-hearing system of trials, which means that a case may be judged at two levels, with the second hearing being final. The Constitution provides that all cases tried by courts should be conducted openly unless otherwise provided for by the law, while the accused is entitled to the right to state a proper defence.[13] Litigation against suspected copyright infringements can be filed at the intermediate and higher levels, as well as in the district courts that have been approved by the SPC.[14] So far, 14 district courts have been designated to hear copyright cases, which are:

- Beijing Haidian District People's Court;
- Beijing Chaoyang District People's Court;
- Shanghai Huangpu District People's Court;
- Shanghai Pudong District People's Court;
- Shanghai Jinan Lixia District People's Court;
- Qingdao Shinan District People's Court;
- Guangzhou Dongshan District People's Court;
- Guangzhou Tianhe District People's Court;
- Guangzhou Baiyun District People's Court;
- Shenzhen Nanshan District People's Court;
- Shenzhen Luohu District People's Court;
- Shenzhen Longgang District People's Court;

---

[12] Ibid., 27.

[13] See Article 125.

[14] The People's Courts are composed of different divisions, including criminal, civil, economic and administrative divisions, which hear cases correspondingly. Copyright infringement cases can be tried only in the specialised intellectual property division set at the courts of intermediate and higher levels, and at authorised district level. For details of court divisions see for example 刘忠, 中国法院的分庭管理, 《法制与社会发展》 2009年第5期第124-135页; Zhong Liu, 'On the Differentiated Tribunals in China's Court', *Law and Social Development* (2009), **5**, 124–35.

- Foshan Nanhai District People's Court; and
- Foshan Chancheng District People's Court.

Should the outcomes of cases fail to satisfy the plaintiff or the defendant, they can be appealed through the national judicial system to the SPC. In 1996, the SPC set up the Chamber of Intellectual Property Rights (IPR) Trials, which consists of five Justices and assistant judges, to offer guidance to and supervision of trials of IPR including copyright cases. Accordingly, collegial panels or tribunals on IP cases were instituted in the civil or economic divisions at the relevant local courts.

In the last few years, foreign companies and governments have strongly lobbied for legislative improvements and clarifications of the Chinese laws to facilitate criminal prosecutions. In December 2004, the SPC and the SPP jointly issued judicial interpretations of the Criminal Code, part of which governs criminal law applications for cases involving copyright infringement. The interpretations clarify and improve the criteria for private prosecutions by lowering the threshold for criminal prosecutions, whereby criminal proceedings relating to copyrights may now commence if the value of the seizures exceeds RMB 50000 yuan or if 1000 units have been manufactured or sold. Providing a clearer definition of "case value" of seizures, the interpretations now state definitively that the plaintiff's market price of the goods should be used to calculate the value of the seizures, where the sales price of the counterfeit products cannot be determined. In accordance with Article 217, criminal sanctions may be applied to copyright-infringing acts done for the purpose of reaping profits such as:

- reproducing and distributing, without the permission of the copyright owner, his/her written works, musical works, cinematic works, television works, video works, computer software and other works;
- publishing a book for which another person has the exclusive publishing rights;
- reproducing and distributing, without the permission of the phonographic or video graphic producer, his or her phonographic or video graphic work; and
- producing and selling a work of art bearing the forged signature of another.

And the punishment for the above criminal conducts, conditional on the circumstances, may include:

- a fixed-term prison sentence of three to seven years;
- the imposition of a fine;

- criminal detention;
- confiscation of all materials, tools, infringing copies, and other property that is mainly used to produce such infringing copies; and
- compensation.

More recently, a new system of IPR judicial protection has been promoted for more effective enforcement, which is called 三审合一, *san shen he yi*, "three procedures consolidate to one", as IP cases have been divided into three categories and tried by the civil, criminal and administrative divisions of the courts respectively.[15]

Efforts are also being made to upgrade the quality of the judiciary: for instance, from 2002 on, people to be appointed judges for the first time should be selected only from among those who have passed the National Judicial Examination (NJE).[16] Nevertheless, the courts at present are still affected by the low educational level of their judges and their low status in the hierarchy of power. Judgeships in China are civil service positions, which are classified into presidents, vice-presidents, chief judges and associate chief judges of divisions, judges and assistant judges of people's courts, and are still of a rather low level of professionalism.[17]

Article 126 of the Constitution authorises that "the people's courts exercise judicial power independently, in accordance with the provisions of the law, and are not subject to interference by any administrative organ, public organisation or individual". However, it also states that the SPC is responsible to the NPC, and that its Standing Committee and local people's courts are responsible to "the organs of state power which created them". Within the structure, each level of court is essentially responsible to local political power at the same level, a responsibility that is reinforced

---

[15] See 陈中利，知识产权司法保护三审合一研讨会，国家知识产权战略网 (2010); Zhongli Chen, 'Seminar on *san shen he yi* IPR Judicial Protection', National Intellectual Property Strategy Office Website (2010); retrieved on 11 March 2011 at http://www.nipso.cn/onews.asp?id=9727.

[16] NJE is currently a paper-exclusive exam and is held annually. It is mainly designed to test candidates' legal knowledge, i.e. legal theory, economic law, international law, international private law, and international economic law and ethics, and their ability to join the legal profession. According to the Chinese Justice Minister Zhang Fusen, a new form may be adopted by adding a personal interview or professional evaluation. http://www.chinadaily.com.cn/english/doc/2005-05/31/content_446995.htm.

[17] See 朱苏力，基层法院法官专业化问题——现状、成因与出路 《比较法研究》2000年14卷3期233-265; Suli Zhu, 'Professionalisation of Judges in China: Its Historical Cause, Current Situation and Future Solution', *Journal of Comparative Law* (2000), **14**(3), 233–65.

by local control over court finances. The courts adopt a vertical management system, which means that lower level courts have to report to higher.
Also, the presidents of courts act as the line managers and supervisors to
all judges and they can not only monitor hearings but also influence judgments. The NPC also has the authority to issue laws binding over all of
China and also appoints the presidents of the SPC and the SPP.

It should be noted that each court case, in theory, stands as its own
decision and will not bind another court, but in practice judges from lower
courts often attempt to follow the interpretations of the law decided by
the higher courts, especially the SPC. Also, higher courts can use the final-
ity of their judgments on appeals as having a binding effect on the lower
courts that issued the first judgment or order. Similar rules apply to cases
concluded by administrative authorities.

2.2   Administrative Enforcement in the Name of the Public Interest

In addition to judicial protection, Article 48 of the 2010 CCL confers
power to the relevant administration departments[18] to enforce the law:
to investigate cases under the circumstances that the copyright-infringing
acts, 同时损害公共利益的, "at the same time breach the public interest".[19]
This public interest clause was not found in the 1990 CCL; it is the legitimate justification provided by Article 47 of the 2001 CCL particularly for
administrative authorities to enforce the law. The revised law weights the
significance of the authorship public interest in the copyright regime, not
only awarding individual authors the exclusive rights to protect copyright
over their works but also granting administrative copyright enforcement,
in which the relevant administration authorities may pursue anyone who
has committed acts of infringement in order to safeguard the authorship
pubic interest.

Administration authorities may impose remedies such as to confiscate
any unlawful income from the infringing act or to impose a fine on the
infringer.

---

[18]   Which include the State Intellectual Property Office, the Trademark
Office under the State Administration for Industry and Commerce, the National
Copyright Administration and the Ministries of Agriculture, Forestry, Culture,
Public Security and Customs – all are responsible for imposing administrative
penalties on IP infringement, and would investigate the infringer's administrative liability after the right owner files a complaint or another person knowing of
the fact informs on the infringer, or after an administrative department takes the
initiative in filing a case.

[19]   See Article 47, 2010 CCL.

> Where the circumstances are serious, the copyright administration department may also confiscate the materials, tools and equipment mainly used for making the infringing reproductions; and if the act constitutes a crime, the infringer shall be prosecuted for his criminal liability.[20]

Chinese lawmakers see the system of administrative protection as necessary in the same way as criminal protection and claim that it is also designed to "safeguard the socio-economic order".[21] The lawmakers point out that adopting administrative enforcement in China is in the public interest (from the authorship aspect), and that it is "important to efficient administrative management and to maintaining social order and protecting citizens' rights".[22] Mr Xu Chao, Spokesman and Deputy Director of General National Copyright Administration of China (NCAC), defends such practice on the basis that,

> although copyright is originally a private right belonging to individuals, it will, when it develops to a certain degree, have a bearing on how to protect the interests of investors in an attempt to promote socio-economic development, and in the public interests.[23]

Article 47 provides lawful justification for administrative enforcement in the copyright regime, yet the "public interest" clause has not been clearly defined by any Chinese legislation and has consequently had a great impact on the enforcement of the law. Since the authorship public interest is opposite to traditional and socialist Chinese culture and is rather foreign to the masses, the interpretation of this clause has been confusing and probably misread as being socialism public interest, which can be seen in the cases discussed later in this chapter. Nonetheless, the "public interest" clause provides a legal basis for administrative enforcement and has conferred upon copyright administrative authorities across the country a quasi-judicial power to enforce copyright law.[24] A Chinese phenomenon such as this is somewhat unique but is not new. Administrative authorities enforcing the law reflect the lengthy past and deep cultural roots from ancient China.

As explained in the first chapter, the tradition of administrative authorities enforcing the law can be dated back to the Qin Dynasty in 221 BC; it

---

20 See Article 47.
21 See Chao Xu, 'Problems in the Practice of Copyright Enforcement', http://www.cpahkltd.com/Publications/Article/Exc992.html, retrieved on 8 March 2011.
22 See http://news.xinhuanet.com/english/2006-05/23/content_4585984.htm.
23 See above, n. 22.
24 Article 47, 2010 CCL and Article 37, Copyright Regulations 2002.

was greatly developed in the Han Dynasty and was adopted thereafter until the last dynasty in China, the Qing Dynasty, in AD 1911. Although the 1911 Xinhai Revolution successfully introduced concepts of democracy and socialism to China, the country once again suffered from wars in the period from 1911 to 1949, which prevented the development of laws and the establishment of a legal system. Modelled from the German and the former Soviet Union legal systems, China began to institute its own system in a socialist setting in 1949; various laws were enacted, including the state Constitution in 1954, for the purpose of serving the dictatorship of the proletariat and the planned economy throughout the country. Nonetheless, Mao initiated the Cultural Revolution in 1966, which interrupted the construction of a modern legal system in China and left Mao and Maoist thought dictating the country for over ten years. It was not until the late 1970s that China started to rebuild its legal system, influenced by international communities and based on principles of international law. Moreover, the 1999 Constitution confirms the rule of law in China for the first time in Chinese history, and intends to foster China as a socialist country governed according to law. It, on the one hand, continues to defend the socialist ideology and system, and, on the other hand, safeguards the individual rights of Chinese people, such as their private property rights, including copyright.

At present, the most important regulatory stakeholders with respect to administrative copyright enforcement are the NCAC and the provincial and municipal Copyright Bureaus that are charged with administering and enforcing copyright protection. The NCAC is responsible for national copyright issues, such as investigations into infringement cases, administration of foreign-related copyright issues and developing arbitration rules and regulations. Other relevant bodies that may also play a role in enforcement include the General Administration of Customs, the Public Security Bureau (the police), Regional IPR bureaus, the State Food and Drug Administration (for pharmaceutical products), the Ministry of Culture (for copyright materials of cultural value), the Administration for Quality Supervision, Inspection and Quarantine (infringements of low quality goods) and their local level offices.

According to the regulations of Articles 48 and 49 of the 2010 CCL and Articles 36 and 37 of the Implementing Regulations 2002, the local administrative authorities are entitled to take legal action against any copyright infringement actively or under a request of the proprietor of copyright in line with the above regulations, and for any foreign proprietor, or under either the Berne Convention or the UCC, of which China has been a member since October 1992.

In 2003, the NCAC issued the Implementing Measures for

Administrative Penalties on Copyright Infringement (Measures 2003) to replace the earlier measures issued in 1997.[25] In line with the 2001 CCL and Implementing Regulations 2002, the Measures 2003 aim to make the provisions more feasible when it comes to administrative enforcement and stipulate that only in cases where the public interest is breached can the copyright administrative authorities take action.[26] However, "the public interest" is not defined.

Detailed procedures to be followed by copyright officials in dealing with infringement cases have been set out. Thus, the procedural rules relating to administrative copyright enforcement are more transparent. In making a request for administrative protection, the interested party should submit a written request, proof of owning copyright and evidence of the infringing act.[27] For copyright disputes, the administrative authorities will make a decision as to whether a complaint will be processed within 15 days of receipt of the request and will inform the applicant of its decision. A written explanation would be given to the applicant if the decision were negative.[28]

Bodies such as the local copyright authorities of the jurisdictions where infringement was committed, the jurisdictions where the infringement took effect, the jurisdictions where the infringing copies were stored, and the jurisdictions where seizure or detention of infringing copies took place, all have the power to take administrative enforcement action. When two or more local authorities have jurisdiction over a case, it will be dealt with by the one first placing the case on file.[29]

Suspected infringers are required to bear the burden of proving that copies of the works have been lawfully authorised. The copyright authorities will give them a specified time within which to produce such authorisation, failing which the copies are deemed to be infringing copies. However, in situations where the infringing goods may be lost as evidence, copyright officials may take action even if the case has not been placed on file, including situations such as a prima facie case.[30]

The local administrative authority has the right, depending on the circumstances, to order the infringer to bear civil liability for such remedies

---

[25] That is, 著作权行政处罚实施办法, which consists of 44 Articles.
[26] See Article 3.
[27] The proprietor of any copyright should carefully collect the information of the infringer and/or infringing goods as direct evidence. Sometimes it is necessary to conduct a professional investigation before submitting a petition to the administrative authority.
[28] Articles 11–13.
[29] Articles 5–7.
[30] See Article 15.

as ceasing the infringement, eliminating the effects of the infringement, making an apology or paying damages the amount of which is no more than the actual injury suffered by the proprietor or of the unlawful income of the infringer. The appropriate fee paid by the proprietor to stop the infringement should also be included in the amount. The infringer may also be penalised in ways such as the confiscation of unlawful income, destruction of infringing reproductions, imposition of a fine not exceeding three times the amount of illegal business turnover or no more than RMB 100 000 yuan, and the confiscation of the materials, tools and equipment mainly used for making the infringing reproductions, if the infringement is serious. "Serious" has been defined as:[31]

- illegal profit exceeding RMB 5000 yuan for individual infringers, or RMB 30 000 yuan for units of business;
- illegal turnover exceeding RMB 30 000 for individual infringers, or RMB 100 000 yuan for units of business;
- sale and supply of more than 2000 infringing copies for individual infringers, or 5000 for units of business;
- repeat infringement;
- other cases resulting in grave influence or serious consequences.

Any party that is unsatisfied with an administrative decision of the administrative authority may institute proceedings with a judicial authority, the People's Court, within three months from the date of receiving the decision. However, as mentioned earlier, it is only courts at the level of intermediate People's Courts or above that are eligible to hear copyright cases, except certain district courts that have been approved by the SPC, usually in big cities. In cases where such proceedings are not instituted and the decision is not complied with within the above period, the administrative authority may approach the People's Court for compulsory execution.[32]

The administrative authority bears full responsibility for the action conducted. In order to prevent governments from abusing the power of administrative enforcement, provisions are made for certain safeguards. Any affected parties may prosecute the related administrative authority for any illegal action or procedure in line with the regulations of the Administrative Procedure Law and the State Compensation Law, which came into force on 1 October 1990 and 1 January 1995 respectively.[33]

---

[31] Articles 4 and 31.
[32] See Article 37.
[33] See Article 37.

3. PRACTICES OF ADMINISTRATIVE COPYRIGHT ENFORCEMENT

While dealing with copyright protection in China, the majority of the concerned parties would choose to take administrative rather than judicial action. Hitherto, most IPR enforcement has been done through the administrative system. For example, according to China's White Paper on IPRs in 2007, 10344 out of 10559 cases, nearly 98 per cent, were concluded by copyright administrative authorities at all levels across the country.[34] Of all the concluded cases, 8524 were concluded with Administrative Punishment Decisions (APDs), 1585 were concluded with mediation arrangements, and 235 were transferred to judicial authorities.[35] The following cases illustrate how administrative enforcement was achieved, the current process and how Article 47, the public interest clause, has been interpreted.

3.1   Illustrative Examples

In July 1995, one of the most well-known companies in the Chinese textile industry, Fuoshan Nanfang Printing and Dyeing Company (Nanfang), filed an administrative complaint at Guang Dong Province Copyright Bureau against Shunde Tenai Textile Design and Decoration Company (Tenai) for the latter's infringement of copyright in its 21 art designs.

After investigation, Guang Dong Province Copyright Bureau issued an APD and confirmed that Nanfang designed *Ju Yuan* and another 19 artworks for textile decoration between 1993 and 1994, registered the copyrights in early 1995 and owned copyright in those art designs. In July 1995, as a newcomer, Tenai participated in the Sixth National Construction and Decoration Exhibitions and presented nine works, with a mark of "Tenai Design", which were exactly the same as *Ju Yuan* and the other art designs. Thereafter, Tenai unlawfully copied *Ju Yuan* and the other 19 of Nanfang's designs and produced 35471.7 metres of decorated textiles for its clients.

In its APD, the Copyright Bureau stated that Tenai copied, exhibited and produced Nanfang's art designs without obtaining designers' and rights owners' permission and therefore had infringed Nanfang's

---

[34]   And over 73 million pieces of various pirated products were confiscated, including over 18 million books, 1.1 million periodicals, 48 million audio-visual products, 2.01 million electronic publications, 3.79 million software discs and 240000 miscellaneous products.

[35]   See State Intellectual Property Office (SIPO) website, www.sipo.gov.cn.

copyright. Tenai was instructed, first, to cease all its infringing acts without delay; second, to hand over all pirated products and the sales gain; and finally, to remunerate Nanfang. Neither party objected to the APD.

Six years later, in December 2001, Tenai, by now an established and strong company in the industry, complained to Guang Dong Province Copyright Bureau, declaring that Xiqiao Henhui Printing Factory (Xiqiao) had illegally copied *ting ting yu li*, an artwork that Tenai designed and owned copyright of. Xiqiao had produced and sold a certain amount of decorated textiles with *ting ting yu li*, infringed Tenai's copyright and seriously damaged Tenai's reputation and business. During the administrative hearing, Tenai's designer presented the draft drawings of *ting ting yu li* and proof of the registration of copyright in September 2000.

In February 2002, based on Article 47(1) of the 2001 CCL, the Copyright Bureau issued an APD and ordered Xiqiao to cease the infringing act immediately, to destroy its 910.9 metres of decorated textile printed with the pirated *ting ting yu li*, and to confiscate its illegitimate gains of RMB 3081 yuan.[36]

Nonetheless, Xiqiao refused to abide by the APD and promptly instituted a legal proceeding with Guangzhou Dongshan District People's Court (District Court), against Guang Dong Province Copyright Bureau. Xiqiao claimed that the decision made by the Copyright Bureau was unlawful since it had no legal basis: Article 47 of the 2001 CCL stated that administrative management departments could investigate cases only when the copyright infringement act has, at the same time, breached the "public interest". Xiqiao argued that its infringement of *ting ting yu li* was on a very small scale and had only an extremely small impact on Tenai; Xiqiao admitted that its infringing act harmed Tenai, one company's benefit, but it did not damage the public interest (in its public welfare aspect). Therefore, the Copyright Bureau had no right to handle this case and its APD should be dismissed. In addition, Xiqiao insisted that the Copyright Bureau should return its 910.9 metres of textile and RMB 3081 yuan because they were Xiqiao's private property, which should be protected by Chinese law.

In the court, the defence of the Copyright Bureau mainly focused on the fact that Xiqiao's infringing act had breached the "public interest" and maintained that the issued APD was lawful and just. The Copyright Bureau pointed out that, without the copyright owner's consent, Xiqiao had copied and produced *ting ting yu li*, in which Tenai had invested not

---

[36] See 粤权(案)[2002]l(2)号 《行政处罚决定书》; Guangdong APD (case) number [2002]l(2).

only money but also human resource and intelligence to research and to design, and then had taken an economic risk to promote the design to the market. Xiqiao's infringing act had, firstly, breached fair competition in the market; secondly, infringed Tenai's copyright and harmed the development of cultural creativity; and thirdly, violated the economic order and brought chaos into the market. Quoting the Office of the State Council's Notice to Further Rectify and Standardise the Cultural Market Order[37] and vice-premier of the State Council Mr Li Lanqing's talk on the National Teleconference on Rectifying and Standardising the Cultural Market Order,[38] the Copyright Bureau highlighted that the creative and cultural market has a great impact on the development of the economy, culture and civilisation in China, as well as on the international reputation of the country. Xiqiao's act had in fact corrupted social values and international harmony, and had thus infringed the "public interest".

The District Court's judgment was granted in the Copyright Bureau's favour. It concluded that Xiquiao's copyright infringement had constituted an act of unfair competition as set out in the competition law,[39] had damaged another party's legal rights in the same trade, and therefore had breached the "public interest".

Xiqiao refused to accept the judgment and appealed to Guangzhou Intermediate People's Court (Intermediate Court) in November 2002. Xiqiao affirmed that the term "public interest" had particular connotations: it meant social and common interest, not individual interest. Xiqiao quoted the *Law Dictionary and Thesaurus* that "the 'public interest' refers to the public order in a society, which, influenced by social and public policy, common morality, and legal principle, should be followed and cannot be changed by any individuals; it is the country and the society's fundamental interest".[40] Xiqiao believed that the intention of adding the "public interest" clause to Article 47 was obvious: it intended to guide the copyright administrative departments to deal with the infringing acts

---

[37]   See 国办发[2001]59 号; General Office of the State Council Official Document Number (2001)59.

[38]   See www.cctv.com/news/china/20010816/450.html, retrieved on 8 March 2011.

[39]   Law of the People's Republic of China for Countering Unfair Competition, 1993.

[40]   曾庆敏, 《法学大辞典》 1998年出版; Zeng Qinmin, *Law Dictionary and Thesaurus* (1998). It consists of 10,837 entries, including constitutional law, administrative law, criminal law, commercial law, economic law, labour law, procedural law, international law, international common and private law, international economic law, maritime law, criminalistic investigation linguistics, forensic science, forensic psychiatry, legal theory, Chinese legal history and Roman law, etc.

that had actually breached the "public interest" but not common disputes of small scale. Furthermore, Xiqiao maintained that both the Copyright Bureau and the District Court had mis-defined the "public interest". Xiqiao pointed out that according to the Copyright Bureau and the District Court's explanations, all copyright-infringing acts in trade had at the same time constituted acts of unfair competition, damaged another party's legal rights and economic order, and therefore breached the public interest. Xiqiao accordingly claimed that the Copyright Bureau and the District Court's generalisation of the concept of the "public interest" was apparently incorrect and had taken no account into the objective of the newly added clause in Article 47.

The Copyright Bureau responded that size and quantity were not the criteria to determine whether an infringement had breached the public interest or not; an ordinary infringing act small in scale may also breach the "public interest". Amended Article 47 certainly in no way meant to limit administrative copyright enforcement but reflected the nation's determination to enhance copyright protection via both systems of judicial and administrative enforcement. In practice, regardless of the scale of an infringing act, the administrative department may lawfully handle any disputes given that such act breached the "public interest". It was a matter of fact that Xiqiao had pirated Tenai's art design, and had unlawfully produced and sold the pirated textile, which had, on the one hand, infringed Tenai's copyright, and on the other hand, disrupted the cultural market and managerial order, thus damaging the "public interest". Hence, the Copyright Bureau's dealing with the case was fair and the APD was lawful.

The Intermediate Court agreed with the defendant's opinion and upheld the District Court's decision in January 2003. Still, Xiqiao was not convinced, especially regarding the explanation of and the inference on the public interest clause of Article 47. In February 2003, Xiqiao held a national press conference, asking the media (both traditional and digital) and lawmakers for further discussions on how the public interest clause should be interpreted and urged future law to take account of such clarification.[41]

These two rather simple cases turned out to be the very first lawsuits in which the public interest clause of Article 47 was considered. However, the explanations on this clause of both the Chinese administrative authority and the courts were imprecise and even confusing. Obviously, Xiqiao

---

41   See www.ycwb.com/gb/content/2003-02/14/content_490267.htm, retrieved on 11 March 2011.

understood the term "public interest" to be the socialism public interest, which was in fact a preconception for most Chinese, and thus deemed that administrative departments might interfere in copyright disputes only when the infringing acts damaged the public welfare or social value. The Copyright Bureau and the courts should, first of all, have made it clear that the public interest clause of Article 47 upholds authorship, which is another dimension of the public interest in copyright, even if it is rather foreign to the Chinese legislation and people.

The latter case has gained great attention from legal practitioners, academia, media and the general public; a sustained debate has gone on ever since. Xinhua, Tianyi, Education China, NCAC, Xinlang, Sohu and other popular Chinese websites have launched a series of forums for discussion on the enforcement of Chinese copyright legislation, particularly the 2001 CCL, the general concept and defence of the public interest in copyright and its implication for copyright and other laws.[42] Some identify the public interest as the benefit that a majority of citizens can enjoy and others think that the public interest is strictly defined in the Civil Code so that the so-called public interest means that all members of society can enjoy the benefits directly. Briefly, as outlined above, the public interest has been defined as the country's interest, the people's interest, the common interest of all members in a society, and, where set in the copyright framework, it refers to the overall situation of the country's fundamental interest, and not just to a particular region's or industry's interest. Among numerous journal papers, three representative views can be identified. Firstly, the public interest currently is positively helping to regulate a delicate balance in Chinese IP including copyright;[43] secondly, the current IP laws in China including copyright have become over-protective for the

---

[42]   See related websites. For example www.ycwb.com/gb/content/2003-02/14/ content_490267.htm and www.southcn.com/law/fzzt/200304290184.htm, retrieved on 11 March 2011.

[43]   See for example 冯晓青, 利益平衡论: 知识产权法的理论基础, 知识产权-2003年6期16–19; Xiaoqing Feng, 'Balance, the Theoretical Foundation of Intellectual Property Law', *Intellectual Property* (2003), **6**, 16–19; 冯晓青,试论以利益平衡理论为基础的知识产权制度,   江苏社会科学-2004年1期210–16; Xiaoqing Feng, 'Studies on Intellectual Property Law', *Jiangsu Social Science* (2004), **1**, 210–16; 韦之, 知识产权神圣不可侵犯, 电子知识产权-2004年3期52–3; Zhi Wei, 'The Sacrosanct Intellectual Property Rights', *E-IP* (2004), **3**, 52–3; 李玉香, 知识产权权利限制制度的法律完善, 人民司法-2004年6期52–6; Yuxiang Li, 'The Perfection of Legal Limitation on Intellectual Property Rights', *People Justice* (2004), **6**, 52–6; 冯晓青, 知识产权法的价值构造: 知识产权法利益平衡机制研究, 中国法学-2007(1)-67–77; Xiaoqing Feng, 'Value of the Intellectual Property Law: Studies on its Balance Mechanism', *China Law* (2007), **1**, 67–77.

rights owners and are impairing the public interest principle;[44] and thirdly, it should be recognised that there is a risk of using public interest as a tool to expropriate people's private rights.[45]

Later, Mr Xu Chao gave open comments on Xiqiao's cases and the arguments involved; he said: "it is evident that the act is a copyright infringement and has damaged the public interest . . . it is very unreasonable to claim for the return of the pirated goods regardless of the size and amount".[46] Mr Xu failed to provide clarification of the public interest clause of Article 47.

It should be mentioned that, although China is not a country governed by case law, cases have always played an extremely important role in its making, enforcement and promotion of laws, for two reasons: the influence of its traditional culture of 事实胜于雄辩, "facts speak louder than words", and the current centralised government of administration and courts. Therefore, it is most common to see that, every year, Chinese courts and administrative authorities at all levels carefully select ten typical IP cases and widely publish them as the "Top Ten of the Year", for the purpose of promoting IP awareness among the masses.[47] As one of the "Ten IP Cases of the Year in Guandong", the Xiqiao cases had a great impact on later IP rulings of both administrative and judicial bodies,

---

44   See 陈传夫, 防止知识产权对公共利益的损害, 情报资料工作-2002年6期5; Chuanfu Chen, 'Prevent Intellectual Property's Damage to the Public Interest', *Information Management* (2002), **6**, 5; 陈传夫,数字时代信息资源知识产权制度的现状与展望, 大学图书馆学报-2003:21(2)-9–14; Chuanfu Chen, 'Intellectual Property Law in the Information Age', *Journal of University Library* (2003), **2**, 9–14; 李国海,析知识产权法中的"公共利益"概念, 中南大学学报: 社会科学版-2003年4期472–5; Guohai Li, 'Analysis on the Concept of Public Interest in Intellectual Property Law', *Social Science* (2003), **4**, 472–5; 王先林,知识产权滥用及其法律规制, 法学-2004年3期107–12; Xianlin Wang, 'Intellectual Property Rights: The Abuse', *Law* (2004), **3**, 107–12; 李强, 认真对待与知识产权有关的权利滥用, 电子知识产权-2006(7)-60–1等。Qiang Li, 'Earnestly Treat the Abuse of Intellectual Property Rights', *E-IP* (2006), **7**, 60–61.

45   See for example 张千帆, "公共利益"的构成——对行政法的目标以及"平衡"的意义之探讨, 《比较法研究》2005年第五期1–14; Qianfan Zhang, 'What Consist of the Public Interest – Aims of Administrative Law and the Balance', *Comparative Law Study* (2005), **5**, 1–14; 刘文静, 公共利益的定义为何不好下, 检察日报2006年8月25日. Liu Wenjing, 'Why Is It Difficult to Define the Public Interest?' *Procuratorial Daily* (25 August 2006), available at www.jcrb.com/n1/jcrb549/ca288582.htm, retrieved on 11 March 2011.

46   See 许超, 关于著作权行政保护的几个问题, 中国版权2004年第一期8–12; Chao Xu, 'Some Issues Regarding Copyright Administrative Protection', *China Copyright* (2004), 1, 8–12.

47   As well as in the other subjects of laws.

particularly on the APDs.[48] In fact, the phrase "the act infringed the public interest" has ever since appeared in all the APDs of NCAC, provincial and municipal Copyright Bureaus. Some of these specific cases have gained great public attention and produced undeniable social effects: they have increased the public knowledge and awareness of copyright. For instance, the 101st Guangzhou Trade Fair, China's largest foreign trade fair, has taken action to strengthen the protection of IPR. In April 2007, three organisations were eligible for removal from the list of trade fair exhibitors owing to their IP-infringing acts.[49]

It may be interesting to note that, with an analysis akin to the rulings of lower courts in the Tenai cases alongside an introduction to the development of and current achievement of Tenai, the High People's Court set out Tenai as an example of how copyright awareness can stimulate a company's business. Repeating the judgment of the Intermediate Court, the legal basis and purpose of copyright administrative enforcement were sketchily given. The High People's Court further noted that copyright administrative departments intend "not only to punish those serious infringing acts according to copyright laws but also to help infringers enhance their understanding of copyright as well as IP in general".[50]

3.2   Administrative Enforcement in Cyberspace

As explained earlier, cyberspace is currently the main domain where most copyright violations occur in China, although Chinese copyright laws have been legitimately in effect on the Internet since the adaptation of the 2001 CCL. In June 2004, a non-governmental organisation, China Internet Illegal Information Reporting Centre (CIIRC), was founded by the Internet Information Service Commission of the Internet Society of China. The CIIRC declares its core mission as maintaining the order of the Internet and upholding the authorship public interest in cyberspace.[51] Administrative authorities also take serious action to reduce software piracy online and offline: the State Council General Office (SCGO) issued a letter to all departments of the central government to promote use of

---

48   See www.gd.gov.cn/govpub/gdyw/200704/t20070425_15503.htm, retrieved on 24 July 2010.
49   See www.chinacourt.org/public/detail.php?id=244434, retrieved on 11 March 2011.
50   See www.gdwto.org.cn/dynamic/img/030416/002.doc, retrieved on 11 March 2011.
51   See the CIIRC website http://net.china.com.cn/, retrieved on 11 March 2011.

legitimate software and demanded all pirated software to be removed.[52] Later on, a similar notification was given to local governments.[53] In 2006, joint notices were authorised by the Ministry of Information Industry, the Ministry of Commerce, the NCAC and the Ministry of Finance to governmental and public institutions at all levels, which intend to cut down downloading of pirated software by enforcing the pre-instalments of legitimate software on all computers made or sold in China and the purchase of legitimate software on pre-installed computers and other equipments.[54] These red-titled notices were soon implemented by administrative authorities.

In April 2006, Autodesk, a US leading design and media software company, made a complaint to Jiangsu Province Copyright Bureau (JSPCB) against Viscount Industries (Kunshan) Ltd (Viscount Industries). Autodesk pointed out that several of Viscount Industries' computers used unauthorised Autodesk software. Together with the local police and Copyright Bureau, and the Industry and Commerce Bureau, the JSPCB inspected Viscount Industries and confirmed that four computers owned by Viscount Industries' Department for Research and Development had downloaded and installed pirated Autodesk software. In December 2007, the JSPCB issued an APD imposing upon Viscount Industries a fine of RMB 800000 yuan, based on the value of the infringing software, and ordered the company to remove the unauthorised Autodesk software from the four computers immediately.[55] It is the biggest fine so far in China regarding copyright infringement. The victory of Autodesk is seen as a boost for the promotion of enterprises using legitimate software throughout the country.[56]

With over 30 per cent of Internet users using Internet cafés to surf online, the very unique Chinese Internet is greatly challenging the late-built system of copyright protection in China, including its system of administrative enforcement. In 2008, 15 out of 29 typical cases announced

---

[52]   See 国办函[2001]57号, General Office of the State Council Letter Number (2001)57.

[53]   See 国办函[2004]41号, General Office of the State Council Letter Number (2004)41.

[54]   See 国权联[2006]1号和信部联产[2006]199号, Guo Quan Lian Document Number (2006)1 and Xinbu Lian Chan Document Number (2006)199.

[55]   In addition, Suzhou Intermediate People's Court also ruled that Viscount Industries should compensate a total of RMB 69400 yuan to Autodesk for its loss and reasonable expense on the case, and pay the costs of the litigation.

[56]   See http://www.sipo.gov.cn/sipo2008/mtjj/2008/200805/t20080523_403811. html, retrieved on 29 March 2011.

by the NCAC are copyright-infringing acts arising on the Internet.[57] Nonetheless, the Chinese administrative authorities believe that to perfect the system of administrative enforcement will help to crack down on online copyright infringement of all kinds and in all fields,[58] including those that used to be treated as materials in the public domain.

Huarong, a county located north of Hunan Province with a population of 703 416 and with rich resources, is a pioneer in demonstrating the determination of the administrative authorities. On 3 August 2007 the Office of Huarong County Government reported to Huarong Copyright Bureau (HCB) that a privately owned website (www.0730hr.com) had infringed copyright in the contents of the official Huarong government portal, www.huarong.gov.cn.[59] After investigation, the HCB proved that www.0730hr.com was owned and operated by Huang Liangyong. Since October 2006, Huang had been copying a large amount of information, mainly of government affairs and news, from www.huarong.gov.cn and had hyperlinked the portal without consent; in addition, using P2P technology, Huang had published over 3100 unauthorised films through his website.[60] On 16 August, based on Article 47 of the 2001 CCL and Article 18(1) of the Regulations 2006, the HCB concluded that Huang's acts breached the "public interest", seriously violated the legitimate rights of the Huarong government portal and other right owners to control the communication of works on the Internet, that is, their public communication right. However, owing to Huang's positive cooperation during the investigation, including publishing a written self-criticism on 4 August,[61] the HCB stated in its APD that Huang had infringed copyright in works published on the Huarong government portal and had breached the public interest; Huang was commanded (1) to publish a copy of his written self-criticism on the Huarong government portal, (2) to cease all his infringing acts immediately, and (3) to pay a fine of RMB 1000 yuan.

The Huarong case, settled in less than two weeks, happened to be the

---

[57]   See the NCAC official publication regarding Chinese copyright cases, retrieved on 24 March 2011 at http://www.ncac.gov.cn/GalaxyPortal/inner/bqj/include/list_column_2.jsp?BoardID=1913&boardid=1150101011161402.

[58]   See 许超，网络著作权保护的三个进步；Chao Xu, 'Three Progress on Protection of Internet Copyright', retrieved on 29 July 2010 at http://news.sina.com.cn/c/2007-04-27/215812883851.shtml.

[59]   See 华版罚[2007]05号, Huarong Copyright Punishment Document Number (2007)05.

[60]   See   http://www.huarong.gov.cn/xwzx/ShowArticle.asp?ArticleID=1457, retrieved on 28 March 2011.

[61]   See   http://www.huarong.gov.cn/xwzx/ShowArticle.asp?ArticleID=1045, retrieved on 28 March 2011.

first court case in China confirming that it is an infringement to copy contents on a government portal without permission. Obviously, the Huarong case intends to establish that governments may own copyright in works published on their portals, which used to be generally seen as works in the public domain. However, Chinese law does not provide copyright protection to documents of a legislative or administrative nature, for the benefit of the general public; therefore copyright in most government departments' works should not be claimed by the state entities.

Hence, several questions arose regarding the decision made by the HCB. Firstly, did or did not Huang breach the Huarong government portal's copyright? The HCB confirmed that Huang mainly copied the Huarong government portal's works of governmental affairs and news, where under Article 6(7) of the Regulation 2006, one of the lawful exceptions is to provide published articles regarding current events to the public through the Internet. Secondly, why was the fact of unauthorised P2P of more than 3100 films not referred to in the HCB's APD? The fact that Huang used P2P to provide more than 3100 films through his website was briefly mentioned once in the APD and the amount of films was described vaguely as "a number of"; the emphasis throughout was on his acts breaching Huarong County Government's copyright. Thirdly, what was the justification for the fine? The HCB imposed a fine of RMB 1000 yuan for Huang's infringement of copyright in works of Huarong government and 3100 films, which makes people wonder about the basis and purpose of this punishment.

In June 2008, the State Council Information Office (SCIO) held a press conference regarding the Issues on National Intellectual Property Strategy Compendium. Mr Xu Chao advocated twofold copyright protections for online works, namely legal protection and technological protection.[62] He highlighted that the challenges of copyright infringement on the Internet in China will remain in the future and optimistically declared that it would be managed by China's dual-track copyright protection system, of which the administrative enforcement was described as "an advanced system even compared to the developed countries including the UK and the US" and thus should be greatly strengthened.[63]

On 12 June 2008, in collaboration with the Ministry of Public Security and the Ministry of Industry and Information Technology, the NCAC

---

[62] See also Xu Chao's speech made at the Sixth China Digital Entertainment Expo & Conference July 2008, http://www.xwcbj.gd.gov.cn/news/html/zxdt/article/1216216895529.html, retrieved on 11 March 2011.

[63] See SCIO online, http://www.scio.gov.cn/syyw/tbtt/200806/t187012.htm, retrieved on 11 March 2011.

officially launched a four-month-long project called Special Action on Striking Online Copyright Infringement and Piracy (Special Action), and set up an integrated office especially for this.[64] According to Mr Xu Chao, the main objective of this Special Action was to prevent illegal broadcasting online of the Beijing Olympics 2008 and to ensure "a normal distribution order on the Internet".[65]

4. DISCUSSION

As has been discussed earlier, historically, China lacked the culture of rule of law. Its administrative authorities have always enjoyed additional judicial power and the jurisdiction over cases was implemented by local civil officials, whose specialities were in Confucianism but never in interpreting and applying laws and rules.

The re-establishment of the legal system along with the Reform and Opening-up Policy has been fairly effective, but problematical. Although the Constitution has confirmed that China adopts the rule of law, to date the Chinese public is more accustomed to administrative enforcement that has continued to be implemented in China within different areas of law including copyright, whilst the central government remains the most trusted institution.[66] Currently, administrative copyright enforcement has certain advantages compared to judicial protection, the process is simpler, the time is shorter and the fee is cheaper. In addition, the administrative authorities may provide authors and copyright owners active protection; either to prevent an infringement or to cease an ongoing infringement instantly, which cannot be offered by judicial protection. Nonetheless, it should be appreciated that there is a growing trend towards judicial protection for copyright as the Chinese legal system evolves. In conjunction with the development of the economy and the gradual improvement of the legal system over the country, judicial protection may become the preferred means for defending copyright in future.

---

[64]   http://www.ncac.gov.cn/GalaxyPortal/inner/bqj/include/detail.jsp?articlei d=14303&boardpid=168&boardid=1150101011160101, retrieved on 11 March 2011.

[65]   See http://www.scio.gov.cn/glfw/dt/200806/t186902.htm, retrieved on 11 March 2011.

[66]   According to the report of a national survey carried out by the Chinese Academy of Social Sciences, published in May 2007, today's Chinese public trust the central government the most, followed very closely by the judges and the police. The trust of local governments was ranked third. See http://news.phoe nixtv.com/mainland/200705/0523_17_122895.shtml, retrieved on 11 March 2011.

The Chinese government maintains that the protective copyright system, particularly administrative enforcement, plays an important role in the promotion of science and technology and in the development of the economy and culture. It is not only a necessary system ensuring the normal functioning of the modern economy, but also stands as one of the basic conditions on which international social communication and cooperation in science, technology, economy and culture have developed. Today, the Chinese government regards the protection of copyright as an indispensable part of its Reform and Opening-up Policy and new legal construction for the twenty-first century,[67] and thus upholds the authorship public interest.

Article 47 of the 2001 CCL has included a public interest clause and, according to Mr Xu Chao, the intention of this is twofold: to clarify the stipulation for administrative liability, and to draw a line between civil liability and administrative liability, and administrative and criminal charges.[68]

However, the purposes may also be understood as follows. Firstly, the amended Article 47 intends to grant administrative protection a legal basis in the name of the authorship public interest, which is the lawful justification for the copyright enforcement function for all levels of administrative departments. As mentioned earlier, administrative power has always been used in China for law enforcement, and adopting administrative enforcement in modern copyright could be viewed as an inheritance of the historical traditions; but no lawful justification was offered prior to Article 47 of the 2001 CCL. It should also therefore be seen as an actual move forward in the development of Chinese law as well as in the lawmaking. Nevertheless, rather than simply insert a clause as such, it would have been better if the lawmaker either could have provided an additional clause for a clearer validation; or could have withdrawn the clause from Article 47 and explained it more clearly in a relevant civil code.

Secondly, the amended Article 47 aims to limit administrative power, namely the administrative authorities' involvement in copyright disputes. It lays down that the administrative departments should engage with copyright disputes in circumstances where the infringing acts have breached the authorship public interest, in order to avoid abuse of the administrative enforcement, which is likely to happen owing to the influence of the

---

[67]   See the Chinese government White Paper, The Conditions of the Protection of the Intellectual Property Rights in China.

[68]   See 许超, 关于著作权行政保护的几个问题 《中国版权》 2004年第1期8–12 页; Chao Xu, 'Some Issues Regarding Copyright Administrative Protection', *China Copyright* (2004), **1**, 8–12.

old traditions. For instance, disputes over uses of copyright works falling within the limitations and exceptions listed in Article 22 should be excluded from administrative enforcement. By limiting administrative enforcement, Article 47 intends to encourage people to guard their lawful rights through legal actions and channels. Indeed, it is taking another constructive step forward in changing the system away from the public notion of the traditional rule of man to the newly established rule of law.

Nevertheless, types of act that breach the authorship public interest and would be taken into concern by administrative authorities should be clarified in line with the Chinese laws. As the 2010 CCL currently provides exceptions for purposes such as research and private study, criticism, review and news reporting, education institutes, libraries and other knowledge providers to balance the rights of the owners and society as a whole, the criteria to determine acts against the authorship public interest may include, primarily, that the infringing act must be undertaken for commercial purposes; and that the infringement has damaged the social order, or has disobeyed common morality, or has harmed consumers' rights in general. Indeed, where an infringing act has also violated the public interest, judicial enforcement should be nevertheless adopted rather than the administrative proceeding, because such acts would damage the interest of the masses and should be decided in line with relevant laws for justice. A further dividing line should be drawn to define whether there should also be criminal enforcement taking account of the consequences of the damage. Hence, Article 48 of the 2010 CCL ought to be improved in future copyright law.

At present, administrative protection is playing a principal and positive role in Chinese copyright enforcement. It provides a simple, efficient and inexpensive service to copyright proprietors, and does stop infringement in one place, albeit temporarily. As revealed in the Autodesk case, the JSPCB inspected the infringer in cooperation with other administrative departments, properly obtained evidence and imposed a fine of RMB 800000 yuan, which, firstly, lawfully punished the infringing acts; secondly, set up a 'stop' sign for other parties who intend to breach the law; and thirdly, presented the Chinese authorities' determination to promote the use of legitimate works.

Furthermore, administrative law and regulations have been greatly developed and offer administrative protection agencies more rules to follow. Indeed, the Chinese government has been actively improving administrative copyright enforcement and has mobilised various sources to crack down on copyright infringement by combining trans-departmental law forces to act together. Coordinated by the authoritative departments of the Central Committee of the CCP, a nationwide working group for consolidating the newspaper, magazine, audio and video market was jointly set up for better copyright protection.[69]

However, the system of administrative enforcement in Chinese copyright still reflects the characteristics of the old legal tradition, the rule of man. It has granted administrative departments a quasi-judicial power, which has led to civil officials acting as judges, but most with very limited knowledge of understanding and implementing laws. This brings the dangers of arbitrary government power, a threat to individual liberty, and deterioration in enforcement of the laws.

As was well illustrated in the Huarong case, the HCB's interpretation of the Regulations 2006 is debatable and its narrow focus on the local government portal's contents, while ignoring the infringing acts in relation to 3100 films, reflects ignorance of copyright, as well as the court's defence over the government's interest and regional protectionism. The latter, commonly seen in China at present, results from the intense regional competition over the country since the adoption of the market economy, and local governments' consequent desires of maximising their own benefits, through employing measures more protective to local business rather than to non-locals, create unfair competition conditions in the market. Regional protectionism also violates domestic laws and WTO treaties, which detracts from state capacity and may eventually cause trade sanctions and so damage the national interest.

Huarong has brought out some basic yet sensible questions for Chinese lawmakers to answer, as follows: What contents on governmental portals are copyrighted works? How can people obtain permission for the use of state-owned copyright? What are the exceptions? These will be discussed in Chapter 6 in comparison with the circumstances in the UK and the US. It is reported that the NCAC is drafting "Regulations on State-owned Copyright Management" and consulting renowned scholars,[70] so the questions above should be answered in the near future.

Nonetheless, such amateur administrative protection may, in fact, weaken the legal enforcement and the development of the rule of law in China. Thus, on the one hand, it is vital to improve the expertise of current copyright administrative authorities, and, on the other hand,

---

[69] The group consists of the Ministry of Public Security, the Ministry of Culture, the Ministry of Broadcast, Film and Television, the Office of Journalism, the State Copyright Bureau, the State Industrial and Commercial Bureau, the Head Office of Customs, the Head Office of Civil Aviation, and the Ministry of Finance.

[70] See http://www.sipo.gov.cn/sipo/xwdt/ywdt/2008/200802/t20080218_23341 4.htm, retrieved on 11 March 2011.

the administrative authorities should be prepared to refrain from law enforcement in favour of the courts in due course.

China ought to develop and perfect its legal system further without delay. Administrative and legal instruments may have to be separate eventually in order to march firmly towards the rule of law. To ensure effective and efficient copyright protection in China, judicial enforcement, both civil and criminal, would be a more appropriate answer. Therefore, it is urgent, firstly, to facilitate Chinese litigation; secondly, to simplify court rules; and thirdly, to professionalise judges, as jurisdiction should be implemented by properly trained legal professionals. In the long term, the administrative departments should be removed from copyright enforcement and be focused on copyright promotion, management and service.

Moreover, the Chinese courts system ought to be reformed. An independent judicial system should be set up to secure justice within the law, which urges that:

- all levels of courts should be independent from governments at all levels;
- lower level courts should not be eligible to report to higher courts; and
- judges should review cases without supervision from presidents of the courts.

As reflected in the above cases, in general Chinese judges currently still lack experience; in addition, all levels of the courts, including their interpretation of the laws, are strongly influenced by the governments at all levels, for their finance is controlled by the latter, which makes the independence of the courts currently impossible. Only an independent court system would be able to implement the laws independently and maintain the justice of the law, which is obviously in the public interest. Further restructuring must be conducted within the court system as set out above, since at present the courts at all levels are run by the power-centralised tradition under which a judge has no authority to enforce the law.

It is not difficult to ascertain the main reasons for concerned parties choosing the administrative channel to enforce copyright laws in today's China. Firstly, the length, cost and publicity of a litigation process and the extensive resources that such a process requires, together with the fact that it puts the burden of proof on the copyright owner, are onerous, whilst the current administrative procedures are comparatively simple and clear; and secondly, the traditional Chinese attitude towards lawsuits probably still has a subconscious impact on the public. However, as the "infringing industry" becomes more profitable, and techniques and networks become increasingly sophisticated, judicial measures may become a preferable option, as, on the one hand, administrative penalties have failed to deter many infringers owing to their professional inadequacy; and as, on the other hand, in practice, there is often more than one administrative department involved in a copyright case investigation, which causes confusion.

Nonetheless, Xiqiao's insistence on demanding the courts' decisions to be reviewed has shown an up-to-date trend in China: to protect lawful rights via means of litigation. The Chinese public, in the past, had been strongly influenced by the Confucian philosophy of *he wei gui*, "harmony should be cherished";[71] thus, seeking mediation between the involved parties would remain the first choice, going to the administrative authorities would be second place, and taking a step forward to the courts would be the least favoured move. Now, legitimate rights including private rights are much more emphasised, laws are increasingly seen as an important means of protecting such rights, and lawsuits are no longer seen as bad luck or evil, but rather as a means to obtain justice or authorised explanations. Furthermore, unlike the period of the Cultural Revolution, concepts of free thinking and freedom of expression have become not only familiar but essential to the general public. That is why Xiqiao organised the press conference as soon as the second judgment was given in the Tenai case, to express disagreement with the authorities' decisions and urge not only the media's concern, but also the public's further discussion and the lawmakers' reconsideration of the public interest in copyright. Most encouragingly, discussions have been intensively carried out in multidisciplinary fields, including academic scholars, legal professionals and the general public, on a national scale; it was unsatisfactory to see the 2010 CCL taking no consideration of these, but hopefully they will stimulate further amendments in the future.

Copyright law grants Chinese administrative authorities the quasi-judicial power to enforce copyright throughout the country, with the purpose of strengthening the authorship public interest. The question is, how far should this quasi-judicial power go or where would administrative enforcement extend to? Indeed, that should be answered cautiously by perusing the public interest in a nation that demands and is pursing the rule of law.

It is thus proposed that China establish a copyright enforcement mechanism with Chinese characteristics. Whilst the independent People's Courts at all levels exercise judicial power for the states in accordance with

---

71 I.e. "礼之用，和为贵"，《论语》; "*li zhi yong, he wei gui*", Analects of Confucius.

the Constitution, a system of judicial copyright enforcement should be matured, where, on the one hand, the relevant courts are staffed by legal professionals with specific knowledge, and, on the other hand, suspected infringers can be proceeded against with appropriate civil or criminal sanctions.

Still, how to define the public interest within the copyright regime is a fundamental question for all. The concept of the public interest is nonetheless at a high level of abstraction and depends on relevance in context. It is impossible to give it an exhaustive definition. It is clear that the public interest concept has offered copyright a firm ground for its launch and development, and that it has been exercised as a tool to maintain a balance between the benefits of the copyright owners and the copyright users with its chief aspects of authorship and access. Studies on the public interest in the context of copyright are vital since it is mainly used as a legal argument in offering the limitations and exceptions of the subjective rights of the copyright owners. Laws are the codes that regulate the behaviour of members of a society and have seldom been neutral. It is thus difficult to believe in the existence of a neutral spectator in defining the public interest. It is, however, possible to try to accept and understand different views on the public interest whilst setting it in different circumstances, including diverse cultural and political backgrounds.

The public interest may be often seen as an accumulation of all items of individual self-interest that, when combined, demonstrate shared values rather than just the aggregation of individual items. The public interest in the context of copyright could be considered to be but in particular circumstances is not equal with the country's interest, nor the majority's interest or common interest (where this does not equate to the concept of combined shared values set out above), which can have numerous definitions. Nonetheless, this legal term should be defined and must be fully functional in order to enable the promotion of learning, the presentation of the public domain and the protection of the right proprietors. The definition of the public interest, on a national scale, should be led by the constitution, be constrained by copyright law, be formed by procedure and be comprehended and corrected by the practice of justice. To determine whether an act, either an infringing act or a legitimate undertaking, is in the public interest should take into account and meet any of the following criteria: firstly, if the act intends to promote the progress of knowledge and learning; secondly, if the act benefits the general welfare or common wellbeing; thirdly, if the act defends lawful private rights; and finally, in China particularly, if the act stimulates a socialist spirit and values.

Certainly, the concept of authorship public interest has not been widely accepted by the Chinese public. It thus should be advocated continuously so people can appreciate this unfamiliar aspect of the public interest in the Chinese context. It should be noted that the main Western philosophy under the principle of "the invisible hand" deems that each individual maximising revenue for himself or herself maximises the total revenue of society as a whole,[72] and thus individual benefits and rights are prioritised in general. On the contrary, the interest of the state has been the overriding principle in Chinese philosophy, and is also the foundation of today's Chinese Constitution and laws; hence, even if the private rights including property rights are authorised, such rights must obey the state's social and collective needs. The doctrine of the public interest in Chinese copyright intends to balance the exclusive property rights of the copyright owners with a social benefit through the free dissemination of information, but additionally it aims to retain and develop China's socialist spiritual civilisation. It thus grants the public interest a threefold dimension: the authorship public interest safeguards rights of copyright owners; the socialism public interest upholds the socialist principle and value; and the access public interest grants individuals the right to use copyright work without owners' consent in certain circumstances, including freedom of information, educational welfare, the spread and availability of knowledge, as well as the state's interests.

In the subsequent chapters, selected aspects will be discussed in order to study copyright and the multidimensional public interest primarily in China. Attention will be drawn to the following sectors: educational institutions, public libraries and public archives, which, on the one hand, fall into the category of the provisions of copyright exceptions based upon the access public interest concept according to copyright laws; and, on the other hand, have been most affected under the development of the modern law of copyright in China.

---

[72] "As every individual, therefore, endeavors as much he can both to employ his capital in the support of domestic industry, and so to direct that industry that its produce may be of the greatest value; every individual necessarily labors to render the annual revenue of the society as great as he can. He generally, indeed, neither intends to promote the public interest, nor knows how much he is promoting it. By preferring the support of domestic to that of foreign industry, he intends only his own security; and by directing that industry in such a manner as its produce may be of the greatest value, he intends only his own gain, and he is in this, as in many other cases, led by an invisible hand to promote an end which was no part of his intention." See Eamonn Butler, *Adam Smith: A Primer* (2007), 100.

4. Public education, copyright and the public interest

No school shall have dangerous buildings, every class shall have a classroom, and every student shall have a desk.[1]

1. INTRODUCTION

Education is crucial to the civilisation of human beings. It has the intention to foster learning, concerns with certain values and is future-oriented: it imparts culture from generation to generation. Education is also a fundamental human right; everyone has the right to education, and to pursue the aim of education for all is an obligation for each state.[2] Such endeavour has, however, the capacity to be affected by copyright. So, for example, in 2000 UNESCO set up an intergovernmental programme to accomplish its determined mission, "Information for All".[3] Moreover, UNESCO set "promotion of the free flow of ideas and universal access to information", especially in education, science, culture and communication, as one of its main strategies in 2002–2007.[4] It was not surprising that this was objected to by the International Publishers Association (IPA) as it is seen to undermine the rights of authors and publishers. The IPA asserts that the strategy conflicts with the international copyright treaties and purports to redefine or renegotiate aspects of them, which UNESCO had no authority to do. In 2008 UNESCO stated its

---

[1] The State Council's Requirements on Conditions of Schools of the People's Republic of China.

[2] See Article 26(1), Universal Declaration of Human Rights. See also Koïchiro Matsuura, 'Education for All: the Unfulfilled Promise', 21st Century Talks Session on Education for All: Always Tomorrow's Concern? (2002), http://portal.unesco.org/education/en, retrieved on 6 March 2011.

[3] See http://portal.unesco.org/ci/en/ev.php-URL_ID=1627&URL_DO=DO_TOPIC&URL_SECTION=201&URL_PAGINATION=30.html, retrieved on 6 March 2011.

[4] See Strategic Objective 10, UNESCO Medium-Term Strategy for 2002–2007, 46.

mid-term strategy was "enhancing universal access to information and knowledge".[5]

Regardless of the diverse systems adopted in different countries, educational activities are exceptions to copyright provided under the access public interest in Western countries such as fair dealing in the UK and fair use in the US, and in countries in the East such as limitations on rights in China. Based on the fair dealing doctrine, the UK CDPA offers certain exceptions for education, which include "things done for purposes of instruction or examination; anthologies for educational use; performing, playing or showing work in course of activities of educational establishment; recording by educational establishments of broadcasts and cable programmes and reprographic copying by educational establishments of passages from published works".[6] The US copyright law states that acts of using copyright works in teaching, scholarship, or research are fair provided the four-factor conditions of fair use are met.[7] And Chinese copyright grants legitimate use of any works for private study, research or compulsory education and the national educational programmes.[8]

Nonetheless, divergence certainly draws forth different provisions and the existence of a dilemma in each system. The UK and the US copyright rules are well established in education institutes and the overall legislative organisms are comparatively mature and systematic. It is recognised in the US that the immediate effect of copyright law is to secure a fair return for authors' creative labour, but the ultimate aim is, by this incentive, to stimulate artistic creativity for the general public good, that is, both aspects of authorship and access public interest are stressed in seeking balance in the regime. The sole interest and primary object of copyright in conferring the monopoly lie in the general benefits derived by the public from the labours of authors.[9] As Justice Ginsburg also notes, the parameters of fair use have to be always respected.[10] Moreover, the authorship and access aspects of the public interest doctrine require a balanced protection for rights holders and users. Lynne Brindley of the British Library reminded us:

> It is the role of a government to weigh the competing interests of a healthy public domain, which engenders education, innovation and creativity, with

[5] See Strategic Objective 12, UNESCO Medium-Term Strategy for 2008–2013, 30.

[6] Sections 32–36.

[7] See Section 107.

[8] Articles 22 and 23.

[9] See *Twentieth Century Music Corp. v Aiken*, 422 US 151, 156 (1975), cited in the MDS case.

[10] See *Eldred v Ashcroft*, No. 01–618 (2003).

the private interests of the individual creator and industry sector to monetize or make profit, healthy living, pension etc. from the fruit of their labours. Copyright law is a complex ecosystem of competing requirements and it is for government, through well-balanced and evidenced public policy formation, to square this set of often conflicting requirements for the greater good of society and the economy.[11]

Obviously, the access public interest sometimes conflicts with the economic rights of copyright owners, which have been strongly emphasised in the law's development. As a result of ongoing advances in IT, in 1996 joint working parties were established in the UK by the Joint Information Systems Committee and the Publishers Association to seek controls over digital exploitation of copyright works in the Higher Education Institutions (HEIs). The access public interest concept has been seen as a threat to certain industries, including publishers.[12] Some other groups strive to promote open source and the free distribution of works – for example, Copyleft makes programs such as Linux or other works free, Open Access offers free access to scholarly articles online, and the Creative Commons believes in free and open exchange of digital content and seeks to create a middle way between "the extremes of copyright-control, and the uncontrolled exploitation, of intellectual property". With all these, the access public interest is strongly advocated for "saving the world from failed sharing".[13] These ideas might sound akin to the Chinese traditional sharing culture, but they have two fundamental differences: the latter did not grant any individual rights other than moral satisfaction and such satisfaction was not secured by licensing, which reflects the absence of the rule of law.

Modern copyright having also been applied in the sought-after educational sectors in China, the interpretation, enforcement and efficiency of the law are developing and are of particular Chinese distinctiveness. This chapter aims to explore these differences, together with the changing position on uses of copyright works in Chinese educational sectors. Since the current copyright and education systems in China were modelled on the West, discussions will start with the UK and the US, and will be focused thereafter on the implementation of Chinese law.

---

[11]   See http://www.bl.uk/news/2008/pressrelease20080109a.html, retrieved on 4 March 2011.
[12]   See *Fair Use Promotes Important First Amendment Values*, House of Representatives, 16 June 2003.
[13]   See http://creativecommons.org, retrieved on 4 March 2011.

2.   THE WESTERN EXPERIENCES

As delivering high quality learning materials is fundamental to all knowl-edge and teaching, in addition to provisions for educational sectors, both the UK and the US have established comprehensive licensing systems and clear guidance on use of copyright works. In general, works of an educa-tional institute are mainly divided into two categories: materials where the copyright is held by the institute and those where it is owned by someone else, when the institute requires copyright clearance. For instance, in the use of text-related copyright works, whilst 14 different copyright licences are available for HEIs in the UK,[14] the US Copyright Clearance Center (CCC) offers 2 licences for academic licensing and permissions, covering all uses of works in HEIs.[15]

2.1   The UK Statutory Explanations

Section 29(1) of the CDPA establishes that "fair dealing with a literary, dramatic, musical or artistic work for the purposes of research for a non-commercial purpose or private study does not infringe any copyright in the work or, in the case of a published edition, in the typographical arrangement", while "research and private study" excludes research and study that is carried out for a commercial purpose. The CDPA, on the one hand, provides an author with the exclusive rights to make copies, to sell or distribute copies of the work in public, to prepare new works based on the copyright work, to perform the work in public and to display the work in public;[16] and, on the other hand, for users such as educational institu-tions, it grants them exceptions for copying an author's work without the author's consent under the fair dealing doctrine but maintains the author's exclusive rights to publish or distribute such works.[17] In addition, sections 35 and 36 provide exceptions for educational institutes recording broad-casts and cable programmes and the reprographic copying of passages from published works.

---

[14]   See E. Gadd, 'An Examination of the Copyright Clearance Activities in UK Higher Education', *Journal of Librarianship and Information Science* (2001), **33**(3), 112–25.

[15]   See http://www.copyright.com/ccc/viewPage.do?pageCode=ac1-n, retrieved on 4 March 2011.

[16]   See Section 16.

[17]   "Fair dealing with a literary work, other than a database, or a dramatic musical or artistic work for the purposes of research or private study does not infringe any copyright in the work." See section 29 and Part 2 of Amendments of the CDPA 1988, the Copyright and Related Rights Regulations 2003.

However, subsection (3) of section 29 grants that certain things done other than by the researcher or student herself/himself are not fair dealing if (a) in the case of a librarian, or a person acting on behalf of a librarian, she/he does anything which regulations under section 40 would not permit to be done under sections 38 or 39 (articles or parts of published works: restriction on multiple copies of same material), or (b) in any other case, the person doing the copying knows or has reason to believe that it will result in copies of substantially the same material being provided to more than one person at substantially the same time and for substantially the same purpose.

In December 2006, a review of the UK IP framework, which was commissioned by the Chancellor of the Exchequer and conducted independently by Andrew Gowers, was published.[18] This was known as the Gowers Review of Intellectual Property (Gowers Review). Amongst 54 other proposals, the Gowers Review recommends consideration be given to the implications of extending the provisions regarding copyright in education in the UK, including amending sections 35 and 36 of the CDPA 1988 to enable educational provisions to cover distance learning and interactive whiteboards,[19] since the "education exceptions are too limited for the digital age"[20] and also "do not apply to secure virtual learning environments (VLEs) or networked computers or 'intelligent whiteboards' within educational establishments".[21] The current section 35 provision only covers the use of copyright works in traditional teaching.[22] The Gowers Review proposed to extend the exception to cover distance learning, for example, to transmit the video of a lecture via the Internet to a student wherever he or she stays. The recommendations also include extension of the right of educational establishments provided by section 36, that is, to include passages from published works in handouts so that the same passages can be presented electronically to both students on campus and in distance learning programmes. Moreover, the Gowers Review points out that the current copyright clearance is "time consuming and expensive".[23]

Taking forward the Gowers Review, the UK IP Office has carried out public consultations on six proposed changes to copyright exceptions,

[18]   See the Gowers Review of Intellectual Property, retrieved on 4 March 2011 at http://www.hm-treasury.gov.uk/independent_reviews/gowers_review_intellect ual_property/gowersreview_index.cfm.

[19]   See the Gowers Review, 48.

[20]   Ibid., 47.

[21]   See 4.15.

[22]   See D. Browne, 'Educational Use and the Internet – Does Australian Copyright Law Work in the Web Environment?, *SCRIPTed* (2009), **6**(2), 449–66.

[23]   See 4.16.

including the two that would expand the fair dealing exceptions for educational institutions.[24] Taking IT development into serious consideration, the consultations investigate the possible impact on both copyright owners and users, and aims to "ensure that copyright law does not place unnecessary administrative burdens on business and can be understood and is respected by the general public".[25]

2.2   Case Law about Photocopying under Licensing

In September 2001, references under Sections 118, 119 and 121 of CDPA 1988 to the Copyright Tribunal led to a rather long discussion of the following three questions on a dispute between Universities UK and the Copyright Licensing Agency Limited (CLA). First, how much money should universities be required to pay under a licensing scheme for the photocopying by their staff and students of the literary and artistic copyright material contained in books and journals? Second, should there be a unitary licensing system, or a two-tier one in which an additional fee and advance clearance are required for course packs? And finally, what was meant by the exclusion from the current licensing scheme of separate illustrations, diagrams and photographs?[26]

The CLA is a collecting society set up by publishers that operates a scheme covering the making of photocopies and scans of parts of copyright works by staff and students in universities and other HEIs.[27] Based on the number of full-time educational students (FTES) at the institution, an annual fee has to be paid to CLA under a licensing scheme called the blanket licence (Current Licence) and the collected fees are then distributed to publishers and authors by CLA. The amount payable for the year 2000/2001 was £3.25 per FTES.

The original argument arose partly because the CLA insisted that the Current Licence did not include artistic works, and therefore requested

---

[24]   The first stage of consultation opened to the public between 8 January 2008 and 8 April 2008; and the second stage was launched on 11 December 2009 and closed on 31 March 2010.

[25]   See the first stage of the consultation paper, 10.

[26]   *Universities UK Limited, formerly Committee of Vice Chancellors and Principals of the United Kingdom v Copyright Licensing Agency, and Design and Artists Copyright Society Limited*, see http://patent.gov.uk/copy/tribunal/uuk-decision.pdf, retrieved on 29 March 2011; see also Copyright Tribunal (2002) RPC 119: 693–727. In addition, this case was analysed in depth by Professor Sol Picciotto: see 'Copyright Licensing: The Case of Higher Education Photocopying in the United Kingdom', *EIPR* (2002), 438–47.

[27]   See http://www.cla.co.uk/, retrieved on 4 March 2011.

additional fees for their reproduction.[28] However, the main reason was the strong concern of Universities UK (UUK) about the ever-increasing cost and bureaucracy of the licence in relation to course packs.[29] In particular, UUK objected to the complexity of having course packs excluded from the licence and subject to a separate clearance scheme, for which additional payment was required. The system for obtaining clearance for course packs was known as CLARCS (Copyright Licensing Agency Rapid Clearance Service). On giving individual clearance, CLA would inform the applicant of the fee payable if clearance was available.

Additionally, the Current Licence excluded separate artistic works from the scope. Later, the CLA introduced an Artistic Works Protocol that allowed copying under the scheme to extend to artistic works found in licensed material. UUK made a number of references to the Copyright Tribunal for decisions relating to aspects of the Current Licence, which included the cost, the format and the scope of the licence.[30] Furthermore, the Designs and Artists Copyright Society Limited (DACS) intervened in the case, arguing that an uplift of 20 per cent would be appropriate if the licensing scheme was to be extended to include artistic works.

Ultimately, a final order was issued by the Copyright Tribunal in April 2002 that:

- the restriction on course pack copying and the requirement for CLARCS clearance be removed from the Current Licence with effect from 1 August 2001;
- the exclusion of separate artistic works be deleted from the Current Licence with effect from 1 August 2001;
- the royalty shall be expressed as a sum per FTES per year, but not be based on any notional number of pages or price per page;

---

[28]   The CLA wanted a large uplift in royalty fees and the maintenance of Course Pack conditions. Costs were to be based on a "fair rate", which began at £13.09 less a discount for "fair deal" copying, which gave a fee of £10.25 + a further uplift for artistic works. The lowest figure quoted by the CLA was £4.44 + uplift for artistic works.

[29]   These were defined as four or more photocopied extracts from licensed material from one or more sources that exceeded 25 pages, intended to be provided to students with a compilation of materials designed to support the teaching of a course of study and prepared and distributed in advance of or during the course of study either piecemeal or in batches. A further requirement was that the copies distributed could not exceed 5 per cent of any published edition or, in the case of a book, not more than one chapter or a single article in a serial publication.

[30]   UUK suggested a figure of £0.60 per FTES with no separate provisions for course packs and a unitary licensing scheme instead of the present blanket licence plus CLARCS.

- with effect from 1 August 2001 the royalty shall be increased to £4.00 per FTES per academic year increasing in line with the increase in the RPI on an annual basis on 1 August each year; and
- the new scheme shall run for five years from 1 August 2001.

Above all, the principles of fair dealing continue to apply to any photocopying carried out in UK educational institutions.

The issue of copying has always been the core of the copyright system. Undeniably, photocopying is still one of the most popular methods within educational institutions with reference to copyright works since it can "greatly reduce both distribution costs, and in effect those of production".[31] Instead of a general licensing scheme, a system called the Blanket Licensing Scheme is adopted between the CLA and educational institutions in the UK, and followed by most industrial countries.

Certainly, the decision of the Copyright Tribunal in *UUK v CLA* has, to some extent, relieved the academic communities in the UK. Apart from reduced costs, it is delightful to see the decisions to permit multiple photocopying, without a bureaucracy-bounded page limit, of extracts from certain published books and periodicals and other printed materials by, and for the benefit of, university staff and students,[32] which includes course pack photocopying. Academics, on the one hand, do not have to waste their time obtaining CLARCS clearance for every piece in a course pack; and, on the other hand, theoretically speaking, they can concentrate on providing the best material for the students instead of wandering around in cyberspace looking for copyright-free material.

Nonetheless, for copies made in support of university courses there are still specific limits for both the proportion of the original source that may be photocopied and the number of copies that may be made. The proportion of any one source of licensed materials that may be photocopied, either singly or aggregately, is set out as follows:[33]

- one complete chapter per book or up to 5 per cent by page count;
- one whole article or up to 5 per cent per issue of a periodical;
- one whole article or up to 5 per cent per set of conference proceedings;
- one short story or poem not exceeding ten pages from any one anthology; or

---

[31] See S. Picciotto, 'Copyright Licensing: The Case of Higher Education Photocopying in the United Kingdom', *EIPR* (2002), 446.
[32] Students enrolled on short-term courses are excluded.
[33] See http://www.cla.co.uk, retrieved on 8 March 2011.

- one report of a case or up to 5 per cent per set of judicial decisions.

Moreover, except for cascade copying from items held in the Heavy Demand Collection[34] (such items still need to be copyright-cleared), the Blanket Licence excludes electronic materials, for which separate and often expensive agreements have to be made. However, it is well known that copying in electronic format is an essential usage in today's life including in the activities of educational institutions, and particularly with Internet-based teaching activities, that is, distance education. It is disagreeable to find that such fair dealing is not included in the Blanket Licence.

It should be noted that the Gowers Review brings some freshness and flexibility into the UK's limited education provisions and has been broadly welcomed by both educational institutions and copyright campaigners,[35] whilst opposed by others, mainly right holders groups.[36] The IPO's consultations on the Gowers Review demonstrate that the UK may take an active and effective approach in turning the recommendation into laws whilst maintaining concern for the particular balance between the interests of the right holders and those of the users in educational institutions. Furthermore, such practice may stimulate evidence-based rulemaking in the future.

2.3   Developments of the Fair Use Doctrine in the US

Reflecting ideas about the public interest, the US copyright law gives an author of a work an economic incentive to create new works and therefore advance the progress of knowledge. Based on the fair use doctrine, the US law provides educational institutes with exceptions to the exclusive rights. It upholds the access public interest and grants that "such use by reproduction in copies or phonorecords" for purposes such as teaching (including multiple copies for classroom use), scholarship, or research,

---

[34]   In order to maximise access for students to essential reading items, those materials that are in heavy demand by students are held under this catalogue and are issued for short loan periods, which include assorted materials such as course notes, sample exam papers, lecturers' notes, and audio and visual materials.

[35]   Such as the Open Right Group, http://www.openrightsgroup.org/2006/12/06/gowers-review, retrieved on 29 March 2011; Creative Comments and Open Democracy   http://www.opendemocracy.net/media-copyrightlaw/gowers_4160.jsp, retrieved on 29 March 2011.

[36]   Such as UK publishers and the British Phonographic Institute.

is not an infringement of copyright, provided that the four factors are considered and satisfied.[37] Fair use permits reasonable uses for non-profit education and research that do not interfere with the copyright owners' normal exploitation of the works or unreasonably prejudice their rights, and is thus compatible with the Berne three-step test.

Dramatic advances in communications technology have offered many exciting opportunities for educational and informational programmes. Academic institutions, either individually or as part of networks, now use satellite and other technologies to distribute instructional programming ("telecourses" is the term used in the US) and share research findings on a regional, national and even international basis. Persons working in remote locations or at full-time jobs or studying at widely dispersed campuses benefit from distance learning by taking courses and earning college degrees, continuing education credits or job-site training via telecommunications.

To meet the demands of the rapid development of digital technology and to implement the WCT that the US signed in 1996, the Digital Millennium Copyright Act (DMCA) was passed in October 1998, and became effective in October 2000. The DMCA addresses a number of issues that are of concern to libraries. The key topics are provisions concerning the circumvention of copyright systems, online service providers' (OSPs) liability, and fair use in a digital environment, including the activities of distance education. Besides, it was not so obvious whether the creation of digital clips from legally-obtained DVDs should be allowed to take place in colleges and universities, for the purpose of classroom teaching and other non-profit educational activities.

Moreover, the Technology, Education and Copyright Harmonization Act (TEACH) was signed into law in November 2001 and enacted in November 2002. TEACH amends the US copyright law[38] to allow non-profit educational institutions to use the Internet to provide copyrighted material to registered students taking part in mediated instructional activities, without permission from the copyright owner and payment of royalties. Apart from expanding the receiving locations greatly, TEACH permits[39]

---

[37] See section 107, Copyright Law of the US.

[38] Section 110 (2) permitted educators to perform only certain types of works and generally allowed transmissions to be received only in classrooms and similar locations.

[39] See http://www.copyright.gov/legislation/pl107-273.pdf, retrieved on 9 March 2011.

- the display and performance of nearly all types of works,
- the digitisation of some analog works, and
- the storage of transmitted content.

On 3 December 2004, the Individuals with Disabilities Education Act (IDEA) came into force, and it further expands authorised reproduction of copyright works for the blind or people with other disabilities on the ground of public interest.[40]

The Copyright Clearance Center (CCC) was established in 1978 at the suggestion of Congress as a not-for-profit corporation to represent authors, publishers and other rights holders in the USA. The CCC serves as a bridge between copyright holders and those who seek to reproduce copyright works, and it operates collective licensing systems that facilitate compliance with the copyright law. These include:[41]

- Transactional Reporting Service, for instant permission to photocopy copyrighted materials;
- Republication Licensing Service, for permission to reproduce copyright works in your own materials from books and journals to email and websites;
- Electronic Course Content Service, for permission to use copyrighted materials in electronic course packs, electronic reserves and distance learning; and
- Academic Permissions Service, covering photocopy permissions for course packs and class handouts.

With regard to reproduction of copyright works, US educational institutes have two options from the CCC, which has now become the world's largest provider of text licensing: in addition to the Pay-per-use License, an Annual Copyright License that permits use of print and electronic materials, from books, scholarly journals, news and trade magazines and newspapers and many others, in course management systems, paper and electronic course packs, e-reserves, research collaborations, etc.[42] In

---

[40]   See http://www.wrightslaw.com/idea/idea.2004.all.pdf, retrieved on 9 March 2011.

[41]   See http://www.copyright.com/ccc, retrieved on 9 March 2011.

[42]   See www.beyondthebookcast.com/wp-images/ALPR_IB0208_Academic_License_Press_Release.pdf, the CCC's News Release; retrieved on 9 March 2011. Other collecting societies in the US include the Artists Rights Society of New York (ARS), the American Society of Composers, Authors, and Publishers (ASCAP), Broadcast Music Incorporated (BMI), Christian Copyright Licensing International (CCLI), and the Society of European Stage Authors & Composers (SESAC).

November 2009, the Copyright Office and the Library of Congress published a circular recounting relevant provisions to guide educators' and librarians' use of copyright works.[43]

2.4   Fair or Not Fair: The Four-Factor Provision

Traditionally, in considering fair use, the four factors specifically set forth in section 107 of the US Copyright Act generally[44] also apply to educational uses of copyright works. It is necessary to conduct an analysis in line with the four factors for any fair use assertion, because each sets different boundaries. Acts satisfying the statute provision should amount to fair use for all interested parties. The questions to be considered are:

- What is the character of the use?
- What is the nature of the work to be used?
- What amount of the work will be used?
- What effect would this use have on the market for the original or for permissions if the use were widespread?

Obviously, not all uses of copyright works are fair use even in educational institutions. In general, an act of using a copyright work in a non-profit educational institution is more likely to be fair use than use of works for commercial purposes, while reproducing a factual work is more likely to be fair use than reproducing an artistic creative work such as a musical composition. Reproducing smaller portions of a work is more likely to be fair use than large or essential portions. Uses that have no or little market impact are more likely to be fair use than those that intervene in potential markets. The four-factor provision has been discussed in depth in several cases.[45] Most relevant for present purposes

---

[43]   See http://www.copyright.gov/circs/circ21.pdf, retrieved on 16 March 2011.

[44]   As discussed in Chapter 2, p. 95.

[45]   See for instance *American Geophysical Union v Texaco (Texaco), INC.*, 37 F.3d 881 (2nd Cir. 1994). The Texaco case is a widely known lawsuit of fair dealing in which a group of publishers sued the Texaco Corporation in 1985 citing infringement by an individual scientist who had photocopied articles from scientific journals. The central issue of the case was whether making a single copy of scientific articles for personal use was considered a fair use. After several levels of appeals, the case was settled in May 1995. This settlement means that the case will not be heard by the United States Supreme Court, which might otherwise have clarified the concept of fair use. However, this case applied only to for-profit corporations and not to educational or non-profit institutions.

is the discussion in *Princeton University Press v Michigan Document Services* (MDS).[46]

The defendant MDS created course packs for professors and students at nearby universities. MDS prepared a master copy of all the materials selected by the professor, created a table of contents, identified excerpts by author and name of the underlying work, numbered the pages, and then bound the copied excerpts together. These course packs were sold to students for use only in a particular course. The course packs were priced on a per-page basis, regardless of the contents of the page. The fee for a page reproducing copyrighted materials was the same as the fee for a blank page.

Furthermore, the professors stated that they received no commissions or other economic benefit from delivering course pack materials to MDS and that in each case they would not have otherwise assigned the various readings if students had to buy the entire publication.

Six excerpts extracted from works to which the plaintiffs held the copyrights were examined by the court and the conclusion was that a range of 5 per cent to 30 per cent of the original works had been copied. All the plaintiffs had their own permissions department to process the evaluating requests, granting permission and charging fees. But the publisher stated that it would not have given permission to copy but would have insisted that students buy the entire book because the requested portion was too large and the price of the book was modest. Nevertheless, MDS did not seek permission or pay royalties for any of its copies.

The four factors were considered. First, the court found that the purpose and character of the use was mixed; although the ultimate purpose of the course packs was to serve the non-profit educational objectives, MDS was seeking to make a profit. Second, with regard to the nature of the copyright work, the court recognised that non-fiction works, which were at issue in this case, may be used or subject to fair use more extensively than fiction. Third, the amount and substantiality of the portion used in this case ranged from 5 per cent to 30 per cent of the original work. Finally, the effect of the use upon the potential market for, or value of, the copyright work was focused upon significantly by the District Court and the entire Sixth Circuit Court of Appeals. Both courts concluded that the market effects based on MDS paying fees to the plaintiffs for permission to make photocopies, and its failure to do so, had an adverse effect on that particular market for the works.

---

[46] See *Princeton University Press, Macmillan, Inc., and St. Martin's Press, Inc. v Michigan Document Services, Inc., and James M. Smith*, 1996 Fed App. 0046P (6th Cir.)

Summary judgment was entered by the District Court against MDS, the court finding that the MDS copying of materials was not fair use, and the publishers were granted a permanent injunction against MDS making any use of any of their works, those existing now and in the future, without their permission.

The first opinion[47] issued by the Sixth Circuit Court overturned the lower court's decision, called the copying "educational", and held that producing course packs for students at the University of Michigan was fair dealing. The court asserted that the four factors are not an exclusive list of the factors relevant to a fair use determination. Thus, an additional factor, incentive to create[48] in this specialised field, was considered, and was thought to "weigh in favour of a finding of fair use".[49] Still, after rehearing the case in April 1996, the entire Sixth Circuit Court vacated the reversal and reinstated the District Court's opinion. The entire court held that MDS's systematic and premeditated copying for commercial motivation was infringing.

An up-to-date copyright system has been established in the US since the DMCA and TEACH were signed into law. While the former was severely criticised in both the legal and Internet communities, it is seen as the "most comprehensive reform of United States copyright law in a generation".[50] Educational institutions are identified as one of the six copyright exceptions in the DMCA,[51] and the Register of Copyrights is required to consider:[52]

- the need for an exemption from exclusive rights of copyright owners for distance education through digital networks;
- the categories of works to be included under any distance education exemption;

---

[47]   The first opinion is called the "Three-judge MDS opinion" and the second opinion is called the "En Banc MDS opinion".

[48]   More than 100 authors declared on record that they write for professional and personal reasons such as making a contribution to the discipline, providing an opportunity for colleagues to evaluate and critique the authors' ideas and theories, enhancing the authors' professional reputations, and improving career opportunities.

[49]   See para E.

[50]   See http://www.educause.edu/issues/dmca.html, retrieved on 16 March 2011.

[51]   The other five are: non-profit library, archive; reverse engineering; encryption research; protection of minors; and personal privacy and security testing. See section 1201 (d)–(j).

[52]   See Section 403.

- the extent of appropriate quantitative limitations on the portions of works that may be used under any distance education exemption;
- the parties who should be entitled to the benefits of any distance education exemption;
- the parties who should be designated as eligible recipients of distance education materials under any distance education exemption;
- whether and what types of technological measures can or should be employed to safeguard against unauthorised access to, and use or retention of, copyrighted materials as a condition of eligibility for any distance education exemption;
- the extent to which the availability of licenses for the use of copyright works in distance education through interactive digital networks should be considered in assessing eligibility for any distance education exemption; and
- such other issues relating to distance education through interactive digital networks that the Register considers appropriate.

The DMCA also required the Copyright Office to conduct a study on how to promote distance learning through digital technologies, while "maintaining an appropriate balance between the rights of the copyright owners and the needs of users of copyright works".[53] After the Copyright Office consultation with representatives of copyright owners and non-profit education and library institutions, as an extension of DMCA, TEACH provides legal guidance to US educational institutions on using copyrighted material in distance education. It states that:

- qualified non-profit educational institutions will receive exemption from copyright law relating to use of copyright materials in distance education;
- students who are officially enrolled in the distance education courses are allowed to be recipients of the copyright materials; and
- guidelines are provided on "reasonable" and "technologically feasible" methods institutions can implement to qualify for exemption.

TEACH offers, with relative clarity and certainty, a right of educational use in the Internet environment. It has confirmed clearly the application of fair dealing to scanning, uploading, downloading and transmission of copyrighted materials for distance education. Furthermore, the Individuals with Disabilities Education Act (IDEA) allows teachers to find

---

[53] See section 403.

the best proper means to help students with different disabilities. IDEA is strongly public-interest-orientated and strengthens academic expectations and accountability for the 15 million children with disabilities in the US.

Nonetheless, the case of MDS provides the most relevant judicial guidance about copyright law as it pertains to multiple photocopying and course packs in educational institutions in general. The courts' decisions indicate that, apart from DMCA, TEACH and IDEA, the making and selling of customised anthologies or course packs without the copyright owners' permission is infringing and oblige those who compile and sell course packs not to change the practice of obtaining permissions from copyright owners when using excerpts of copyright works.

Fair use doctrine is what the US educational institutions rely upon in use of copyright works. The four-factor provision is vital in determining whether such a use is fair and the factors constantly interplay with each other. The law is broad and flexible and requires a thoughtful analysis of each of the four factors based on specific circumstances. In applying the four fair use factors, each is relevant in order to determine whether a particular use is a fair use. A final determination on fair use depends on weighing and balancing all four factors against the facts of an individual situation. A non-profit purpose under the first factor has traditionally affected the consideration of the weight of the third factor, how much one may copy, and the fourth factor, the effect of the proposed use on the market for the copyright work.

Although MDS did not create or publish anthologies, all selection and arrangement of content was determined by the professors and the materials were not sold to the public. The lost revenues were emphasised. Numerous academic authors claim that they do not write primarily for money and that they want their published writings to be freely copyable within educational institutions. However, they were not the copyright holders, but the publishers. As Judge Nelson noted in his dissent, the publishers obviously need economic incentives to publish scholarly works, even if the scholars do not need direct economic incentives to write such works.[54]

It is said that the current state of educational fair use is troublesome as it provides educators with no identifiable standards and rules, by which they may operate "to maintain fidelity to the law of fair use, and to facilitate the learning process without fear of litigation by publishers and copyright owners".[55] Seeing the uniqueness and importance of education,

---

[54]   See paras 164–5.

[55]   See D.A. Simon, 'Teaching Without Infringement: A New Model for Educational Fair Use', *Fordham Intellectual Property, Media & Entertainment Law Journal* (2010), **20**, 561.

"an executive agency devoted exclusively to administering fair use within the education sector" has been proposed,[56] based upon the advocate of the creation of an agency to administer fair use generally,[57] to create a "workable, flexible and coherent legal framework" for assessing whether particular educational uses are fair.[58]

On 14 August 2008, the Higher Education Opportunity Act (HEOA) was signed into law after five years of consultations, which re-authorised the Higher Education Act (HEA) of 1965 and the regulations for implementing the HEOA were issued by the Department of Education on 29 October 2009. Embracing the economic and technological situations, the lengthy HEOA modernises the HEA. In addition to provisions such as state higher education spending,[59] increasing federal Pell Grant maximums,[60] improving transparency in tuition increases for consumers,[61] and requiring institutions and lenders to adopt, publicise and enforce a code of conduct for student loan,[62] the HEOA deals with unauthorised file sharing on campus networks and imposes three general requirements on colleges and universities, which are:

- an annual disclosure that explicitly informs students on copyright law and campus policies related to the law;[63]
- a plan to effectively combat the unauthorised distribution of copyrighted materials through the use of a variety of technology-based deterrents;[64] and
- a plan to offer alternatives to illegal downloading.[65]

---

[56]   Ibid., 528.

[57]   See J. Mazzone, 'Administering Fair Use', *William and Mary Law Review* (2009), **51**, 395–415.

[58]   See above, n. 55, at 528.

[59]   See Section 137.

[60]   See Section 401.

[61]   See Section 111.

[62]   Sections 421–466.

[63]   See Section 488P(i)–(iii).

[64]   See Section 493(29)A; according to the Managers Report that accompanied the HEOA, the technology-based deterrents are of four categories: (1) bandwidth shaping, (2) traffic monitoring to identify the largest bandwidth users, (3) a vigorous programme of accepting and responding to the DMCA notices, and (4) different commercial products designed to reduce or block illegal file sharing.

[65]   See Section 493(29)B.

3.   MADE IN CHINA

3.1   A Brief Introduction to Chinese Education[66]

Historically, education has been prioritised in China, so that teachers were called "father" in the past and "the engineers of the human soul" today, and have been highly respected in society.[67] The traditional Chinese culture believes that 万般皆下品，唯有读书高, "education is the only decent business among ten-thousand of such". Moreover, education has been regarded as an extremely important means leading towards personal achievement and career success.

Chinese school education has had a record of several thousand years ever since the Xia dynasty (c.2100–1800 BC), when education was controlled by governmental official schools set up for the nobles. Confucius, the greatest Chinese educator and philosopher, initiated private schools and advocated free teaching and learning, which broke the noble monopoly of education and made it possible for ordinary people.[68] Thereafter, private schools developed as part of the Chinese educational system side by side with official schools. The primary objective of feudal education was to train officials, and the imperial examination system was an important form of education in the feudal society from the Sui dynasty on. As mentioned in the first chapter, Confucianism and the Confucian classics were the main contents of education throughout Imperial China until 1911. Modern schools were introduced to China in the 1860s, which included schools specialising in foreign languages, military and technical education. In 1905, the imperial examination system was abolished. A "new educational system"[69] was established that was based on Chinese traditional learning together with Western knowledge to be acquired for practical purposes, although ancient classics continued to be read and Confucianism extolled. In 1912, the newly founded Republic of China reformed the educational system and set the aim as being to develop students in a balanced manner. After the anti-imperialist and anti-feudal May 4th Movement in 1919,

---

[66] See 王炳照、郭齐家、刘德华、贺晓夏、高奇 (2006) 《简明中国教育史》 (修订版) Bingzhao Wang et al., *The Compendious History of Education in China* (2006).

[67] A quote in the Records of the Grand Historian, which is widely known in China: 一日为师, 终身为父, "being a teacher for one day, being the father for life". And Neo-Confucianism claims that 天地君亲师, "teacher" has the same social status as "the heaven" and "the king".

[68] Confucius, 551–479 BC, had more than 3000 students.

[69] This was divided into three stages:. nine years of primary, five years of secondary and seven years of higher education.

Confucian classics were withdrawn from school education. Western teaching theories and methods were introduced and education became more oriented towards the common people and more practical. In addition, girls were allowed to be enrolled in schools, so girls' education thus started in China.[70]

In 1949, a system consisting of pre-school, regular and adult education began to take shape, with an emphasis on gender equality. In 1957, Mao proposed that the Chinese educational policy must enable everyone who receives an education to develop morally, intellectually and physically, and to become a worker with both socialist consciousness and culture. This policy guided the development of education in China until the mid-1980s. During the Cultural Revolution of 1966–1976, the concept of education was upturned and its development was broken off: enrolment in higher educational institutions ceased, teaching and learning in primary and middle schools were disrupted, and textbooks were full of political slogans. People were fed the concepts of "learning is useless" and "intellectuals are *chou lao jiu*", (intellectuals, including all teachers, deserved low social status). After the Cultural Revolution, the reform of the educational system was carried out following the Reform and Opening-up Policy. Education-related modern laws and regulations were enacted in China for the first time, including Regulations on Academic Degrees 1980,[71] Compulsory Education Law 1986, Teachers Law 1993, Education Law 1995, Vocational Education Law 1996, Higher Education Law 1998 and Regulations on Chinese-Foreign Cooperation in Running Schools 2003, together with 16 administrative regulations and more than 200 administrative rules. A legal framework for education has thus taken shape.[72]

At present, the Chinese educational system is divided into four stages: basic education, middle-level vocational education, higher education and adult education.[73] Basic education includes programmes of pre-school, six-year primary school, three-year middle school and three-year high school or middle-level vocational school. A nine-year compulsory schooling policy is adopted, which means that all children are required to complete at least both the primary school programme and the middle

---

[70] See 施正良, 传统德育经验传承中的现代转换, 《中国教育导刊》 2007年12期 17–19页; Zhengliang Shi, 'The Modernisation of Traditional Moral Education', *Journal of China Education* (2007), **12**, 17–19.

[71] This was amended at the 11th Session of the Standing Committee of the 10th National People's Congress on 28 August 2004.

[72] See the MoE website, http://www.moe.edu.cn/english/laws_e.htm, retrieved on 16 March 2011.

[73] See http://www.moe.edu.cn/edoas/website18/09/info4009.htm, retrieved on 16 March 2011.

school programme for free. An entrance examination is set for high schools or middle-level vocational schools. Higher education is possible only for those students who have passed examinations at all lower levels. Moreover, for admission to universities, the National College Entrance Examination (NCEE) has to be taken. The once-a-year NCEE is considered the most important examination in China: people believe that it can change examinees' lives in today's competitive society. In June 2009, 10.2 million examinees took the NCEE, whilst around 6 million were able to enter universities or colleges at all levels and of all kinds.[74] Undergraduate programmes take four or five years, masters' degree programmes three years, and doctoral programmes another three years.

A fees system has been adopted since 1995, instead of the previous free university education that had lasted since 1949. The average of tuition fees plus on-campus dormitories has reached RMB 4000 yuan annually, which is ten times larger than the average income increase.[75] Although fees can be paid for by all levels of governments, the rapid growth has been seriously criticised by many interested parties and individuals. In January 2007, the Ministry of Education (MoE) announced that a regulation on higher education fees would be enacted in the near future,[76] although it is still awaited.

Chinese adult education overlaps with all the above programmes. Adult primary education includes workers' primary schools, peasants' primary schools, and literacy classes. Adult secondary education includes radio and TV specialised secondary schools, specialised secondary schools for cadres (officers of public institutions), specialised secondary schools for staff and workers, specialised secondary schools for peasants, in-service teacher training schools and correspondence specialised secondary schools. Adult higher education includes radio and TV universities, cadre institutes, workers' colleges, peasant colleges, correspondence colleges, and educational colleges. Most of the above programmes offer both two and three year short-cycle curricula; only a few also offer regular undergraduate curricula.

Furthermore, distance learning plays a significant role in Chinese education because of the massive demands and the poor economic foundation.

---

[74] See http://www.gov.cn/jrzg/2009-06/02/content_1330614.htm, retrieved on 16 March 2011.

[75] See http://finance.people.com.cn/BIG5/1037/5282438.html, retrieved on 16 March 2011.

[76] See http://news.xinhuanet.com/edu/2007-01/04/content_5562872.htm and http://www.china.com.cn/news/txt/2007-01/09/content_7628071.htm, retrieved on 16 March 2011.

Most HEIs in China offer distance learning programmes; depending on means of communication, distance learning is distinguished as mail, radio, television and Internet-based. The rapid development of IT, especially of the Internet,[77] has greatly stimulated the progress of Chinese education. To 2008, the gross enrolment ratio in higher education reached 23 per cent, compared to 6.5 per cent in 1995.[78] Constructed and operated by Tsinghua and other leading universities, the China Education and Research Network (CERNET) has been founded.[79] CERNET now connects 1 million computers in 900 universities over 100 cities.[80] According to the MoE, over 10 per cent of universities and colleges in China now have campus networks, whilst 60 per cent use various technologies.

Currently, education is seen as a foundation to promote the cultural and economic development of the country, and thus the educational sector still has a much higher esteem than others. Regarding copyright, both educational institutions and the public are used to education privileges, a particular Chinese concept that is almost equivalent to 'copyright free'. Indeed, the concept of education privileges has been widely accepted by the Chinese. For instance, ask anyone in China whether or not it is fair to make free use of copyrighted materials in the classroom, and his or her answer would most likely be, "Of course it is!" If you ask further why, the answer probably would still be the same as the person takes this for granted and would tend not to give you an explanation. Not only most of the public, but also the majority of educators recognise that education has important social benefits and that the relevant uses of copyrighted materials should be exempt from the usual legal obligations.

---

[77] China launched its Copyright Registration System in March 2009 and, according to the official website www.copyright.com.cn, all copyright registrations can be filed online, including software copyright, software transfer and licence contract, works copyright registration, copyright contract recordation, and copyright pledge contract.

[78] See http://www.moe.gov.cn/edoas/website18/level2.jsp?tablename=1261364 343113580, retrieved on 17 March 2011. Note that firstly, the gross enrolment refers to the percentage of total number of students at school to the population of school age students prescribed by the government; and secondly, higher education includes graduate education, regular institutions of higher education undergraduates, adult institutions of higher education undergraduates, military institutions of higher education undergraduates, degree and diploma education, television higher education, and self-taught higher education.

[79] This was the first nationwide education and research computer network and has been funded by the Chinese government and directly managed by the MoE since July 1994.

[80] http://www.edu.cn/cernet_jian_jie_1327/20060323/t20060323_91159.shtml, retrieved on 6 March 2011.

3.2 Provisions for Education

The Chinese law states that copyright owners, in exercising their rights, shall never prejudice the public interest. It provides educational institutions with the right to access copyright work "without permission from, and without payment of remuneration to, the copyright owner".[81] However, no other specific provisions were offered in the CCL 1990 with regard to the educational uses of copyright works apart from the section of limitations on rights, which mentioned that teachers may reproduce or translate a small quantity of copies of published works, in classroom teaching, without the copyright owners' permission.[82]

The CCL 2001 provides an additional Article stating that parts of published works, short written works, musical works or single copies of works of painting or photographic works may be compiled into textbooks for the nine-year compulsory education and the national educational programme without consent from the authors, except where the authors have declared in advance that the use thereof is not permitted. The law meanwhile asserts that remuneration must be paid for such uses; also, the name of the author and the title of the work must be indicated, without prejudice to other rights enjoyed by the copyright owners.[83]

Collective management of copyright and copyright clearance is currently under development. In accordance with the CCL 2001, the Regulations on Collective Management of Copyright were adopted in December 2004 to facilitate copyright owners and owners of rights related to copyright to exercise their rights and users' rights to use works.[84] The Regulations define "organisation for collective administration of copyright" as "a mass organisation which is legally established for the benefit of right owners and which, with the owner's authorisation, collectively administers their copyright or rights related to copyright".[85] The Regulations also approve the "agreement for reciprocal representation", agreements between a Chinese collective society and overseas organisations of the same kind mutually authorising the other party to carry out activities of collective administration of copyright in the country or region to which the other party belongs.[86] This responds to China's role as a part of the international community and to the need to protect and manage foreign

---

[81] See Article 22.
[82] See Article 22(6).
[83] See Article 23.
[84] See Article 1.
[85] See Article 3.
[86] See Article 22.

copyright owners' lawful rights in China. The requirements for setting up such an organisation are:[87]

- the initiators should be Chinese citizens, legal entities or other organisations that enjoy copyright;
- the number of owners who initiate the establishment of such an organisation should not be less than 50;
- the envisaged operating scope of such an organisation should not overlap or coincide with that of another registered organisation of the same kind;
- the organisation must be able to operate on behalf of the interests of the relevant owners nationwide; and
- the statute, the rates for collecting licensing fees, and the methods for distribution of licensing fees among the owners of the organisation must have been regulated.

The Music Copyright Society of China (MCSC), established in 1992, is the oldest and most active collecting society in China.[88] Representing musical work copyright owners, the MCSC focuses on reproduction and performing rights, taking action on infringement for commercial purposes primarily, such as pirated discs, illegal downloading on the Internet and background music playing in business premises.[89] At present, hotels, department stores and supermarkets in China have started to pay royalties for playing copyright music, whilst most television and radio stations are still using music works for "free".[90] Although licensing and assignment contracts are approved by the law, the CCL 2001 confirms that "a user of a work of another shall be in possession of a concluded licensing contract with the copyright owner, except where no license is required by this

---

[87]   See Article 7.
[88]   See http://www.mcsc.com.cn/index.do, retrieved on 17 March 2011. Other collecting societies are the Written Works Copyright Society of China (WWCSC), which was founded in December 2008 and the Sound and Visual Copyright Society of China (SVCSC) that was set up in May 2008 mainly for the purpose of regulating the karaoke industry; see http://news.xinhuanet.com/newmedia/2008-05/29/content_8274247.htm, retrieved on 17 March 2011. On behalf of hundreds of Chinese writers, the CWWCS accused Google Book of copyright infringement in October 2009 and its negotiation with Google on compensation to authors is underway notwithstanding the search engine giant's apology made in January 2010 over unauthorised scanning of tens of thousands of books; see http://www.prccopyright.org.cn/News_View.asp?NewsID=101, retrieved on 17 March 2011.
[89]   See http://www.mcsc.com.cn/xhjj.htm, retrieved on 17 March 2011.
[90]   See   http://www2.chinadaily.com.cn/china/2007-09/02/content_6073626.htm, retrieved on 17 March 2011.

Law".[91] The approaches adopted in practice are twofold: to obtain permission individually and to obtain permission collectively. In the former users try to find the copyright owners to get permission; in the latter copyright owners search for prospective users to negotiate their rights to use works.

3.3　A Warning to All Chinese Education Institutes and a Debate on Whether Exam Questions Should Be Copyrighted

The use of copyright works of any kind in Chinese educational institutes was not challenged until 2001, and then by a foreign organisation.

On 30 January 2001, the Educational Testing Service of the US (ETS) issued a letter to all American universities to urge them to treat each and every GRE and TOEFL test score from China with caution, as "certain individuals may have gained unfair advantage through intensive coaching that included exposure to undisclosed exam questions".[92] The ETS, "the world's largest developing, achievement, occupational, and admissions tests for clients in the areas of education, government, and business",[93] deals with the Graduate Record Examination (GRE) and the Test of English as a Foreign Language (TOEFL) in 181 countries across the world. During 1998 and 1999, 11 million people took part in the examinations held by the ETS.

The institute that offered "intensive coaching" named by the ETS in that letter was Beijing New Oriental Private School (New Oriental) – a Beijing-based test-preparation education group – one of the most successful private educational institutions in China. It owns first-class chain-schools providing after-class lessons mainly for the purpose of study abroad or improving foreign language skills in the major cities across the country.

Earlier, on 4 January 2001, the ETS litigated in Beijing First Intermediate People's Court (Intermediate Court) against New Oriental, for the infringement of copyright in the ETS' old exam questions.[94] A dispute that involved only foreign copyright works was thus brought into the

---

[91] See Article 24.

[92] See Xinhua News Agency http://202.84.17.11/english/htm/20010221/376092. htm, retrieved on 26 March 2011.

[93] See http://www.ets.org, retrieved on 6 March 2011.

[94] See *Educational Testing Service v Bei Jing New Oriental Education Group*, the Beijing First Intermediate People's Court Judgement Number (2001) FI 35 (given on 27 September 2003). Please note that the original appeal involved both patent and copyright infringement, even though only the latter is discussed in this chapter. In addition, the Graduate Management Admission Council (GMAC) also sued New Oriental on the same day in the same court and for the same infringements.

Chinese courts. The ETS claimed that New Oriental had been reproducing, publishing and distributing, without lawful authorisation, the copyright exam questions and test forms ever since the mid-1990s. The ETS demanded that New Oriental (1) immediately cease all the infringement, (2) confiscate all the infringing materials including all the old questions of TOEFL and GRE stored on its PCs, (3) make an apology in a national published outlet, (4) cease all the effects of the infringement, (5) pay the ETS a damage of RMB 12936906.25 yuan, and (6) bear the fee of RMB 1418197.09 yuan that the ETS spent to stop the infringing acts and all the lawsuit cost.

In fact, prior to that litigation, the ETS authorised a local company, respectively in January 1996, January 1997 and November 2000, to file complaints with a Beijing administrative authority on New Oriental's unlawful copying of the TOEFL exam tests. Correspondingly, the administrative authority confiscated New Oriental's illegal copies and issued two APDs, in February 1997 and November 2000 respectively, to order New Oriental to stop the infringing acts. This was followed by continued non-compliance. Obviously, exam questions are the result of some element of creativity and include the result of some creative or intellectual activity, and are subject matter protected by the Berne Convention, which states that copyright works "include every production in the literary, scientific and artistic domain, whatever may be the mode or form of its expression".[95] Thus, for example, in the UK copyright protection over exam questions, despite the low level of originality, was established in the early twentieth century case *University of London Press v University Tutorial Press*.[96]

In the court, New Oriental explained that, along with the development of the economy in China since the 1980s, the demand for studying abroad had been increasing hugely, while taking the ETS's TOEFL or GRE test had become one of the few lawful paths to studying in the US. New Oriental's professional and innovative training created a brand new business in China, offered students a needed aid, and therefore had expanded rapidly. Admitting its acts of publishing and distributing the collected questions of the old TOEFL and GRE test without permission had infringed the plaintiff's copyright, New Oriental nonetheless defended on the basis that, on the one hand, New Oriental as well as other Chinese institutions had been trying to contract with ETS for copyright authorisation since the mid-1990s, but had never received any feedback.

---

[95]   See Article 2.
[96]   See *University of London v University Tutorial Press* (1916) 2 Ch. 601.

Its infringing acts were in fact also a consequence of the ETS's unfair rejection of authorising any uses of the old exam questions in China's mainland. On the other hand, the majority of New Oriental's uses of the old exam questions were based on teaching activities in classrooms, which would be fair use according to Article 22 of the Chinese Copyright Law and thus should not be totally stopped.

In September 2003, in the first instance the judgment was given in favour of the ETS. The Intermediate Court required New Oriental to (1) cease the infringement and hand in all the infringing material to the court for confiscation within 15 days of the effect of the judgement; (2) make an apology regarding its infringement in the *Legal Daily*, a well-known national Chinese newspaper, within 30 days of the effect of the judgment; (3) pay RMB 5 000 000 yuan in damages to the ETS for using pirated copies of the copyright old tests and employing agents to collect exam questions that were still used in the ETS's exams, plus RMB 522 000 yuan for the cost of the litigation.[97]

New Oriental appealed to the Beijing High People's Court (High Court) in October 2003. The case was heard on 28 April 2004. New Oriental argued that (1) exam questions were not covered by the Chinese Copyright Law as one of the protected works, therefore ETS's copyright on the exam questions should not be recognised in China; (2) New Oriental mainly used the exam questions for teaching purposes and this was fair dealing according to the copyright law in China; (3) the First Intermediate Court confirmed that New Oriental copied some TOEFL exam questions for publishing in 1997 and 2000 respectively, but the ruling of a damage of RMB 5 000 000 yuan lacked legal grounds; (4) the judgment of an apology in the *Legal Daily*, a very well-known nationwide published newspaper, was unfair since New Oriental had sold its course materials mainly to its students and to a small number of others only.

A detailed judicial interpretation was given regarding foreign copyright owners' lawful rights under the provisions of both the Berne Convention and the CCL 2001. The High Court explained that, according to the Berne Convention, literary and artistic works shall include every production in the literary, scientific and artistic domain, whatever may be the mode or form of its expression.[98] Additionally, New Oriental had avoided two APDs issued by the local administrative authority, and its infringing acts lasted for almost a decade, which greatly infringed the plaintiff's copyright and should therefore be penalised. In the meantime, the High Court

---

[97] See 北京市第一中级人民法院判决书 (2001) 一中知初字第35号民事判决, Beijing First Intermediate People's Court Judgment Number (2001) 35.
[98] See Article 2 (1).

pointed out that acts of New Oriental using exam questions in its class-room teaching activities were fair use as stated in Article 22 of the CCL 2001 and did not violate the plaintiff's copyright.

On 27 December 2004, the High Court ruled that New Oriental must (1) cease all the infringing acts and hand in all the infringing materials to the court for confiscation within 15 days of the effect of the judgment; (2) publish an apology regarding its infringement in the *Legal Daily* within 30 days of the effect of the judgment; (3) pay the ETS a reduced damage of RMB 3 740 186.2 yuan and RMB 22 000 yuan for the cost of litigation within 15 days of the effect of the judgment.[99]

Before *ETS v New Oriental*, the public interest concept in the Chinese educational section was interpreted as freedom to access and use copyright materials provided that the use was restricted to educational purposes. This confusing concept was also what New Oriental had relied upon since the mid-1990s and it comes from the influence of the long history of Chinese culture and tradition.

ETS v New Oriental offers a profound lesson on the uses of copyright materials for educational purpose. It warns all Chinese educational insti-tutes to study copyright law, to understand the relevant provisions, and to review whether their uses of works are fair. The High Court's judgment and final decision not only correct misunderstanding on uses of copyright works in educational institutes but also show the emergence of the then new CCL 2001 in a court case. The ETS has registered its TOEFL exam questions with the US Copyright Office and therefore evidently owned copyright over TOEFL in the US. In accordance with the CCL 2001, works that are published or authorised in other countries are also protected by the Chinese law, which is one of the amendments made by the CCL 2001.

The reduction of damages in the final decision has been seen by many Chinese as a sign of, on the one hand, a maturing court that is not only driven by international parties; and, on the other hand, as the access public interest concept being applied within the established infringement. While the ETS published its exam questions with copyright authorisation in the US and other countries but avoided the repetitive requests from all Chinese institutes and refused to authorise any publication of the exam questions in China for a rather long period of time, the exam questions became irreplaceable yet unobtainable in the Chinese market. Under such circumstance, how should the law balance the interests of the copyright owners and those of the broader public? Would it be in the public inter-

---

    99   See 北京高级人民法院判决书 (2003) 高民终字第1393号, Beijing High People's Court Final Judgment Number (2003) 1393.

est to make the works available? Should the copyright owners' interest be limited to protect the public interest? If yes, how should it be done and what would be the jurisdiction? Maybe the Chinese courts should have answered these questions.

The judgment fails to clarify if copyright protection for exam questions also applies to interested Chinese institutes and individuals. Currently, the CCL 2001 and relevant regulations do not provide any clarification with regard to the protection for exam questions, while the practice has long seen exam questions as exempted from copyright in an understanding of the public interest. For instance, after each NCEE, the exam questions of every subject would be published by Chinese media, offline and online, analysed by experts and renowned teachers, and used by schools and students – all for free. Hitherto, it is still discussed whether exam questions should be copyright or not in China: Chinese tradition supporters emphasise the significance of exams in China, especially the NCEE, and insist that exam questions should be excluded from copyright in defence of the public interest; and copyright supporters argue that exam questions are intellectual works and are protected by copyright laws in developed countries such as the UK and the US. China should learn from others and also grant exam questions copyright to stimulate creativity on the one hand and to encourage lawful exploitation on the other.[100] To provide exam questions with copyright protection or to exclude them: Chinese law should make this clear.

3.4 A Changing Community

The copyright awareness of the Chinese public in general is strongly influenced by the traditional culture and the state socialist system, which results in somewhat different conceptions compared to the West, including those relating to money.

For instance, Zhang Xinmin, a professor at Guizhou Normal University, sued Professor Chen Guosheng in Chong Qing First Intermediate People's Court for his breach of copyright in October 2002. The court found that in the defendant's article, published in a nationally renowned periodical, more than 50 per cent of the words were plagiarised from the plaintiff's work. However, in respect of the plaintiff's plea that "the lawsuit aims to call for the esteem to be given to academic research and to copyright, therefore, I claim 1 Yuan ONLY for compensation", the court ruled that the defendant should (1) cease the infringing

---

[100]   See   http://www.sipo.gov.cn/sipo2008/yl/2007/200804/t20080402_365958. html   and   http://sx.sooxue.com/gaokao/gkkd/gkzc/200711/63865.html,   retrieved on 4 March 2011.

act, (2) publish an apology, and (3) pay 1 yuan for the infringement of copyright.[101] Professor Zhang's act of seeking justice but not money, and seeking moral rights but not economic benefit, represents the influence of traditional Chinese philosophy on people's (not only scholars' but also ordinary people's) values today.

While educational free use has been widely accepted by the Chinese for centuries, the modern concept of copyright has brought about a great break in these privileges. Nevertheless, Article 22(6) of the law offers a rather simple and vague provision for uses of copyright materials in the education sector, which continuously encourages the Chinese public's belief in free use for educational purposes as well as freedom to use educational materials. The situation is changing along with the advance of IT, and the increasing consciousness of private rights; protections for works in the educational sectors are becoming narrower and more specific, as shown in the cases discussed below.

Seeing that the development of IT has also made copying a work much easier in all ways, in December 2008 the China National Knowledge Infrastructure of Tsinghua University developed a polygraph software, 学位论文学术不端检测系统 (TMLC), to "combat" plagiarism in China.[102] The TMLC has been adopted in some established HEIs ever since.[103] Moreover, China officially launched its Copyright Registration System in March 2009, which allows copyright registrations to be filed and searched online.[104] Certainly, the traditional culture of sharing and copying is bowing to modern copyright, a law that encourages creativity and learning via securing private property rights.

3.4.1   Are lectures protected? *Luo Yonghao v eNet.com*[105]

Luo Yonghao, nationwide known as *lao luo*, senior Luo, was one of the most popular English teachers in New Oriental. On 8 March 2006 Luo Yonghao sued eNet.com, a Beijing-based e-commercial company, in Beijing Haidian District People's Court (Haidian court) for breach of copyright in his lectures.

---

[101]   See http://www.chinacourt.org/public/detail.php?id=13920&k_title=张新民&k_content=张新民&k_author=, retrieved on 4 March 2011.

[102]   See http://check9.cnki.net/Article/news/2009/03/26.html, retrieved on 10 March 2011.

[103]   See for example http://www.edu.cn/gao_xiao_zi_xun_1091/20091207/t20091207_428045.shtml and http://news.haedu.cn/SNZX/633985356159218750.html, retrieved on 10 March 2011.

[104]   See www.ccopyright.com.cn, retrieved on 10 March 2011.

[105]   See 北京市海淀区人民法院判决书 (2006) 海民初字第9749号, Beijing Haidian District People's Court Judgment Number (2006) 9749号.

Luo Yonghao stated that the defendant copied 43 recordings of his lectures without consent, compiled the recordings into "Ana of the New Oriental's Lao Luo" and uploaded it on eNet.com between 21 January 2005 and 20 February 2006, for users' free downloading. The defendant's deed, Luo Yonghao claimed, had infringed his rights of use and remuneration over his 43 oral works. He thus made a plea for a written apology that would be published on the homepage of eNet.com for 30 days and RMB 10 000 yuan damages.[106]

The defendant admitted the unauthorised compilation and online publication, but argued that, firstly, not all contents in those 43 recordings should be seen as copyright works; and, secondly, that eNet.com had no intention to breach the plaintiff's copyright as it neither recorded his lectures nor continued its online publication after the plaintiff's alert. In addition, the defendant expressed its strong interest in reaching an amicable settlement, which was declined by the plaintiff.[107]

On 17 July 2006, the Haidian Court ruled that eNet.com had breached Luo Yonghao's right of communication of information on networks and must pay Luo Yonghao RMB 7900 yuan.[108] The judgment stresses that copyright law in China has defined oral works as copyright works that are created in spoken words such as impromptu speeches, lectures and court debates.[109] Hence, Luo Yonghao's lectures were certainly works protected by the law. The judgment further pointed out that all Internet companies such as eNet.com must be cautious in uploading any documents, should censor their uploadings, and actively take steps to avoid copyright infringements.[110]

Nevertheless, Luo Yonghao's plea for a written apology was not supported, the Haidian Court explained, as the infringing act was related to the plaintiff's intellectual property rights but not to his personality rights.[111] Luo Yonghao was unsatisfied with that decision and announced on his blog that "the written apology is the key" and he thus "has appealed to the higher court".[112] The plaintiff's insistence on a court judgment other than a settlement has demonstrated the increasing public awareness of protecting their rights by means of law, including in the educational sector.

---

[106] Para 2.
[107] Para 3.
[108] Para 12.
[109] See Article 4(2), Implementing Regulations 2002.
[110] Para 10.
[111] Para 11.
[112] See http://luoyonghao.blog.sohu.com/10904378.html, retrieved on 4 March 2011.

Luo Yonghao's case has, for the first time, confirmed teachers' copyright over their oral works (lectures) including the recordings of such works. Chinese law confirms that recording rights are initially owned by performers and may be licensed to a third party. Moreover, these rights have officially extended to all the personality rights and property rights on the Internet after adaptation of the CCL 2001 and Regulations 2006. However, recording rights have not been mentioned at all by the court in this case, either with regard to licensing or contracts.

3.4.2 Who owns copyright over lesson plans? *Gao Liya v Sigongli Primary School* (Sigongli)[113]

Gao Liya was just a very ordinary primary teacher in Sichuan Province until February 2006, when she became a celebrity after the conclusion of a long-lasting lawsuit over her copyright to her lesson plans. After four years of struggle, the final judgment was given in Gao Liya's favour.

The plaintiff taught the Chinese language in Sigongli from January 1990. Following the school's managerial code, she handed in her lesson plans for assessment at the end of each term. In April 2002, she realised that her lesson plans, which in total were 48 notebooks over the decade, had not been returned to her as they should have been. She then requested their restoration. However, only 4 notebooks of her lesson plans were returned, and the remaining 44 notebooks, she was told, had either been lost or recycled by the school. She, of course, was not happy with what she heard and insisted that the school should have valued a teacher's work more and respected the intellectual property rights therein.

During the dispute, Gao Liya was surprised by the school's peremptoriness. She thus sued Sigongli in Chongqing Nanan District People's Court (District Court) on 30 May 2002, demanding restoration of her 44 notebooks of lesson plans together with compensation of RMB 8800 yuan. On 24 October 2003, the District Court turned down the plaintiff's plea mainly because, firstly, the 44 notebooks were notebooks formatted especially for lesson plans, and were bought and distributed by Sigongli, which granted the defendant property rights over the notebooks rather than the plaintiff.

---

[113] See 重庆市南岸区人民法院 (2003) 南民初字第903号民事判决书, Chongqing Nanan District People's Court Judgment Number (2003) 903; 重庆市第一中级人民法院 (2004) 渝一中民终字第232号民事判决书, Chongqing First Intermediate People's Court Judgment Number (2004) 232; 重庆市第一中级人民法院 (2005) 渝一中民再终字第357号民事判决书, Chongqing First Intermediate People's Court Judgment Number (2005) 357; 重庆市第一中级人民法院 (2005) 渝一中民初字第603号民事判决书, Chongqing First Intermediate People's Court Judgment Number (2005) 603.

Secondly, the plaintiff's lesson plans followed a predetermined format and did not fall into the scope of works protected by copyright. And thirdly, no agreement had been signed between the two parties to adjust ownership of the filled-in notebooks.

Gao Liya soon appealed to Chongqing First Intermediate People's Court (Intermediate Court). The Intermediate Court stated that the plaintiff's lesson plans were copyright works owing to the individual's intellectual creativity in writing them. Nevertheless, those works were created by the plaintiff in the fulfilment of tasks assigned to her by the defendant, which according to Article 16 of the CCL 2001 should therefore be deemed as works created in the course of employment, with the copyright being owned by the defendant. Hence, the District Court decision was upheld on 29 March 2004.

The plaintiff did not give in. She called upon Chongqing People's Procuratorate (Chongqing Procuratorate) for a prosecution in May 2004. On 25 November 2004, Chongqing Procuratorate prosecuted in Chongqing High People's Court (High Court), pointing out that the first judgments failed to provide coherent and clear explanations on whether lesson plans were copyright works, while the second judgment, which would be the final decision, barred the plaintiff's right to seek copyright protection.

Then, the High Court ordered the Intermediate Court to re-hear the case. On 30 May 2005, the Intermediate Court once again upheld the original judgment. The Intermediate Court stated that the plaintiff, from the beginning, had made two requests, namely, recalling of the 44 notebooks of lesson plans and compensation of RMB 8800 yuan. If the plaintiff would claim her copyright over the lesson plans, a separate case must be filed.

Supported by Chongqing Procuratorate, Gao Liya filed another case in the Intermediate Court on 7 September 2005, against Sigongli's copyright infringement on her lesson plans. She requested the court to confirm that she would be the copyright owner for the lesson plans and demanded that Sigongli (1) admit its infringement, (2) compensate her damage of RMB 6000 yuan, and (3) bear the litigation fees.

Sigongli defended on the basis that its loss of those lesson-plan notebooks did not form any copyright infringement since the defendant owned the notebooks as well as the lesson plans. Also, the defendant claimed that, according to the school's practice, teachers should hand in the lesson plans at the end of a term and withdraw them again at the beginning of the next term, a practice of which the plaintiff had been informed. The school had no responsibility to keep lesson-plan notebooks for any teachers, and the fact of losing notebooks had nothing to do with breach of copyright.

Based on Article 2 of the Implementing Regulations 2002,[114] the court explained that lesson plans, including the plaintiff's, were copyright works and should be protected by the law because they were original intellectual creations. Further, the court confirmed that Gao Liya's lesson plans were works created in the course of employment, therefore the copyright should be owned by the author, the plaintiff in this case. Nonetheless, based on Article 16 of CCL 2001, Sigongli, the employer, should have a priority right to exploit the works within the scope of its professional activities. That, the court affirmed, was for the public interest (socialism aspect).

On 9 December 2005, the Intermediate Court pronounced that (1) Sigongli breached Gao Liya's copyright over her lesson plans, (2) Sigongli must compensate Gao Liya RMB 5000 yuan, and (3) Sigongli must pay the litigation fees of RMB 1625 yuan.

Sigongli refused to accept the judgment and appealed to the High Court. But it failed to pay the litigation fees within the effective period. Thus, on 27 February 2006, the High Court ruled that the Intermediate Court's order came into force instantaneously. The small but dramatic case was finally concluded.

Gao Liya's case has settled that lesson plans are protected by Chinese copyright if they are sufficiently original and creative, and fixed in a tangible medium. Moreover, the Chinese court has established that teachers shall be the lawful copyright owners of their lesson plans, always provided that the school has a priority right to exploit the lesson plans within the scope of its professional activities. The validation for that conclusion is allocated to the public interest concept. But the court has failed to clarify the term "professional activities". Will projects of distance learning fall into the category? What about overtime teaching or publication of compilations of lesson plans?

Regarding works created in the course of employment, on the ground of the public interest Chinese copyright law has adopted a different attitude from the Anglo-American approach, in which copyright created by employees in the course of employment will be owned by the employer unless there is an agreement in place to the contrary. So the UK CDPA 1988 states that the employer is the first owner of any copyright in a work when the work is made by an employee in the course of the employment;[115] and the US Copyright Act 1976 confirms that, "in the case of a work made for hire, the employer or other person for whom the work was

---

[114] The term "works" used in the law shall mean original intellectual creations in the literary, artistic and scientific domain, insofar as they are capable of being reproduced in a certain tangible form.

[115] See Section 11.

prepared is considered the author".[116] The Chinese law prefers to follow the Continental traditions and confer copyright on the author, not the employer (except for software and databases). Article 16 of the CCL 2001 declares that copyright created in the course of employment shall be held by the author, who shall not, without the consent of the employer, author- ise a third party to exploit the work in the same way as the employer does within two years after the completion of the work.

Nonetheless, the Chinese law states that in certain circumstances copy- right shall be held by the employer, including works created in the course of employment mainly with the material and technical resource of the employer, or where there are laws, administrative regulations or contracts in place to assign the copyright to the employer.[117] Material and techni- cal resources have been defined as the "funds, equipments or materials provided expressly for the creation of a work".[118] Obviously, Gao Liya's lesson plans were created with the material and technical resources of her employer, Sigongli. Why then should she enjoy the copyright rather than Sigongli? The court should answer this question and provide a convincing justification in accordance with the law.

3.4.3 Is a state organ's violation in the public interest? *Hu Haobo v National Education Examinations Authority of the Ministry of Education (NEEA)*

On 23 July 2007, Beijing Haidian District People's Court heard a case filed in the name of the public interest. The plaintiff, Hu Haobo, a journalist of China Central Television (CCTV), took the NEEA, a department of the MoE, to the court for its copyright infringement. Hu Haobo insisted that his lawsuit was not interested in any monetary compensation but aimed only at defending the public interest, which intended to stop those "common violations done by state organs in the name of fulfilling their official duties".[119]

The NEEA, appointed by the MoE, was the exclusive authority in China undertaking official educational examinations, including the NCEE, the only examination for admission to universities or colleges in China.[120] In 2003, the NEEA used the plaintiff's paper, 'Current Global Warming

---

[116] See Section 201(b).

[117] See Article 16(2).

[118] See Article 11 of the Implementing Regulations 2002.

[119] See http://news.xinhuanet.com/edu/2007-07/24/content_6420220.htm, ret- rieved on 4 March 2011.

[120] See http://www.neea.edu.cn/buttom/english.htm, retrieved on 4 March 2011.

and Future Disaster', which was originally published in the opening issue of *Science & Technology Pictorial* in 1996, as one of the main reading exam questions. However, the author's name was acknowledged neither on the test paper nor after the NCEE. The plaintiff found out about such use in May 2007 and contacted the NEEA for acknowledgement but was rejected.

In November 2007, judgment was issued in favour of the NEEA. It confirmed that the plaintiff was the author of the paper used in NCEE 2003. However, the judgment explains, the CCL 2001 has stated that a work may be exploited without permission from and without payment of remuneration to the copyright owner by a state organ for the purpose of fulfilling its official duties.[121] The NEEA's use of the plaintiff's work was for non-commercial purposes, thus falling into fair dealing under which the plaintiff's work may be used without permission or remuneration.

Furthermore, as regards whether the name of the plaintiff should be mentioned, the court held that, although protection of the author's interest should be one of the main purposes of copyright law in China, the public interest should be another very vital factor to take into account. The public interest defence may override the copyright owner's rights in certain circumstances where "the public interest is more important than the right owner's", in order to facilitate a proper balance between private interest and the public interest. In addition, the NEEA may amend works to meet the need of being in the NCEE exam questions for the public interest. Such use of a copyright owner's works would not breach copyright law, for example in Mr Hu's case.

But the court suggests that the NEEA may consider acknowledging and appreciating copyright owners for using their works, immediately after the NCEE was held, with the intention of showing respect to the right owners.[122] In response to the suggestion, the NEEA officially replied to the court on 28 November, and said that, every year after the NCEE, the NEEA would, on behalf of the MoE and all the examinees, acknowledge and thank relevant copyright owners for using their works as the NCEE exam questions.[123]

Hu Haobo was not persuaded and he appealed to the Higher Court to

---

[121]   See Article 22(7).

[122]   See北京市海淀区人民法院民事判决书 (2007) 海民初字第16761号, Beijing Haidian District People's Court Judgment Number (2007)1676; and also http://news.xinhuanet.com/legal/2007-11/29/content_7165428.htm, retrieved on 4 March 2011.

[123]   See http://news.xinhuanet.com/edu/2007-12/28/content_7330848.htm, retrieved on 4 March 2011.

continue his fight against "the common violations done in the name of fulfilling state organs' official duties".[124] The court confirmed that it is in the public interest to permit the NEEA to use works without copyright owners' authorisation as it ensures efficient and fair preparation for the NCEE. However, Hu Haobo asked, how would adding an author's name on the exam question or acknowledging the name after the NCEE be in conflict with the public interest? The legal suggestion to the NEEA issued by the court has approved that adding the author's name on the exam question or issuing an acknowledgement after the examination would be in the public interest. In addition, Article 22 of the 2001 CCL states clearly that for the purpose of fulfilling a state organ's official duties,

> a work may be exploited without permission from, and without payment of remuneration to, the copyright owner, *provided that the name of the author and the title of the work shall be mentioned* and the other rights enjoyed by the copyright owner by virtue of this Law shall not be prejudiced.

It offers a strong basis for Hu Haobo's claim. Then why did the court not support such a claim?

It may be understood as follows. Firstly, the NEEA has been using works for exam questions without any acknowledgments ever since 1950. Innumerable copyright infringing acts had been conducted if the judgment was given for Hu Haobo. Imagine what chaos would occur if all the copyright owners took legal actions against the NEEA. Chinese courts, which are financially controlled by governments, would always want to avoid bringing such trouble to a state organ if possible. Secondly, the court was fully attentive to the copyright provisions as well as to the need to safeguard people's lawful rights. As explained in the third chapter, owing to the influence of traditional culture, cases are of extreme importance in Chinese legal practice although China is not a case law country officially. Therefore, the court found a very Chinese solution: to reject Hu Haobo's claim yet also issue the NEEA with an official suggestion. So, the NEEA would be happy with the judgment and most members of the public would be happy with the legal suggestion, especially if the NEEA acted promptly in positive response. Indeed, the judgment shows a mix of the rule of man and the rule of law, which represents current enforcement in China generally as well as in Chinese courts.

It is not difficult to foresee that the outcome of Hu Haobo's appeal in the Higher Court will not be too different from the first judgment

---

[124]   See http://blog.sina.com.cn/s/blog_448b7469010089po.html, in an interview with "Rule of Law in China" on 2 January 2008, retrieved on 4 March 2011.

unless he gets attention from an even higher authority that is determined to implement the rule of law despite causing potential damage to state organs.

3.5   Updates on the Subject of Photocopying

Chinese law has not given any guidance to educational institutions regarding photocopying other than declaring that photocopying is part of the right of reproduction owned by copyright owners.[125] It seems that the public as well as different institutions have taken such issues easily until quite recently, when publishers in China have become attentive to the long ignored practice of photocopying.

For instance, on 12 June 2006 the NCAC issued an official document in reply to an enquiry made by the Higher Education Publisher (HEP) on 1 June 2006, asking if acts committed by copying shops surrounding university campuses, such as photocopying an entire textbook and selling the copies to students, were infringements.[126]

The NCAC stated that, according to Article 47 of the CCL 2001, anyone who engages in reproduction and distribution without consent commits infringement and shall bear civil liability; and in addition be subject to administrative penalties imposed by a copyright administration department if such acts breach the public interest. Acts committed by copying shops around university campuses, such as photocopying textbooks and selling the copies to students, breach the publishers' and authors' legal rights, and therefore should bear the relevant liability. Of students, it is suggested that universities should strengthen the management of rights; emphasis should be put on positive education to students and cracking down on those copying shops primarily engaged in providing services of copying entire textbooks.

3.6   Findings of the Empirical Study

In order to examine the adaptation of copyright laws in Chinese education institutes, and to determine the extent of genuine knowledge about the use of copyright works in these sectors, a small-scale survey was conducted in 2008. The findings of the survey are summarised below.

Copyright exceptions for educational uses are strongly advocated by those surveyed. The term of the "public interest" is influential to

---

[125]   See Article 10(5).
[126]   See 权司[2006]48号; NCAC Documents Number (2006)48.

the majority, but while the access and socialism aspects are recognised, the authorship dimension is unfamiliar. The country's socialist policy was often mentioned during the interviews, which is understood by the majority as one of the main grounds for allowing free educational uses. Moreover, collective benefit is emphasised not only by the older but also the younger generation. Most of the participants would be happy to have their works distributed as long as their names were acknowledged. Recognition rather than monetary gain would be their foremost motivation. With regard to using others' works, the majority misunderstands acknowledgements as copyright permissions.

Courseware is usually prepared by teachers for students in Chinese education institutions and few survey participants knew that it is illegal to photocopy a big proportion of a work or an entire book. Evidently, copyright notices have not been introduced and are unknown in practice since the requirement has not been adopted by the current legislation. In addition, copyright has not yet become the main concern while photocopying and downloading; instead cost is the primary concern. The demand for digitisation of works is surprisingly strong. Regarding digitising copyright works, no copyright permission is obtained in advance in most cases.

There is certainly a gap between the SZU and Baotou, mainly regarding the facilities and resources that reflect the regions' relative economic strength. For instance, 7 schools in Baotou still use printing machines as an alternative to photocopiers and 11 schools have no Internet connection. Bear in mind that Baotou is seen as a developed city in China; thus, the aspiration that "no school shall have dangerous buildings, every class shall have a classroom, and every student shall have a desk" is not so much the requirements of the Chinese State Council but more China's goal in the massive poorer areas, where copyright might appear the least important issue to the public as well as to local governments.

Echoing the desk research, the empirical study illustrates that the existence of copyright has become known to most participants. However, the knowledge of copyright law and its educational provisions is very limited, especially amongst those of the younger generation. One of the reasons may be the education and promotion of the law over the country – several students pointed out in the interviews that they never had any lectures on the subject of copyright and the law, either at school or at university. The study tells us that the administrative departments are still the first choice of enforcement for the majority and courts would be the option only if the problem could not be solved. The study also suggests that providing relevant training to schools' leaders, law professors and students would help to promote the law.

4.   DISCUSSION

Current laws provide exceptions for educational uses of copyright works and the provisions are somewhat different one from the other. The UK law grants fair dealing to individuals in educational institutions, which gives detailed guidance regarding what uses are fair; whilst the US law offers a four-factor provision for the institutions and the courts to determine whether a use is fair; and the Chinese copyright law allows uses including reproduction in educational institutions commonly on condition that the reproduction should not be published or distributed.

Dilemmas have occurred in industrial countries: on the one hand, the exercise of the access public interest is a social need and has therefore been talked about very much as essential to public discourse and democratic vitality; and, on the other hand, the influences of powerful commercial organisations and the very essence of capitalism have enlarged the monetary function of copyright as an aspect of the authorship public interest, which has been gradually accepted by the majority including educational institutions.

Therefore, the educational institutions within the UK and the US have always to justify carefully their uses of works in various educational activities, and be extremely alert to all the legitimate provisions and court cases, in order to stay clear from any possible infringement. For instance, copying for third parties is restricted in HEIs. Moreover, a strange fact emerges, that is, that all the distance learning projects in the UK are currently violating copyright unless licensed since the law neither offers provisions like the US legislation that covers education on the Internet nor gives a loose clause like the Chinese law in the name of the public interest. Nevertheless, the Gowers Review has recommended a straightforward solution for the awkward situation with a sensible balance of interests. Further, the UK IPO's profound consultations indicate that Gowers' recommendations may be adopted by the UK law under the plea of the public interest.

Distance learning is becoming topical in educational institutes in the West because of the great monetary potential. Ongoing discussions include the types of work that the exception should cover, the methods of communication that should be permitted to present works, and whether safeguards are required to ensure that only the designated ones may access the work.

As for China, public welfare and social value have been historically stressed in Chinese culture, and education has been set as a national priority for its development. The access and socialism public interests are widely recognised in the Chinese system and often override copyright in the educational sector. Besides, collective benefit, the socialist concept, has been accepted by the public across the nation, still including the young generation. Chinese copyright is in favour of the concept that public benefit should take precedence over financial gain, particularly in educational institutions.

Thus, the educational institutions in China enjoy a rather convenient environment regarding uses of copyright works of all kinds for educational doings. The education privilege has been well received in Chinese society, as shown by the empirical studies. It may explain why no litigation has been taken so far against any educational institutions concerning photocopying, digitisation or file sharing. Nonetheless, the NCAC's official reply to the HEP regarding photocopying in shops around campuses has confirmed that it would be copyright infringement if a shop copied an entire textbook and sold students the photocopies without authorisation. Maybe court cases eventually will occur. Would any publishers file lawsuits against those small stores? Or would the publisher target universities since the NCAC has allocated the managerial responsibilities to universities?

Regarding exam questions, Chinese courts have reached a controversial conclusion, allowing the free use of exam questions without clarification under the current copyright law. However, as the Berne Convention requires and the CCL 2001 has confirmed, works published or authorised in other countries are also protected by the Chinese law, and the courts therefore ruled that foreign exam questions are protected by Chinese copyright. The logically next question, whether Chinese exam questions will be given copyright or not, remains unanswered at this stage.

If Chinese exam questions are not protected by copyright, as it is now, then it sets a double standard in the Chinese copyright system: one for foreign right holders and the other for the Chinese, and the foreign right owners could thus be able to enjoy more protection than the Chinese holders in China, which is not in conformity with international law. What would be the justification for excluding locally produced exam questions and what would be the legal basis for this double standard? The latter question also applies to other aspects, for instance translation of works – Chinese law has granted exceptions to translations of any works owned by Chinese citizens or institutes from the Han language into any minority nationality language, in the name of the public interest. The current double standard may be understood as follows. Along with its entry into the world economy, China has to obey the signed international treaties, which in this case require protection over exam questions that are given by other countries. However, exam questions in China are of significance to every family for the reason mentioned earlier; hence it is in the public interest to allow people free access to exam questions. The principle of socialist policy that is adopted in China rejects placing individual rights or commercial benefit prior to the common interest and social welfare, which is in accordance with Confucianism, the prioritisation of collective interest.

Or, should exam questions be clearly included amongst subject matter protected by Chinese copyright, providing exceptions have been authorised for teaching, research and private study? This would set China free from the double standard and allow acts for the benefit of education such as use of exam questions, as well as providing rightful protection to copyright owners. The only question arises whether this limitation to the exclusive rights could rest upon the Berne three-step test. The answer would be yes for the following reasons: firstly, the scope of this limitation would be known and particularised; secondly, such limitation would have no conflict with the technological and market developments of the work, including commercial gains from exam questions in general; and thirdly, such prejudice would balance the exclusive rights of copyright owners and the access rights of users. A fair provision like this may effectively prevent infringement of the public interest, in both its authorship and access aspects.

Exam questions are rather a narrow issue in the context of education as a whole. Recent Chinese cases mentioned above also show that the awareness of copyright and the demands of the rule of law are continually increasing over the country. Lawsuits are no longer seen as "evil" or "bad luck". They are becoming a strong means for defending people's legal rights. Furthermore, as also reflected in the fieldwork, Luo Yonghao and Gao Liya have raised two important questions the answers to which are currently not clearly known and would normally be ignored by people in the educational sector. These are landmarks in the development of copyright protection in China.

Nonetheless, the Chinese courts are still struggling to integrate enforcement of the rule of law into the current yet traditional system that is strongly influenced by the tradition of the rule of man. The judgment in the *Hu Haobo* case reveals a typical Chinese compromise and also a small step forward towards the rule of law: on the one hand, an individual has challenged a powerful state organ without fear; and, on the other hand, the court has issued a legal suggestion to the NEEA and such suggestion has been adopted, affirming that copyright ought to be acknowledged and respected even when the NCEE represents the interest of millions. Indeed, Hu Haobo's petition represents Chinese people's requisite of individual rights, which is also the foundation of the public interest, and should be confirmed by Chinese lawmakers in the near future.

The empirical study has illustrated that the understandings of copyright laws and uses of copyright works in Chinese educational institutions are somewhat loose, and that the comprehension of the law is rather inadequate. In order to raise awareness and strengthen enforcement, it is urgent to supply correct knowledge of the law. It is suggested to set up a subject of IP including copyright in school education as well as a university training programme. Moreover, copyright notices might be adopted as a practical method in China to help promote the law more (although the Berne Convention puts an end to such). In addition, users in educational institutions should be aware that acknowledging the source of copyright materials does not substitute for obtaining permission. In most cases, since sometimes the distinction between fair dealing and infringement may be unclear and difficult to apply, getting permission from the copyright owner before using the works would be the best method of avoiding copyright violation.

At present, general copyright clearance is just establishing itself in China and copyright permissions are usually obtained individually. Most educational institutions adopt the library provision of notice to delete (that is, go ahead with reproduction unless and until challenged by the right holders; this procedure will be discussed in the next chapter) and it has worked well so far. Nonetheless, the Western licensing system has been gradually accepted by Chinese copyright, has been implemented in commercial sectors and may be popularised in educational institutions in the future.

Evidently, uses of copyright materials in Chinese educational institutions are changing – from a world of copyright-free to copyright-enforced – and China is in for a long haul. Adopting the access public interest concept, Chinese copyright creates education privileges that fall within the Berne three-step test and provide educational institutions with a rather comfortable context for all educational activities, in both classroom and distance learning. In the meantime, it is believed by the majority that for the benefit of the masses certain works such as exam questions should not be copyrighted. Regarding that, Chinese lawmakers have not yet provided a rational answer. Other questions ought to be answered in line with international treaties, which include: how to promote copyright correctly and effectively to the educational sectors at the same time as advocating the access public interest tradition and socialist values; how to improve the enforcement of copyright over the sector while giant gaps exist between rich and poor; and how to correct the unequal standard of protection between foreign and Chinese right owners.

In accordance with the Berne Convention and TRIPS, Chinese copyright law provides exceptions for certain uses of works in sectors including education. Such exceptions promise rights of access to and use of copyright works, including digitised works, and contribute to a well-informed citizenry and educated population in society. The CCL 2001 offers educational exceptions in Article 22(6) and Article 23, although they are rather vague and incomplete. The Chinese education privileges at present are based more upon the long-lasting practice of prioritising education than the access public interest concept. These education provisions should be made clearer and more rational to legalise the nationally accepted education privileges, including learning, teaching, study and assessment in both actual and virtual environments; this ought to be in accordance with the Berne three-step test. While the public interest often grants users rights to access and use works and overrides copyright owners' rights of profit in the education sector, Chinese copyright law should encourage the establishment and advancement of collective societies and licensing to balance the two interest groups, the copyright owners and the users. In addition, education should be future-oriented and concerned with value. Copyright and other laws should be embraced within China's education curricula in schools and universities to promote creativity and the culture of the rule of law, together with its public interest-oriented tradition, thus providing the rule of law with a solid foundation in a Chinese setting amongst future generations.

5.   Public libraries, copyright and the public interest

1.   INTRODUCTION

The opening ceremony of the Beijing Olympics 2008 caught the world's attention, as did the song mimed by a nine-year-old girl, "Ode to the Motherland", which may be unknown in the West but is familiar to most Chinese people. However, not many know that Professor Xin Wang, the song writer, has assigned his copyright over that song to the people of China and its scores have been kept by public libraries over the country for free exploitation.[1]

Public libraries, which exist in most countries of the world nowadays, contribute greatly to promoting learning, and spreading and sharing knowledge. They care for and allow access to works: on the one hand, they collect new works to fulfil acquisition and preservation functions; and, on the other hand, they make collections available to the general public to ensure access to information and recorded knowledge in the broadest possible way, regardless of the media format. They become deeply involved with copyright issues when they make copies of works for the purposes of preservation, research, private study, teaching, sending, or receiving in the name of inter-library loans, whilst all reproductions must abide by international instruments.

Copyright provides certain exceptions for the uses of copyright works in libraries, subject to the three-step test, which are explained in and permitted by the Berne Convention and TRIPS. While the Convention concerns exceptions that allow users to make copies without the copyright owners' permission, TRIPS applies more generally to all forms of

---

[1]   老作曲家王莘教授郑重宣告— 《歌唱祖国》 版权属于人民, 《人民日报》 网络版1999年8月13日整点新闻: 'Copyright for the "Ode to the Motherland" Belongs to People – An interview with Professor Wang Xin', Hourly News, *The People's Daily* (13 August 1999), retrieved on 21 March 2011 at http://web.peopledaily.com.cn/zdxw/18/19990813/19990813181.html. A propos, the song was written in 1950 and Professor Wang passed away on 15 October 2007.

copyright.[2] Article 10 of the WCT 1996 focuses predominantly on the protection of copyright content in the digital networked environment, allowing copyright exceptions, including those for public libraries, on the Internet, although it does not prescribe limitations subject to the three-step test. Certainly, the impact of digital technology on the development of libraries and on uses of copyright works in the library sector is enormous, which raises the technological concern in applying the three-step test.

Libraries have immense value in educational institutions as teachers and students rely on their resources to accomplish research, teaching and learning. Furthermore, libraries, especially public libraries, play an important role in trying to maintain a balance of interests between copyright owners and users. Library exceptions are extremely important for public libraries and users, and demonstrate that the law is imbued with the access public interest, which upholds the rights of the authors/copyright owners and the rights to access in the context of libraries. Such privileges allow libraries to be the public's access points to knowledge and for learning both actual and virtual, and these free of charge access points are particularly critical for the people who lack resources elsewhere, like many in developing China.

Chinese copyright grants certain exceptions for the use of copyright works in public libraries, a sector that has been playing a significant and unique role in education and learning in New China. Since the concept and system of public libraries were introduced to China from the West and are ongoing, and a Chinese library law has not been established, a brief study of the developments in the UK and the US has been carried out, in order to help make an effective library law and set up a more efficient system in China. In addition, the adaptation of laws and the balance of the interests in public libraries along with the development of digital technology are examined, together with discussions on how copyright law and the multidimensional public interest are enforced in the Chinese sector and how the relevant concepts and implementations have been changing.

2. DEVELOPMENT OF PUBLIC LIBRARIES AND THE PROVISIONS IN THE WEST

In the West the origins of libraries, as old as the origins of written records, began with the practice of collecting the writings of others. Ancient

---

[2] See Article 9.2, the Berne Convention; and Article 13, TRIPS.

libraries, some of which date back to three thousand years before the Christian era in Assyria, Egypt and Greece, were the custodians of the knowledge of their day.[3]

Centuries later, the invention and widespread use of printing led to a revolution in the book industry and made the establishment of public libraries materially possible; furthermore, the development of education and the demand for reading matter urged and stimulated the evolution of public libraries, which has been seen as part of the great social movement for making knowledge available to the poorer classes.[4]

2.1 Public Libraries

A library is "a place in which literature, musical, artistic, or reference materials (as books, manuscripts, recording, or films) are kept for use but not for sale",[5] and it has vital connections with books. The English word "library" derives from the Latin word for book, *liber*, as the French *bibliothèque* (library) comes from the Greek word for book, *biblios*. *Liber* and *biblios* are etymologically linked, denoting the ancestry of library.[6]

Public libraries may be defined as a collection of information for public use, subject to public control and support.[7] The establishment and growth of public libraries can be regarded as part of the great social movement for the spread of knowledge.[8] With information stored and preserved, public libraries uniquely endeavour to make information available to the public, just as they open their doors to all persons. Their main functions can be divided into three parts:[9]

- collecting, storing and preserving information material;
- organising, cataloguing, and providing means for the process of information navigation and discovery; and
- providing access to information.

---

[3] J. Minto, *A History of the Public Libraries Movement in Great Britain and Ireland* (1932).

[4] Ibid.

[5] *Encyclopaedia Britannica* (1998).

[6] E. Rose, *The Public Library in American Life* (1954).

[7] See G.P. Cornish, 'Libraries and the Harmonisation of Copyright', *EIPR* (1998), 241.

[8] See above, n. 6.

[9] See ACLIS (Australian Council of Libraries and Information Services) Submission to the CLRC Review and Simplification of the Copyright Act, 1995.

2.1.1   United Kingdom, the cradle of the modern library system

The oldest public library in the UK, the Bodleian Library (Bodleian) of Oxford University, was founded in 1602 with about 2500 books and 1 professional librarian.[10] The Bodleian Library is named after its founder Sir Thomas Bodley, who made an astute agreement with the Stationers' Company in 1610, whereby they undertook to send the Bodleian a copy of every new book registered with them. This means it became effectively a copyright deposit library a century prior to the first copyright law act in 1709. Under the legal deposit principle confirmed by law,[11] a copy of every newly published work must be sent to the British Library, the Bodleian, the Cambridge University Library, the Library of Trinity College, the National Library of Scotland, the National Library of Ireland and the National Library of Wales (with certain exceptions).[12] Nonetheless, the Bodleian is not a lending library, which means that all the materials must be used on the premises. In 1653, an open-to-public library called Chetham's Library was founded in England; later, Innerpeffray, the oldest, free, lending library in Scotland, was started in about 1680. These two libraries are both independent and charity-funded, and they remain open to readers and visitors free of charge to date.[13]

In fact, charity played an influential role in the growth of public libraries, while Andrew Carnegie (1835–1919), the famed steel magnate, played a very significant role in their development in the late nineteenth and early twentieth centuries. With the belief in a society based on merit where anyone who worked hard could become successful, he considered public libraries as instruments for the elevation of the masses of the people and focused his philanthropy on founding libraries.[14] With the philosophy of "free to all" and "place within its reach the ladders upon which the aspiring can rise", he was determined to use his enormous wealth to establish free libraries that could offer opportunities to the poor.[15] More than half the towns in the UK received a donation from him.[16] The first was

---

[10]   See http://www.bodley.ox.ac.uk, retrieved on 28 March 2011.

[11]   It is under the terms of the Legal Deposit Libraries Act 2003, which supersedes the Copyright Act 1911, and the Irish Copyright Act 1963. Section 15 of Copyright Act 1911 requires "the publisher of every book published in the United Kingdom shall, within one month after publication, deliver, at his own expense, a copy of the book to the trustees of the British Museum".

[12]   See G. Jefferson, *Libraries and Society* (2000).

[13]   See the websites http://www.chethams.org.uk and http://innerpeffraylibrary. co.uk.

[14]   See P. Krass, *Carnegie* (2002).

[15]   Ibid., 243.

[16]   That is, 213 out of 437 in England and Wales, 50 out of 77 in Scotland, and

in his home town, Dunfermline, which opened in 1881; later his support extended to other parts of the UK, the USA and elsewhere. By 1919, he had donated 2811 libraries at a total cost of $56 704 188.[17] Apparently, he succeeded in creating a high level of popular and civic commitment to free public libraries that persists after over a century. His contributions were always accompanied by the condition that an undertaking should be given to maintain the library from local funds. This was adhered to by the adoption of the Public Libraries Act 1850, which was previously only applied to the municipalities with populations of over 10 000. Carnegie made a great increase in the number of places adopting the Act, and therefore stimulated widely the growth of public libraries.[18]

The Public Libraries Act gave power to town councils to establish public libraries and museums. This was the first national library legislation in the world and is seen as the foundation of modern library laws. Nevertheless, the progress of public libraries was fairly slow then.[19] In 1870, the Education Act ratified the system of compulsory education, and, together with the formation of a Board of Education in 1899, introduced the idea of raising literacy levels, which offered the necessary condition for the expansion of public libraries in the country. The promotion of public libraries moved from a philanthropic position towards being a government responsibility under legislation, which allowed greater opportunity for municipal library development and coverage of rural areas.[20]

Thus, the promotion of public libraries was expanded and became the most developed in the UK. In addition, the Library Association was inaugurated in 1877, committed to the delivery and promotion of high quality information services responsive to users' needs.[21] By the end of 2002, 4614 public libraries, 6 national libraries, and 875 university and higher

---

47 out of 58 in Ireland. Carnegie's motivation of philanthropy has always been an interesting point to contemplate; nevertheless, his dictum that "the man who dies thus rich, dies disgraced" has presented his own answer. Ibid., 243.

[17]   Ibid., 502; see also the Carnegie United Kingdom Trust website, http://www.carnegieuktrust.org.uk.

[18]   W.R. Aitken, *A History of the Public Libraries Movement in Scotland to 1955* (1971).

[19]   See J. Minto, *A History of the Public Libraries Movement in Great Britain and Ireland* (1932). The Act was introduced in the House of Commons by William Ewart and enthusiastically promoted by Joseph Brotherton, as well as Edward Edwards.

[20]   See above, n. 12.

[21]   See the Library Association website, http://www.la-hq.or.uk, retrieved on 17 March 2011.

education libraries had been set up, with 25 797 librarians and 34 101 042 registered users.[22]

Along with the maturity of the system of public libraries in Europe came the legal idea of Public Lending Right (PLR), initiated in Denmark in 1941. Although it was not active until 1946 because of World War II, the idea spread slowly from country to country. In many nations, PLR programmes have developed fairly recently. For instance, the PLR scheme was implemented in Norway in 1947 and in Sweden in 1954.[23] In the UK, the PLR, which gave authors a legitimate right separate from copyright, to receive payment for the free lending of their books by public libraries was confirmed by the Public Lending Right Act 1979 (PLRA). Only the lending out of printed books by public libraries is covered.[24] The PLRA also establishes a Registrar of PLR appointed by the government to maintain a register of eligible authors and books, and to supervise the administration of PLR. The operation was set out in more detail by the 1982 Scheme. The Registrar of PLR received grant-in-aid of £7.63 million in 2007–2008, whilst £6.66 million was distributed to some 24 000 authors.[25]

Lending and rental right is an exclusive right generally. In the UK copyright in a work of any description is not infringed by the lending of a book by a public library if the book is within the PLR scheme, which was updated by the CDPA 1988,[26] where the rental right in sound recordings, films and computer programs is created; and it is further amended to comply with the 92/100/EEC, the EU Directive on Rental and Lending Right. The Directive was passed in 1992 and is a key development in relation to the PLR's legal status in Europe. It has established the PLR as a part of copyright protection, which is defined as an exclusive right to prohibit or authorise public lending with or without payment.[27] Nevertheless, it allows member states a number of derogations and other flexibilities when it comes to implementing the Directive, including the option not to recognise an exclusive right as long as right owners would be remunerated for the loan of their work; it also allows states to exclude certain categories of library from the PLR, and to give priority to their own cultural objectives in setting the PLR systems. For instance, instead of an exclusive

22   See   http://www.lboro.ac.uk/departments/dils/lisu/list03/list03.html,   the Library and Information Statistics Table 2003.
23   See J. Griffiths, 'Copyright and Public Lending in the United Kingdom', *EIPR* (1997), 499.
24   W.R. Cornish & D. Llewelyn, *Intellectual Property: Patents, Copyright, Trade Marks and Allied Rights*, (2007, 6th edn).
25   See http://www.plr.uk.com, retrieved on 17 March 2011.
26   See Section 40A: Lending of copies by libraries or archives.
27   See Article 2, 92/100/EEC.

right, or after its exhaustion, a remuneration right for the public lending of protected works has been granted in Austria, Denmark, Finland, Germany, Luxembourg, the Netherlands and Sweden.[28]

The PLR in the UK grants an exclusive lending right to British authors, performing artists, phonogram producers and film producers and gives them the legal right to receive payment from government funds (the PLR Central Fund) for the free borrowing of their works from public libraries.[29] Furthermore, copyright is not infringed by the lending of copies of a work by educational establishments or by the lending of a book by a public library if the book is within the PLR scheme.

Moreover, the Copyright Licensing Agency (CLA), a reproduction rights organisation, was set up in 1982 by the Authors' Licensing and Collecting Society Ltd and the Publishers' Licensing Society Ltd. The CLA represents the interests of copyright owners, and licenses businesses, education and government to copy extracts from books, journals, magazines and periodicals in the UK. The CLA provides collective licensing to secure copyright royalties due to registered authors and publishers for the reproduction of their works, including digital materials.[30]

2.1.2 The US public libraries

The development of public libraries in the US was historically stimulated by, and relies upon, the desire for education. The demand for learning in the early US followed closely the physical need for shelter and food.[31] Harvard University Library was instituted in 1636 by vote of the Great and General Court of the Massachusetts Bay Colony and was named after its first benefactor, John Harvard, a young minister who, upon his death in 1638, left his library and half his estate to the new institution. It later grew to be extraordinarily helpful to the advancement of higher education

---

[28] See Report from the Commission of the European Communities on the Public Lending Right in the European Union, 2002.

[29] The UK government produced the PLR Scheme, which passed through Parliament in 1982. The Scheme sets out more detailed rules for the operation of PLR in the UK and covers such areas as author and book eligibility, selection of libraries and payment calculations. The payment is in accordance with how often the works are lent out from a selected sample. Besides, to qualify for payment authors must apply to the Registrar of the PLR who is appointed by the government to maintain a register of eligible authors and books, and to supervise the administration of the PLR.

[30] See CLA's website, http://www.cla.co.uk, retrieved on 17 March 2011. According to the CLA accounts, the distributions to the rights holders in 2006–2007 were £47.8m, of which over £9.9m for copying in HEIs.

[31] See above, n. 6.

in the USA. It is now the oldest library in the United States and the largest university library in the world.[32] In addition, the library at Yale University has also become one of the most successful institutions in the world. These college libraries, which served similar purpose as the UK council libraries, aimed to stimulate the need and knowledge of reading, and offered the use and study of their collections to people of their communities.[33]

In 1800, the Library of Congress was founded. It claims to be the oldest public library in the USA and it is now the largest library in the world. The Library serves as the research arm of Congress and to "make its resources available and useful to the Congress and the American people and to sustain and preserve a universal collection of knowledge and creativity for future generations".[34] The opening of Boston Public Library in 1854 and the formation of the American Library Association in 1876 further motivated the spread of US public libraries, together with the idea of use being free to people.

As with the development of public libraries in the UK, the name of Andrew Carnegie, the Scottish immigrant, is inseparably connected with the development of public libraries in the US. Carnegie developed the idea of establishing free public libraries to make available to everyone a means of self-education, one of his lifelong interests and enduring actions. For instance, as one-time gifts in March 1901, Carnegie offered the city of New York $5.2 million for the construction of 65 branch libraries.[35] Altogether, Carnegie donated over $41 million for 1689 free public library buildings in 1419 communities around the US.[36] One condition of every Carnegie grant was that a community must pledge an annual amount of 10 per cent of the grant, from tax monies and not from endowment or gift, to maintain the library. This has been successful in the promotion of government financing of public libraries.[37]

The Library Services and Construction Act, the first national library law in the USA, was passed in 1956. It set up a government fund for the establishment of public libraries. The Act hastened the expansion of public libraries, not only in number, but also in respect to their fields of activity

---

[32]   See the Harvard University Library website http://hul.harvard.edu, retrieved on 17 March 2010.

[33]   Ibid.

[34]   See the Library of Congress website, http://www.loc.gov, retrieved on 10 March 2011.

[35]   See above, n. 14, at 419.

[36]   Ibid., 422–3.

[37]   See E. Stone, *Historical Approach to American Library Development* (1967), http://www.ideals.uiuc.edu/bitstream/2142/3995/2/gslisoccasionalpv00000i00083_ocr.txt, retrieved on 19 March 2011.

and function. As at April 2008, there are 123 291 libraries of all kinds in the USA, of which 12 851 are public libraries.[38]

In addition, the Copyright Act of 1976 authorised the library legal deposit, which requires that all works published in the US shall be deposited in the Copyright Office for the use or disposition of the Library of Congress. Two complete copies of the best edition, or, if the work is a sound recording, two complete phonorecords of the best edition, together with any printed or other visually perceptible material published with such phonorecords, shall be sent in within three months after the date of such publication.[39]

2.2   The Copyright Laws

Uses of copyrighted works by libraries and archives have led to controversy in many countries.[40] On the one hand, libraries, especially public libraries, press governments for copyright exceptions owing to the fundamental role of libraries as obviously beneficial for the whole of society, and urge that this argument should be taken into account more by copyright, in striking a balance between the right holders and the public. On the other hand, right holders argue that their works should not be used to subsidise the educational and informational roles of these institutions.

Nonetheless, the Berne Convention has provided the minimum standards of copyright protection and an overriding qualification to the permitted exceptions, the three-step test, the application of which in the library sector may be seen as follows:

Firstly, uses of copyright work must be in special cases, which should specify the types of uses in libraries and define the limits. For example, it is generally clear that photocopying a whole book in general circumstances would be excluded from the exceptions; however, such action in some particular circumstances, that is, libraries' or archives' photocopying for preservation purposes or making copies of some special collections for non-commercial research purposes, would be appropriate and lawful.

Secondly, the cases of exception must not conflict with the normal exploitation of a work, which presumably has included library use hitherto and means that competing economic and non-economic norms must be considered within the provision, mainly the extent of the exceptions. Thus, exceptions should be granted to libraries when they do not conflict with the right holders' reasonable exploitation of the work, which might

---

[38]   See http://www.ala.org, retrieved on 19 March 2011.
[39]   See section 407.
[40]   WIPO Standing Committee on Copyright and Related Rights 2003.

be, without asking for permission and without paying royalties, a walk-in user making a copy of the work for purposes of private study and other fair dealing.

Finally, the uses of libraries must avoid unreasonable prejudice to the legitimate interests of the right holder. In case of photocopying, this depends on the amount that may be taken, the persons by whom the photocopying can be done, and whether or not the photocopying is subject to an obligation to pay fair compensation. As in downloading, such an act might be permissable for private use and for non-commercial purposes.

2.2.1   The UK law

The CDPA 1988 admits library privileges and offers certain statutory exceptions that permit copying without prior permission such as archiving, lending and inter-library loans.[41] As regards photocopying in the library context, it lists a variety of circumstances in which the law applies, which includes the copying of articles in periodicals, or parts of published works, together with a restriction on production of multiple copies of the same material; the supply of copies to other libraries; replacement copies of works; certain unpublished works and copies of works required to be made as condition of export.

While the request for copying must satisfy the librarian that the copy is for the purpose of research or private study only, a librarian may make a single copy in circumstances that would fall within the exception for fair dealing for research or private study as if it had been the user rather than the librarian making the copies. As a general rule, libraries must make a charge for copying, which should cover the actual cost of making the copy, plus a contribution to the general expenses of the library but not the author. All copies must be done either with the copyright owners' permission or under the CLA licensing scheme.

The Copyright (Librarians and Archivists) Regulations for Copying of Copyright Material came into force in 1989. These regulations, known as the "library regulations" or the "library privileges", apply to libraries photocopying on behalf of users and for other libraries.[42] The library privileges permit public libraries to make and supply copies of copyrighted works (1) to users for the purposes of research or private study, (2) to other libraries or archives requiring copies of such works for reference purposes, and (3) to replace lost or damaged items in their permanent collection where it is not reasonably practicable to purchase the items.

---

[41]   Sections 37–43.
[42]   S. Norman, *Copyright in Public Libraries* (1999).

However, users requiring copies of works must deliver a signed declaration to the librarian to the effect that the copies are required for research or private study purposes, and, in the case of a request for a copy of an article in a periodical or of a part of a published work, that the requirement for the same is not related to any similar requirement of another person.

The CDPA 1988 was amended by the Copyright (Visually Impaired Persons) Act 2002, which was implemented on 31 October 2003. The Act allows the accessible copy of literary, dramatic, musical and artistic works, both published and unpublished, to be made for, or by, a visually impaired person in a format they can use. It is therefore no longer necessary to obtain permission from the rights holder to produce an accessible copy; besides, multiple copies can be made lawfully and the complete work or any part can be copied always with a copyright statement attached.[43]

In 2001, the European Community Directive 2001/29/EC on the Harmonisation of Certain Aspects of Copyright and Related Rights in the Information Society (InfoSoc Directive) was implemented. The Directive specifies that acts of reproduction made by public libraries under the exception must not be for direct or indirect economic or commercial advantage.[44] Hence, the CDPA 1988 was once more amended by the Copyright and Related Rights Regulations (2003 Regulations), which came into force on 31 October 2003 and now take account of the comprehensive nature of the legal protection required for technological measures used by copyright holders to protect their works against unauthorised reproduction and other copyright infringements. Changes made within the 2003 Regulations are various; but are of particular relevance in the field of photocopying and scanning of published books, magazines and journals covered by CLA licences that are in the exceptions to copyright.

The exception for photocopying in the 2003 Regulations provides that copying by librarians is limited to research or private study that is for non-commercial purposes and that single copies made under the library privileges are also restricted to the non-commercial.[45] Businesses that obtain copies from libraries and document suppliers for commercial purposes will need to pay a copyright fee. In addition, when further

---

[43] An accessible copy, which includes hard and soft copies of a work, is defined as "a version which provides for a visually impaired person improved access to the work", and also "an accessible version may include facilities for navigating around the version of the copyright work".

[44] See Article 5(2)(c).

[45] Regulation 14 and Schedule 1.

copies of the document supplied are requested, a CLA business licence is required.[46]

In the business of press cutting services, whether copying an article constitutes a substantial part of the published edition is the key. On 12 July 2001, the House of Lords dismissed Newspaper Licensing Agency Ltd (NLA)'s appeal,[47] and declared that Marks and Spencer Plc's acts of copying and internal distribution of newspaper articles provided by a press cutting service, which had a licence from the NLA to copy newspapers, did not infringe the copyright in the typographical arrangement of the published editions of the newspapers, as Marks and Spencer did not reproduce anything that could be regarded as "either resembling the newspaper concerned or having newspaper-like qualities".[48]

Nevertheless, the Directive 2001/29/EC requires member states to safeguard the exclusive right of copyright owners to authorise or prohibit direct or indirect, temporary or permanent reproduction by any means and in any form, in whole or in part.[49] The law will be continuously challenged, especially while online cutting services are now developing rapidly.[50]

Public libraries may offer copying services to walk-in users, by signing a declaration form to state that the copy will be used only for research or private study, that it will not be further copied and that it is not related to a similar request from anyone with whom the requester worked or studied.[51] The act of copying must fall within certain limits, and the exception only applies to copies made for non-commercial purposes. While walk-in users who do self-copying of copyright materials for a direct or indirect commercial purpose, the CLA Sticker Scheme, which is developed for public libraries to cover copying for walk-in users, should be used, as it provides a simple way in which the user can pay a copyright fee (£9.00 inc VAT per item) and lawfully copy a work for commercial purposes.[52] Under the

---

[46]   The Copyright and Related Rights Regulations 2003, Part 2, Acts permitted in relation to copyright works and rights in performances 14.

[47]   See   http://www.publications.parliament.uk/pa/ld200102/ldjudgmt/ jd010712/news-1.htm, retrieved on 19 March 2011; in this case, the NLA made no claim "based upon literary or artistic copyright in the articles or photographs which have been copied", para 4.

[48]   Para 27.

[49]   See Article 2.

[50]   See   http://www.marketingservicestalk.com/news/web/web103.html, retrieved on 19 March 2011.

[51]   See http://www.cla.co.uk, retrieved on 19 March 2011.

[52]   See Article 5, Copyright (Visually Impaired Persons) Act 2002. The new CLA licence (back-dated to be in effect from 1 August 2001) is the blanket photocopying licence that covers photocopying undertaken by students registered and staff employed by the university.

scheme, the amount of an extract from a book, magazine or journal that can be photocopied for commercial purposes is the same as for research or private study purpose:

- no more than 5 per cent of any published edition or, in the case of a book, one complete chapter;
- in the case of an issue of a periodical, or in a set of conference proceedings, one whole article;
- in the case of an anthology, one short story or poem not exceeding ten pages;
- illustrations that are an integral part of articles/chapters.

In December 2006, in order to enhance the flexibility of the library privileges, the Gowers Review of Intellectual Property recommended further amendments, which include allowing fair dealing copying to cover contents in digital format,[53] permitting libraries to copy the master copy of all classes of work in their permanent collections for archival purposes and also allowing format shift and further copies to be made from the archived copy,[54] and providing a provision for and facilitating access to orphan works.[55] This will be discussed in the next chapter.

2.2.2 The US provisions

Copyright in the US recognises the special role of libraries in society, and reasonable access to copyright materials is thus facilitated on the ground of fair use. Once a work is published, copies of the work must be deposited with the Library of Congress for the benefit of the public.[56] While the US public libraries can avail themselves of fair use under Section 107 of the US Copyright Act 1976, specific library exemptions are granted in Section 108.

Williams & Wilkins Co. v United States concluded that it was a fair use for libraries to photocopy articles for use by patrons engaged in scientific research.[57] Section 108 permits public libraries, archives and their employees to reproduce and distribute copyrighted materials for the following non-commercial purposes:

---

[53] See Recommendation 9.
[54] Recommendations 10a and 10b.
[55] Recommendations 13, 14a and 14b.
[56] See Section 407, and also the American Library Association website, http://www.lala.org.
[57] 420 US 376 (1975).

- replace damaged or lost copy;
- backup copy; and
- private scholarship or research.

In addition, it requires libraries to carry out reasonable investigations to determine that (1) the work is not subject to normal commercial exploitation, (2) a copy cannot be obtained at a reasonable price, and (3) the copyright owner has not provided a notice to the Copyright Office showing (1) or (2). Satisfying the three conditions above, libraries may digitise and put works that are in the last 20 years of copyright protection on the web. Nevertheless, "reasonable investigation", "normal commercial exploitation" and "reasonable price" are not defined or clarified by the law.

Although there is no limitation on the kinds of works that are covered under the permitted libraries archival and preservation acts,[58] the exemptions granted under Section 108 do not apply to (1) musical works; (2) pictorial, graphic, or sculptural works or (3) motion pictures or other audiovisual works, except news programmes. Because of the massive economic involvement, the US law has explicitly placed more limitation on the use of music, films, photos and maps rather than textual sources.

On 27 October 1998, the Sonny Bono Copyright Term Extension Act (SBCTEA) was enacted, which extends the term of copyright protection to 70 years post mortem auctoris in the USA. The SBCTEA permits libraries, archives and non-profit educational institutions that function as such to reproduce, distribute, display, or perform in facsimile or digital form a copy or phonorecord of works in their last 20 years of protection for purposes of preservation, scholarship, or research, on condition that such work is not subject to normal commercial exploitation and a copy or phonorecord of the work cannot be obtained at a reasonable price.[59]

The first sale doctrine permits copyright owners to control only the commercial rental right of a work. This is the basic legal foundation of the US public libraries system. Section 109 permits the owner of a lawfully made copy to dispose of it by lending or any other means. It also allows book owners to sell their books at garage sales without permission from or payment to the copyright owner. But the right to dispose of a copy does not include the right to make more copies.

For the purpose of bringing copyright law into the digital era and implementing the WIPO treaties, the DMCA came into force in 1998. Regarding library exceptions, the DMCA clarifies that a qualified library

---

[58]   See Section 108 (b) and (c).
[59]   See Section 104.

must open its collections to the public or make the collections available not only to researchers affiliated with the library or with the institution of which it is a part, but also to other persons doing research in a specialised field.[60] The DMCA amended Section 108 of the exemptions for libraries to accommodate digital technologies and evolving preservation practices.[61] In relation to copying copyrighted works for purposes of preservation or inter-library loan, the DMCA permits qualified libraries to make up to three digital archival copies of both published and unpublished works for storage and retrieval. However, such digital copies have to be made and kept only within the premises of libraries and should not be otherwise distributed in that format or made available to the public in that format outside the premises of the library or archives.[62] Such requirements have limited the accessibility of remote users.

The DMCA also gives more detailed guidance about copyright notices. It states that copyright notices must be imposed on all library copies or phonorecords and requires that any copyright notice originally on a work should be included on the copy or phonorecord; and in the case that no such notice can be found, the library must include a legend stating that the work may be protected by copyright law.[63] The amended section allows libraries to copy a work into a new format if the original format becomes obsolete, which includes the possibility that the machine or device necessary to render perceptible a work stored in that format is no longer manufactured or is no longer reasonably available in the commercial marketplace.[64]

Furthermore, Section 1201 provides prohibition on acts of circumvention of copyright protection systems. It grants an exception to non-profit libraries to gain access to the commercially exploited copyrighted works solely in order to make a good faith determination of whether to acquire lawful copies of the works.[65] The provision also allows exemptions from the prohibition on circumvention of technological protection measures for good faith uses and classes of works.[66] In addition, it requires that, to be reviewed every three years, the Librarian of Congress, upon the recommendation of the Register of Copyrights, shall consult with the Assistant Secretary for Communications and Information of the Department of

---

[60] See Section 1201(d)5(A)and(B).
[61] See Section 404.
[62] See Section 404 (2)(C).
[63] See Section 404(1)(C).
[64] See Section404(3)(E).
[65] See Section 1201(d).
[66] See Section 1201(a)(1).

Commerce and report and comment on his or her views in making such recommendation. This must examine the following matters:[67]

- the availability for use of copyrighted works;
- the availability for use of works for non-profit archival, preservation, and educational purposes;
- the impact that the prohibition on the circumvention of technological measures applied to copyrighted works has on criticism, comment, news reporting, teaching, scholarship, or research;
- the effect of circumvention of technological measures on the market for or value of copyrighted works; and
- such other factors as the librarian considers appropriate.

The first recommendation relating to Section 1201 was published on 27 October 2000, giving two classes of works that would be subject to exemptions from the prohibition against circumvention of technology that controls access to copyright works:[68]

- compilations consisting of lists of websites blocked by filtering software applications; and
- literary works, including computer programs and databases, protected by access control mechanisms that fail to permit access because of malfunction, damage, or obsolescence.

On 28 October 2003, four new exemptions were enacted: the first exempted class allowed interested parties to circumvent technological measures to gain access to the complete list of blocked websites that a filtering software program may block for the purpose of reviewing the lists of blocked websites; the second class allowed computer program users to overcome damaged access control measures to gain access to the underlying programs; the third class intended to provide exception to libraries and archives in the preservation activities; and the fourth class intended to assist the blind and visually disabled people to gain access to digital materials.[69]

---

[67] See Section 1201(a)(1C).

[68] See the Statement of the Librarian of Congress Relating to Section 1201 Rulemaking, http://www.copyright.gov/1201/anticirc.html, retrieved on 19 March 2011. These exemptions did not apply to the prohibitions on trafficking in circumvention devices and remained in effect through 28 October 2003.

[69] See http://www.copyright.gov/1201/docs/librarian_statement_01.html, retrieved on 19 March 2011. These exemptions remained in effect until 27 October 2006.

Then, on 27 November 2006, the third recommendation ruled that six classes of works are exempt from Section 1201:[70]

- audiovisual works included in the educational library of a college or university's film or media studies department, when circumvention is accomplished for the purpose of making compilations of portions of those works for educational use in the classroom by media studies or film professors;
- computer programs and video games distributed in formats that have become obsolete and that require the original media or hardware as a condition of access, when circumvention is accomplished for the purpose of preservation or archival reproduction of published digital works by a library or archive. A format shall be considered obsolete if the machine or system necessary to render perceptible a work stored in that format is no longer manufactured or is no longer reasonably available in the commercial marketplace;
- computer programs protected by dongles that prevent access owing to malfunction or damage and that are obsolete. A dongle shall be considered obsolete if it is no longer manufactured or if a replacement or repair is no longer reasonably available in the commercial marketplace;
- literary works distributed in e-book format when all existing e-book editions of the work (including digital text editions made available by authorised entities) contain access controls that prevent the enabling either of the book's read-aloud function or of screen readers that render the text into a specialised format;
- computer programs in the form of firmware that enable wireless telephone handsets to connect to a wireless telephone communication network, when circumvention is accomplished for the sole purpose of lawfully connecting to a wireless telephone communication network; and
- sound recordings, and audiovisual works associated with those sound recordings, distributed in compact disc format and protected by technological protection measures that control access to lawfully purchased works and create or exploit security flaws or vulnerabilities that compromise the security of personal computers, when circumvention is accomplished solely for the purpose of good faith testing, investigating, or correcting such security flaws or vulnerabilities.

---

[70] See http://www.copyright.gov/1201/docs/2006_statement.html, retrieved on 19 March 2011. These exemptions have remained in effect since 27 October 2009.

It should be noted that the Technology, Education and Copyright Harmonization Act (TEACH), which was passed in 2002 and regarded as an act balancing the interests of copyright holders and users in educational sectors, has amended sections 110, 112 and 802. TEACH is a key act for distance learning as it allows for more flexibility in the digital environment for educators and learners. It expands formats of distance learning from using satellite in a classroom to using the Internet and digital transmission to learners wherever located.

TEACH also specifies requirements for educational institutions including public libraries that serve educational activities especially distance learning: to ensure copyright works used in all distance learning programmes are legitimately obtained;[71] to provide notice to students that copyright materials may be included in the course of distance learning;[72] and to adopt technological measures to make the materials available only to students "officially enrolled" in the courses[73] and for the necessary period of time,[74] and to avoid further copies and reproductions.[75]

Moreover, for the purpose of preserving digital content for future generations, the Library of Congress set up a collaborative project, the National Digital Information Infrastructure and Preservation Program (NDIIPP) in December 2000.[76] Working with partners including libraries, the NDIIPP intends to "develop a national strategy to collect, archive and preserve the growing amounts of digital content".[77]

The library sector provides essential access points for a wide range of information products. Digital technology has made access broader and easier, as well as creating many more economic pressures and opportunities. Thus, judicial discussions on library uses, in both traditional and digital environments, of copyright works have been ongoing.

2.2.3   Case law on uses in the traditional settings: *American Geophysical Union v Texaco*[78]

Before the passage of the DMCA, the application of the exceptions was brought before the US courts with reference to a special kind of research library in the *Texaco* case, where the defendant was a research

---

[71]   See Section 2(2).
[72]   See Section 2E(i).
[73]   See Sections 2E(ii) and 3C(i).
[74]   See Section 2D.
[75]   See Section 3f(1).
[76]   See http://www.digitalpreservation.gov/library, retrieved on 19 March 2011.
[77]   Ibid.
[78]   *American Geophysical Union, et al. v Texaco, Inc.*, 60 F.3d 913 (2nd Circ. 1995).

corporation employing 400 to 500 research scientists. The corporation library purchased numerous subscriptions to many journals and routed them to the employees who requested them. Texaco scientists would often copy articles from a journal for their own use in their office. The plaintiffs, American Geophysical Union and 82 other publishers of scientific and technical journals, sued Texaco in 1985, claiming that individual scientists at Texaco had photocopied articles from scientific journals and not paid royalties to the publishers for copying. In order to spare the enormous expense of exploring the photocopying practices of each of them, Dr Chickering was chosen at random as the representative of the entire group. It was found that he had photocopied several journal articles that contained information relevant to the research he was conducting.

The case was decided by the Federal District Court in favour of the publishers in 1992. The judge ruled that Dr Chickering violated Section 107 when he copied articles without providing the appropriate fee to the publishers. Among other defences, Texaco claimed that its copying fell within fair use under Section 107 of the Copyright Act since the copies were made in pursuit of research, not for commercial gain. The court ruled that the profit motive of the company was a relevant consideration in the analysis of the purpose of the use.

The decision was upheld by the Court of Appeals in 1994, which held that companies in the for-profit sector that make copies of copyright scientific and technical journal articles violate fair use under the Copyright Act of 1976. In its analysis of the case, the court established that:

- The for-profit motive of the company is a relevant consideration in the analysis of the purpose of the use. The fact that the researcher copied the articles and placed them in his files for future reference duplicated the archival function of the library and therefore was not "fair use" as established by copyright laws.
- Copying the article as a unit, rather than considering the article as a portion of a volume of the journal, violated "fair use" in the amount and substantiality of the portion used in relation to the copyrighted work as a whole.
- While the publishers of the journal had not lost subscriptions, they had lost the right to license the work for reproduction. Texaco could have acquired a license through the CCC; therefore, the market was affected.

Based on Section 107, the court looked at the following four factors to determine if a particular use constitutes fair use:

- The photocopying was done personally in the library, made for future retrieval and reference; and the copies were for practical purposes (easier to carry around separate pieces of paper rather than an entire book). However, it is for a commercial purpose as Texaco is a for-profit corporation.
- The photocopied articles were essentially factual in nature.
- The amount of the copyrighted work: the articles were copied entirely and each article is a whole work.
- The market was affected because Texaco could have paid royalties through the CCC.

The Court considered the character and nature of the use to be non-transformative and, therefore, archival copying. The Court also considered the fourth factor of fair use analysis; that is, the copyright holder would suffer harm if this kind of copying were widespread. The decision strongly endorsed the CCC and the role it has played in the development of a viable market for mechanisms to photocopy works and pay publishers.

In April 1995 Texaco petitioned the US Supreme Court to review the case, together with an amicus brief of the American Association of Law Libraries, the Special Libraries Association, and other members of the university and library community, including the American Council of Learned Societies and the National Humanities Alliance. The amicus seeks to elucidate and reaffirm fair use rights permitted to scholars and researchers in the conduct of research and education as provided in the Constitution and in law. On 15 May 1995 the case was brought to a close with the announcement of a settlement by Texaco and a steering committee representing the publishers. In it, Texaco agreed to pay over $1 million to the publishers in the suit and to enter into a standard licensing agreement with the CCC for five years.

It should be noted that the Texaco case was decided on a very specific set of facts that do not have general application to all instances in which works are copied in libraries. The judges held the ruling only applied to "archival copying" for placement of the material in the library for future use. Texaco applies neither to photocopying done in non-profit educational institutions for educational purposes nor to photocopying done by libraries and archives.

Texaco is an important case testing the fair use clause in the US Copyright Act, and is of concern to the libraries that serve academic research institutions and corporate research centres. It distinguishes spontaneous copying by a researcher related to a current specific project or a teacher's copying for non-profit classroom use, from the copying of materials to be added to an office library. It speaks volumes to librarians for it involves fair use, which library uses of works depend upon. When does fair use end and copyright violation begin? Texaco defines the limits so that the commercial purpose behind uses of work has been clearly excluded from the fair use provision. Nonetheless, two questions remain. In the case that a publisher had not registered with CCC, would it lose the right to claim market effect? What about copying outside of archiving?

The *Texaco* case narrows down the fair use provision. While the interest of publishers is promoted, the boundaries of fair use are more narrowly defined. The library sector in the US, which is sensitive to the rights and restrictions in Sections 107 and 108, is increasingly required to assume an assertive, educational role in the community about applications of fair use. In addition, the libraries' amicus brief has confirmed the libraries' firm position of defending the public interest in copyright.

2.2.4 Uses in the digital environment: Google Books Library Project (Google Library)[79]

While making photocopies available to the public created disputes about fair dealing in the traditional context, the digitising of works and making them available to Internet users is merely under discussion in the spotlight of today's digital environment.

Founded by two Stanford PhD students in 1998, Google has become the most powerful Internet search engine in the world.[80] The Google Library Project was initially called "Google Print". It intends to have every book ever printed available for viewing online, either in its entirety if the copyright has elapsed or as a summary, if not. It also hopes to assist publishers to market books and other offline materials over the Internet.[81] On 14 December 2004 Google launched its programme of "Google Prints for Libraries", which was joined by the university libraries of Harvard, Stanford, Michigan, Oxford and the New York Public Library, to digitise library books and make them searchable online.[82] Using technological measures, Google, on the one hand, limits the number of viewable pages and attempts to prevent page printing and text copying of material under copyright; and, on the other hand, allows works in the public domain and other non-copyright material to be downloaded in PDF format.

---

[79] See http://books.google.com/googlebooks/library.html, retrieved on 29 March 2011.

[80] See http://ap.google.com/article/ALeqM5jy9NYSibUWEKVrY8BYF2rVn 3WbqgD930L4H00, retrieved on 19 March 2011.

[81] See http://www.google.com/press/pressrel/print_library.html, retrieved on 19 March 2011.

[82] Ibid.

Of course, such a project has led to a controversial debate, especially on copyright issues. In May 2005 the Association of American University Presses issued an objection to Google's digitisation, and in August 2005 Google halted the project allowing publishers to agree on whether they want their titles to be excluded from Google Library.[83] In September 2005 the Authors Guild announced that it has filed a class action suit in a New York federal court, alleging that Google has been engaging in "massive" "unauthorised scanning and copying" at the expense of the rights of individual authors.[84] In October the Association of American Publishers took action against Google in New York for the same unauthorised acts.[85] Google defended the case on the ground that its use is "fully consistent with both the fair use doctrine and the principles underlying copyright law itself, which allow everything from parodies to excerpts in book reviews".[86] In November, offering authors and right owners freedom to opt out of the project, Google Library was resumed.

In June 2006 Copiepresse, a news agency in Belgium, filed a lawsuit in the Court of First Instance in Brussels to stop Google including snippets of its articles on the Google News search pages. In September the court handed down an injunction against Google using Copiepresse's materials, which Google appealed but the injunction was upheld in February 2007. The Belgian court ordered Google to remove the plaintiff's materials within 24 hours or to pay fines, and to publish the entire intervening judgment on the home pages of google.be and of news.google. be for a continuous period of 5 days within 10 days.[87] Nevertheless, the courts support Google's opt-out procedure, according to which the copyright owners are responsible for notifying Google of the acts of infringement.[88]

Again in June 2006, La Martiniere Group, a French publisher, sued in Paris against Google's "contrefaçon" and "atteinte au droit de propriété

---

[83]   See http://googleblog.blogspot.com/2005/08/making-books-easier-to-find. html, retrieved on 19 March 2011.

[84]   See the Authors Guild news release online http://www.authorsguild.org/ advocacy/articles/authorsguildsuesgooglecitingmassivecopyrightinfringement. html, retrieved on 19 March 2011.

[85]   See http://news.bbc.co.uk/1/hi/business/4358768.stm, retrieved on 19 March 2011.

[86]   See http://googleblog.blogspot.com/2005/09/google-print-and-authors-gui ld.html, retrieved on 19 March 2011.

[87]   See http://www.copiepresse.be/13-02-07-jugement-en.pdf, retrieved on 19 March 2011.

[88]   Ibid. And Google has appealed in June 2007.

intellectuelle".[89] It claimed that Google Library had digitised at least 100 titles from its catalogue without consent and demanded 100 000 euros for each digitised book.[90]

Yet in the same month Google obtained its first victory in the Hamburg court, where Wissenschaftliche Buchgesellschaft (WBG), a scientific publisher, asked for an injunction to stop its books from being scanned in Google Library but later withdrew its application on 28 June 2006, as the court held that WBG failed to bring arguments in support of its action and informed WBG that it would have only a poor chance of winning, notwithstanding its being backed by the German publishers association. The Hamburg court concluded that the development of Google Library did not violate copyright on the basis of the fair use doctrine.[91] Rather, the court drew attention to the fact that copyright law is territorial and embraced the US copyright law to examine Google Library's acts as the scanning of books occurred and will occur in the US.

In October 2009, on behalf of hundreds of Chinese writers, the WWCSC accused Google Library of copyright infringement and its negotiation with Google on compensation to authors is still underway, notwithstanding Google made an apology over unauthorised scanning of tens of thousands of books in January 2010.[92] Moreover, Google Library was brought to the Beijing Haidian District People's Court by Mian Mian, a popular fiction writer, in May 2010, for unauthorised scanning of one of her books, *Salt and Sour Lover*.[93]

Authors Guild et al. v Google inc.[94] nonetheless has developed into an actual drama. After over three years of negotiation, the plaintiff and defendant reached a USD 125 million settlement agreement on 28 October 2008, which also included licensing provisions. On 9 November 2009 the parties amended the settlement agreement (ASA) because the Department of Justice filed a brief suggesting that the initial agreement may violate US anti-trust laws. Following that, the court held a Fairness Hearing

---

[89] See http://www.zdnet.fr/actualites/imprimer/0,50000200,39355239,00.htm, retrieved on 19 March 2011.

[90] See http://news.bbc.co.uk/1/hi/entertainment/5052912.stm, retrieved on 19 March 2011.

[91] See http://www.guardian.co.uk/technology/2006/jun/29/news.google, retrieved on 29 March 2011.

[92] See http://www.prccopyright.org.cn/News_View.asp?NewsID=101, retrieved on 29 March 2011.

[93] See http://epaper.bjnews.com.cn/html/2010-05/27/content_105020.htm, retrieved on 29 March 2011.

[94] See http://thepublicindex.org/docs/amended_settlement/opinion.pdf, retrieved on 29 March 2011.

on 18 February 2010, and on 22 March 2011 Judge Denny Chin issued a ruling rejecting the ASA, which was concluded to be not "fair, adequate and reasonable".[95] While admitting "the digitization of books and the creation of a universal digital library would benefit many", the judgment pointed out that the ASA "would simply go too far" to permit the online giant to implement a business arrangement that "would grant Google significant rights to exploit entire books, without permission of the copyright owners".[96] Judge Denny Chin urged that the ASA be revised from "opt-out" to "opt-in" and set a "status conference" on 25 April 2011 at which to discuss next steps.[97] At the moment it is not clear what action Google will take.

Following Google's lead, the European Commission launched its online library in May 2005 to "preserve Europe's cultural heritage" by making the materials in Europe's libraries and archives accessible to all.[98] In December 2006 Microsoft launched a similar project, Live Search Books, which included books from the British Library, the University of California and the University of Toronto.[99] However, the project was abandoned in May 2008 since Microsoft believes that "the best way for a search engine to make book content available will be by crawling content repositories created by book publishers and libraries".[100] Obviously, Microsoft has no interest in being an online librarian. However, Google Library seems determined to continue its mission of digitising books as it deems that making the world's knowledge more accessible will benefit everyone.[101]

Recognising the power of the Internet, Google Library is seen as a great threat to the rights of publishers and copyright holders on the Internet, and at the same time is seen as a huge step forward for developing digital libraries and benefiting Internet users all over the world. The topical debates on Google Library illustrate the conflicting interests between those two groups. The tension is growing along with the advance of IT. It appears that Google Library, representing digital libraries, has taken the

---

[95] See para 1.
[96] See para 2.
[97] See Conclusion.
[98] See http://news.bbc.co.uk/1/hi/technology/4512831.stm, retrieved on 29 March 2011.
[99] See http://news.bbc.co.uk/1/hi/technology/4377984.stm, retrieved on 29 March 2011.
[100] See http://blogs.msdn.com/livesearch/archive/2008/05/23/book-search-winding-down.aspx, retrieved on 29 March 2011.
[101] See http://googleblog.blogspot.com/2006/06/germany-and-google-books-library.html, retrieved on 29 March 2011.

traditional public libraries' position in upholding the access public interest and the balance of copyright. What would French judges say about the German approach? Would Google Library satisfy the four-factor provisions in the US courts and thus be affirmed as fair use? Would fair dealing exceptions in the UK permit online libraries to provide copyright works, including music and films, to Internet users? It is worth noting that Google adopted an approach of "notice to withdraw" while digitising works rather than the established copyright tradition of "obtaining permission to use" in the West. *Authors Guild et al. v Google inc.* certainly denied such an approach and has an immediate impact not only on the Google digital library project but also on the US digital libraries in general, and it may well affect digital libraries in the West.

3.   THE CHINESE VERSION

The origin of Chinese libraries may be traced back to the Zhou Dynasty 600 BC, the *collection chamber*. The Zhou *collection chamber*, located in the king's palace, kept literature together with valuables and was allowed for use only by the king's families and the ministers.[102] After the Zhou, for a period of more than 2000 years, the library was named *cang shu ge*, "book-concealing chamber", describing perfectly its primary function: to collect and to store books. Moreover, the book-concealing chambers have always been privately owned and they were also seen as giving status. The oldest existing library in China, *Tianyi Ge*, was built in 1561 by a Mandarin noble, Fan Qin.[103] In the 1700s, Zhou Yongnian, the founder of China's public libraries, opened his book-concealing chambers to the public for the purpose of the distribution of literature.[104] Thereafter, more and more book collectors started to share their collections with the public. Indeed, private collectors and their promotional activities have played a vital role in and made great contributions to the growth of public libraries in China.[105]

---

[102]   See 钟守真 《中西图书馆起源之比较研究》 图书馆理论与实践1992(4):41; Shouzhen Zhong, 'A Comparative study of the Origin of Libraries in the West and East', *Library Theory & Practice* (1992), **4**, 41.

[103]   Ibid. Fan Qin was the vice minister of Military Ministry in the Ming Dynasty and his collection was up to 300 000 books.

[104]   See 赵尔巽、柯劭忞等 《清史稿·周永年列传》; Erxi Zhao, Shaomin Ke et al. compiled *The Draft History of Qing – The Bibliography of Zhou Yongnian*; available at http://www.tianyabook.com/lishi2005/qingshigao/index.htm, retrieved on 19 March 2011.

[105]   See the Report of the National Library of China 2003.

3.1 Public Libraries

Most Chinese public libraries, including their collections, are comparatively new owing to their late commencement. The modern term "library" was introduced from the West to China in 1896, the period of the late Qing Dynasty. Library in Chinese is *tu shu guan*, which means "a place for drawings and books" and holds not only books but also drawings and other materials. Spread of the term was encouraged by the establishment of the first national public library, *jing shi tu shu guan*, in 1909.[106] A year later, the Qing government passed its first library law, the Regulations of Jingshi Library and Provinces' Libraries, for the purpose of stimulating the spread of public libraries.[107]

In December 1927 the Statute of Libraries was promulgated in the Republic of China, approving public libraries funding and making compulsory the establishment of libraries by universities. Moreover, the Statute was revised in 1930 and it ratified legal deposit by the additional Rules of Legal Deposit of New Books.[108]

All previously published laws were abolished in 1949; and, as noted in Chapter 2, the current legal system in China was rebuilt in 1978. Although an initial network of public libraries, including state-owned public libraries, school and university libraries and research libraries, had been set up, expansion is far behind demand, mainly because of the financial difficulties, not only in almost all the countryside, but also in most cities.[109] A number of administrative regulations have been published by different state departments in mainland China. A Library Law was publicised in Taiwan China in January 2001, which affirms local government funding for the establishment and development of public libraries.[110]

In the early 1990s, only 3.4 per cent of Chinese had the chance to

---

[106]　See 汪家熔，两件图书馆史史料，《图书馆学通讯》 1983(2):88; Jiarong Wang, Two Historical Materials of Library History, *The Library Science* (1983), **2**, 88.

[107]　Ibid.

[108]　See 董乃强 2002 《中国高等师范图书馆史》 Naiqiang Dong, *The History of Libraries in Chinese Higher Education* (2002).

[109]　See 刘楚材，现代观念与现代图书馆: 深圳图书馆十年改革实践及其引发的思考，《中国图书馆学报》 1997年23卷3期71, 54–7; see Chucai Liu, 'Modern Concept and Modern Library – Ten years Reform and Practice of Shenzhen Library', *Journal of the Library Science in China 23* (1997) **3**(71), 54–7.

[110]　See 孙利平，卢海燕，台湾地区图书馆法立法回眸 《大学图书馆学报》 2001 第 6 期; Liping Sun & Hiayan Lu, 'The Retrospection on Library Legislation in Taiwan Region', *Journal of Academic Libraries* (2001), **6**, 25–33. See also, http://law.moj.gov.tw/Scripts/Query4A.asp?FullDoc=all&Fcode=H0010031, retrieved on 19 March 2011.

receive higher education.[111] Very many people in China carry on their *zixue kaoshi*, "self-study examination", to gain certificates, diplomas or degrees; and most of them greatly depend on public libraries, which serve people including school children from poor families and provide places to study.[112] Therefore, public libraries are also called *dier ketang*, "the second classroom",[113] by the public and are seen as social welfare, playing an important part in people's lives.[114] Indeed, Chinese public libraries serve as the nationwide reading platform.[115] In 2001, for example, 2696 public libraries received 208 760 000 readers, which was more than 15 per cent of the population.[116] To the end of 2006, around 2778 public libraries were established throughout mainland China, among its 1.3 billion population[117] and the number of public libraries reached 2850 by December 2009.[118]

Owing to the great imbalance between the limited number of libraries and the massive population and demands, as well as the lack of considerable funding, public libraries in China have adopted a membership system, and many also provide specific services for profit. The use of technology is also a core part of the institutional mission of libraries, essentially the computer-based systems.[119] Since the mid-1980s, Chinese public libraries

---

111   See http://www.moe.edu.cn/edoas/website18/87/info33487.htm, retrieved on 19 March 2011.

112   See 刘精明, 杨江华, 关注贫困儿童的教育公平问题 《华中师范大学学报》 2007年第2期120–28页; Jingming Liu & Jianghua Yang, 'Attention to Equal Education for Children in Poverty', *Journal of HuaZhong Normal University* (2007), **2**, 120–28; see also http://www.sociology.cass.net.cn/shxw/zxwz/t20080310_15937.htm, retrieved on 19 March 2011.

113   Another unique phenomenon resulted from China's economy, which was often talked of as a rapid development. Whilst it became the second biggest economy in the world in 2010, its GDP per capita in 2006 was about 1700 US dollars, equal to the level of the US in the 1940s, and in 2010 was around 7000 US dollars and ranked 127th.

114   See http://www.ncac.gov.cn, retrieved on 19 March 2011.

115   See P. Yu & D. Davis, 'Arthur E. Bostwick and Chinese Library Development: A Chapter in International Cooperation', *Libraries & Culture* (1998), **33**(4), 389–406.

116   Statistical Yearbook of Chinese Culture 2002.

117   See Basic Statistics on Public Libraries, http://www.stats.gov.cn/tjsj/ndsj/shehui/2006/html/0307.htm, retrieved on 19 March 2011.

118   See 国统制[2009]72号, National Bureau of Statistics Document Number (2009), 72.

119   Lorna Hughes, *Digitizing Collections – Strategic Issues for the Information Manager* (2004). See also Terras, Melissa, 'Review of Lorna M Hughes "Digitizing Collections – Strategic Issues for the Information Manager'. *Literary and Linguistic Computing* (2007), **22**, 105–6.

have made efforts in the research and application of IT in their services. For instance, Shenzhen Library (SZL) currently keeps 1.8 million books and periodicals, and 1 million electronic and network resources, and set up its Newspaper Cutting Centre in 1992, gaining many subscribers by providing various information in the fields of general merchandise, real estate and finance and stock, with revenue of about RMB 0.4 million yuan for three years in succession;[120] the centre has been renamed the E-press Clipping Service since 1999 and provides e-versions to members.[121] SZL also holds the *Fashion Collection, Law Collection* and *Commerce Collection*, where readers can use a mixture of information on the selected topic and obtain professional lectures and personnel training services on the basis of paying membership fees.[122] In addition, other than reading or studying in the library, readers may book facilities and equipment on the Internet to learn languages, or appreciate music and films on the library intranet.[123]

The development of IT, especially the Internet, has made notable impacts on the growth of public libraries and has shifted the modern library sectors from providing documentary services only to providing wide-ranging information services. Such changes have strengthened public libraries' role of information holder in society, as well as of knowledge provider and promoter.

3.2   Digital Libraries

The spread of the Internet has also brought Chinese people a fresh view on libraries, including developing digitisation initiatives and digital libraries. With various understandings,[124] "digital library", or "electronic library",

---

[120]   See Xiaolin Li, 'Shenzhen Library Promoting Self-Development through Serving the Society', *Chinese Culture* (1996), **5**(1), 1.
[121]   See http://www.szlib.gov.cn/english/serv/feaserv.html, retrieved on 19 March 2011.
[122]   See http://www.szlib.gov.cn/newsshow.jsp?itemid=204, retrieved on 19 March 2011.
[123]   See http://www.szlib.gov.cn/cgi-bin/OPAC/TopicLibrary.cgi?id=VODS YS, retrieved on 19 March 2011.
[124]   According to the Graduate School of Library and Information Science's survey (http://web.simmons.edu/~schwartz/462-defs.html), more than 65 different definitions were collected in 1999. Nevertheless, the Digital Library Federation (DLF) has given a comprehensive definition as follows: "Digital libraries are organizations that provide the resources, including the specialized staff, to select, structure, offer intellectual access to, interpret, distribute, preserve the integrity of, and ensure the persistence over time of collections of digital works so that they are readily and economically available for use by a defined community or set of com-

or "virtual library" – the once new concept – has populated the country, along with the advance of ICT, by offering convenient and free or cheap materials to the public.[125]

The term "digital library" was introduced to China in September 1995 by three joint projects of digital libraries set up between IBM China Research Laboratory and Tsinghua University, Fudan University, and Chinese National Petroleum Corporation respectively, which were intended to build up stand-alone mass data processing systems for images and multimedia information resources.[126]

Aiming to establish an experimental digital library system with collaboration, resource sharing and unity, China launched its first national level digital library project, China Pilot Digital Library Project (CPDLP), in 1997, which was jointly undertaken by the National Library of China (NLC) and six major Chinese public libraries, namely, Shanghai, Shenzhen, Zhongshan, Liaoning Provincial, Nanjing and Guilin.[127] The CPDLP was completed in May 2001 and is now open to the public, offering services of reading, retrieval and researching documents of special subjects online.

A Documents Digital Centre was established in the NLC in March 1999, and by December 1999 a total of 30 million pages of the NLC collections had been digitised and could be read on the Internet, whilst 600 GB of databases, catalogues, titles and full text were available on the NLC intranet.[128] Following the success of the CPDLP, the China Digital

---

munities;" see D.J. Waters, 'What are Digital Libraries?' *CLIR* (1998), 4, http://www.clir.org/pubs/issues/issues04.html, retrieved on 19 March 2011.

[125]   See for example 胡新平; 沈洪妹; 张志美;数字图书馆: 让所有人平等获取信息 《情报理论与实践》 2011年2期77–80, 84页, Xinping Hu, Hongmei Shen & Zhimei Zhang, 'Research on the Construction of the Regional Cloud Digital Library', *Information Studies: Theory & Application* (2011), 2, 77–80, 84; 祝坤, 孔敏, 安英浩, 中小型公共图书馆的职能问题 《图书和情报》 2006年4期85–87页, Kun Zhu, Min Kong & Yinghao An, 'The Functions of Small- and Medium-Size Public Libraries', *Library and Information* (2006), 4, 85–87; 范并思, 论加强公共图书馆问题研究 《图书馆》 2000年6期1–4页; Bingsi Fan, 'On Emphasizing the Research of Public Libraries', *Library* (2000), 6, 1–4.

[126]   See 杨雨师、董陆驷, 浅析IBM数字图书馆方案 《图书馆学研究》 2002年10期27–28页; Yushi Yang & Lusi Dong, 'Analysis on IBM Digital Library Projects', *Researches in Library Science* (2001), **10**, 27–8.

[127]   See http://www.nlc.gov.cn/old/old/dloff/scientific6/sci_7.htm, retrieved on 19 March 2011.

[128]   See 邓胜利, 我国数字图书馆的发展现状调查 《情报资料工作》 2000年6期14–17页; see Shengli Deng, 'A Survey on the Development of Digital Libraries in China', *Information and Documentation Services* (2000), 6, 14–17.

Library Project (CDLP) was set up in April 2000.[129] As of the end of 2002, allying members of the CDLP had reached 117, under the practice code of "planning cohesively, standardised management, team working and resource sharing".[130]

In December 2000 the China-US Million Book Digital Library Project initialised its "Chinese American Digital Academy Library", which is supported by the State Development and Reform Commission, the Ministry of Education and the Finance Ministry.[131] In December 2004 the NLC Phase II and the National Digital Library of China Project were officially inaugurated; the intention is eventually to have its 12 million item collections digitised, including drawings, photos and other special collections.[132]

Apart from the efforts of government-funded public libraries, there have been hundreds of digital library projects initiated by business corporations and individuals, most notably书生之家 (http://edu.21dmedia.com), 中国 (http://www.d-library.com.cn), 方正 (http://apabi.lib.pku.edu.cn), 超星 (http://www.ssreader.com) and 同方知网 (http://www.cnki.net/gycnki/gycnki.htm).[133] These new digital libraries retain not only works in the public domain but also contemporary and popular works, and allow people to exploit their collections either for free or with very low membership fees, and are thus quickly appreciated by Chinese Internet users.

Since the collections can be made accessible via digital surrogates and are in an enhanced format that allows searching and browsing via the Internet, digital libraries have been generally supported in China, alongside great discussions over digital works, especially the digitisation of copyright materials.[134]

---

[129]   Ibid.; see also http://english.peopledaily.com.cn/english/200004/20/eng20000420_39348.html.

[130]   See at http://www.nlc.gov.nc/newgygt/ndbg NLC Annual Report 2003, retrieved on 20 March 2011.

[131]   See http://www.cadal.zju.edu.cn/Index.action, retrieved on 20 March 2011.

[132]   See http://www.nlc.gov.cn/GB/channel1/index.html, retrieved on 20 March 2011.

[133]   See http://news.xinhuanet.com/it/2002-05/27/content_411044.htm, retrieved on 20 March 2011.

[134]   See for example 张彦博, 罗云川, 王芬林, «数字图书馆资源建设和服务中的知识产权保护政策指南» 解读, «中国图书馆学报» 2011年 01期59–63页, Yanbo Zhang, YCh Luo & FL Wang, 'Interpretation of "A Guide to Intellectual Property Protection Policy in Digital Library Resources Development and Services"', *Journal of Library Science in China* (2011), **1**, 59–63; 姚春杰, 数字图书馆建设中面临的知识产权问题及对策, «图书馆论坛» 2007年 02期97–99, 51页, Chunjie Yao, 'The IPR Issues in Digital Library', *Library Tribune* (2007), 2, 97–99, 51; 沙志龙, 数字图书馆建设中的知识产权问题及对策 «大学图书情报学刊» 2009年 02期3–5页, Zhilong Sha, 'Problems and Measures of the Intellectual Property

3.3 Copyright Provisions

Under the strong influences of Confucianism, copying for collection was seen as appreciating works; it has been the main philosophy employed by Chinese libraries.[135] Up to the mid-1990s, most libraries held a certain amount of gravure collections such as pirated reproductions of foreign language books, periodicals, software, database or audio-video publications; and those collections were officially in use before copyright law came to be enforced.[136]

The 1990 CCL authorised copyright owners' personality rights and property rights while naming 12 specified uses of protected works as fair dealing. Amongst these uses were included "use of a published work for the purposes of the user's own private study, research or self-entertainment", and "reproduction of a work in its collections by a library, archive, memorial hall, museum, art gallery or any similar institution, for the purposes of the display, or preservation of a copy, of the work".[137] Article 5(1) of the Implementing Regulations 1991 defined reproduction as "the act of producing one or more copies of a work by printing, photocopying, copying, lithographing, making a sound recording or video recording, duplicating a recording, or duplicating a photographic work, or by other means".

In order to meet the minimum requirements set by the WCT 1996 and the TRIPS, the law was first revised before China acceded to the WTO in 2001 and the second amendment came into effect in 2010, without much change. The 2010 CCL confers upon right holders the right of communication of their work to the public through an information network.[138] Besides, it states that anyone who has intentionally circumvented or sabotaged the technological measures adopted by the right owner of copyright and neighbouring rights to protect his work or the sound

---

Rights in the Construction of Digital Libraries', *Journal of Academic Library and Information Science* (2009), **2**, 3–5; 陈志宏, 新形势下图书馆业务涉及到的知识产权问题的思考 《情报探索》2003年3期14–17页; Zhihong Chen, 'IP Questions Raised by New Services in Public Libraries', *Information Research* (2003), 3, 14–17; 吴永臻, 数字图书馆建设的版权问题 《情报科学》2001年 08期801–3, 808页, Yongzhen Wu, 'Copyright Problems in Digital Library Construction', *Information Science* (2001), **8**, 801–3, 808.

[135] See also N. Wingrove, 'China Traditions Oppose War on IP Piracy', *Research Technology Management* (1995), **38**, 6.

[136] See 陈志宏, 新形势下图书馆业务涉及到的知识产权问题的思考 《情报探索》2003年3期14–17页; Zhihong Chen, 'IP Questions Raised by New Services in Public Libraries', *Information Research* (2003), **3**, 14–17.

[137] Article 22 (1) and (8).

[138] See Article 38, the 2010 CCL.

recording or audio-video recording, or removed or altered any electronic rights management information attached to the copyrighted works and other objects, without permission of the right owners, should bear civil or criminal liabilities, or be punished by the copyright administration, except where otherwise provided for in laws or administrative regulations.[139] The definition of reproduction was entirely removed from the statute when the Implementing Regulations 2002 came into force.

However, the law does not offer concrete and operable guidance for copyright protection in the network environment, which has generated numerous disputes over use of copyright works on the Internet.[140] Thus, as mentioned in Chapter 2, the 2006 Communication Right Regulations were enacted, in light of the WCT 1996 and with the intention of balancing the interests amongst copyright holders, ISPs and large-scale Internet users. In accordance with the regulations, libraries may digitise their collections for display or archiving, and provide the digital materials to readers within their premises, without permission from the copyright owner and without remuneration, on condition that no economic profits are involved.[141] The regulations also offer libraries a safe harbour by imposing the "notice to remove" liability on the network intermediaries. "Notice to remove" has confirmed the right owners' burden in any objection of uses of copyright works and is of particular importance for digital libraries to avoid online copyright infringement disputes. Where an interested party considers that a digital library infringes the Internet communication rights, he/she may send the library a written notice to request that it deletes the collection or disconnects the link to the infringing material; and the library shall immediately delete the infringing collection or disconnect the link on receipt of such notice. To help public libraries understand the relevant laws, the Ministry of Culture issued the Guide to the Policy of Intellectual Property Protection in Digital Library Resource-Development and Services on 15 July 2010, which consists of 17 Articles primarily related to copyright protection and emphasises the implementation of the 2006 Communication Right Regulations[142] and the balance of the interests.[143] The 2010 Guide holds "three principles" on the topic of IP protection in digital libraries, namely, 公益性原则, "principle of public welfare", 利益平衡原则, "principle of balance of the interests", and 实用性原则, "principle of

---

[139]   See Article 47.
[140]   See http://www.gov.cn/zwhd/2006-05/29/content_294127.htm, retrieved on 20 March 2011.
[141]   See Article 7.
[142]   See Article 10.
[143]   See Article 3.

practicality".[144] Though the actual effect remains to be seen in the coming years, such administrative supervision may constructively assist the expansion of digital libraries over the country, although the definition of public libraries as well as digital libraries is absent.

3.4 Legitimate Trials

At present, the traditional public libraries' digitisation in China is mostly focused on two types of works, that is, works that fall into the public domain and those in the library catalogue, including information about works such as title, author, publisher, price and the year of publication. The majority of Internet readers are not satisfied with accessing only works in the public domain and the library catalogue but want more works of today. So some new digital libraries have played an important role as knowledge providers in this sense. While most adopt the "notice to remove" procedure for copyright works, their libraries are open to all Internet users either by registering as members for free or by paying a membership fee. However, many Chinese scholars and lawmakers question whether they are public libraries as they are funded by private organisations or individuals, unlike most traditional public libraries in China, which are publicly funded and owned by governments at all levels. Whether they should enjoy the library exceptions as other "real" public libraries is thus being questioned and claims are most often brought by right holders rather than would-be users or the digital libraries themselves. To date, disputes over copyright issues mainly occur within these non-public funded digital libraries: since *Chen Xingliang v China Digital Library* in 2001, numerous litigations have been brought about by the copyright owners.

3.4.1 *Zheng Chengsi v Shusheng Digital Library*[145]
On 21 October 2004 Beijing Shusheng Digital Technology Limited Company (Shusheng) was sued in Beijing Haidian Court by Professor Zheng Chengsi and six other well-known IPR experts; seven cases were filed on the same day against the infringing digitisation of their works in Shusheng Digital Library.[146]

---

[144] Ibid.
[145] See 北京市第一中级人民法院民事判决书 (2005)一中民终字第3463号, Beijing First Intermediate People's Court Judgment Number (2005) 3463.
[146] Reported on 24 October 2004, China Intellectual Property Newspaper. See also, http://chinanews.sina.com/tech/2004/0917/0339118411.html, retrieved on 20 March 2011.

In March 2004 Professor Zheng and the other six experts discovered on the Internet that Shusheng, a software company involved in developing software for digital libraries, digitised a number of their books in its own digital library without their authorisation. Relying on Section 41 of the Copyright Law 2001, Professor Zheng and the other six experts requested, respectively, judgments to order the defendant to cease its infringing acts, publish apologies and pay compensation for the damage caused.

Shusheng defended on the basis that, as stated on its website, the company "is making diligent efforts towards signing an authorisation with each author. But because the subject works are massive, it is difficult to sign treaties with all authors at once". Regarding the unauthorised uses of books, it added that "any authors of the works collected who have not received the reward, please contact us; please inform us if you do not want your work used by the digital library, we shall remove your work within 24 hours".[147] Shusheng pointed out that its uses of works were lawful in harmony with the 2001 CCL: its digital library project was meant to contribute to society and to promote reading, and thus was in the "public interest". More interestingly, Shusheng maintained that, adopting proper technological measures, its digital library was primarily for research and illustration purposes, and could be accessed only via the company's own software, Shusheng Reading, which was available only to its registered digital library readers.[148]

In the court, amongst other arguments, discussion on the nature of Shusheng Digital Library was the focus. Being in agreement with the plaintiff, the court deemed that the defendant's digital library was not a public library, for it was neither funded by public money nor owned by public institutes; besides, it was not large enough in scale to benefit the masses. Therefore, exceptions provided in Article 22 and the "public interest" defence did not apply to its uses of the plaintiff's works. Based on Article 10(12) of the 2001 CCL, "the right of communication of information on networks", and Articles 47(1) and 48, "the legal liabilities and enforcement measures", judgment was given in favour of Professor Zheng on 20 December 2004, commanding Shusheng (1) to delete all infringing works in 7 days, (2) to publish a written apology, which must be censored by the court, in the *Legal Daily* in 37 days, and (3) to pay the plaintiff a damage of RMB 56 500 yuan and his litigation fee RMB 5554 yuan in 17

---

147 See www.21dmedia.com, retrieved on 20 March 2011.
148 Shusheng also argued that Professor Zheng and the six other experts' uses of its software without consent had breached Shusheng's copyright and demanded litigation. The court accepted Shusheng's request and filed a separate lawsuit.

days. Shusheng appealed to the First Intermediate People's Court but failed. The first judgment was upheld in full on 10 June 2005.[149]

Zheng Chengsi v Shusheng Digital Library is seen as the logical extension of *Chen Xingliang v China Digital Library*, which was discussed in Chapter 3. Although the facts of the cases are not unique, they have brought digital libraries into question, especially the definition of a digital library.[150] As an IP authority, Professor Zheng's notion on public libraries and copyright in the Internet-based libraries, with which the courts also appear to agree, influenced many: relying on the investigations on funding, ownership, scale and benefits for people, Shusheng and several other open-to-public, non-state-owned digital libraries were at once accused of being "Internet Pirates".[151]

So, what is a public library? Must a public library be funded and controlled by a public body? Must a public library be of large scale to benefit the public? As a developing country with a huge problem of poverty, these seemingly simple questions ought to be answered, only with care. Other questions arising include: may digital libraries fall into the same copyright exceptions as the traditional libraries? What are the requirements for enjoying the privileges? Will legal clarifications be set forth in the near future?

Anyhow, the courts then did not offer clear interpretation or definition for either traditional or online public libraries, or about copyright owners' right of communication of their works on the Internet. In addition, the courts paid no attention to Shusheng's "notice to remove" and "notice to remunerate", which was later granted by Communication Right Regulations in 2006, and failed to offer any guidance to digital libraries regarding these copyright procedures.

There have been numerous cases involving copyright infringement disputes in the digital library sector thereafter; the courts in these cases have given different and even contradictory judgments. One example is China National Knowledge Infrastructure (CNKI), an ambitious digital library project established by Tong Fang, a sub-company of Tsinghua University.

149　See 北京第一中级人民法院判决书(2005)一中民终字第3463号; the Beijing First Intermediate People's Court Final Decision Number (2005) 3463. Same results with the six other experts' pleas.

150　Reported on 24 October 2004, China Intellectual Property Newspaper.

151　See for example, 周林, 法院终审判决 书生公司败诉; see Zhou Lin, 'How Shusheng Failed Its Appeal', retrieved on 18 September 2010 at http://www.iolaw. org.cn/showNews.asp?id=12406; 郭兴业, 网络盗版者与数字图书馆的区别 «中国工商管理研究» 2005年9期 62–3页; Guo Xingye, 'The Difference between Online Copyright Infringers and Digital Libraries', *Research on China Administration for Industry & Commerce* (2005), **9**, 62–3.

Claiming to be the leading digital library in China, CNKI started its business with e-journal products and expanded to cover newspapers, dissertations, proceedings, yearbooks and reference works, for sale. Indeed, as stated on its English website, CNKI is an e-publisher which "now serves more than four hundred universities, public libraries, research institutions, enterprises, and hospitals in more than twenty countries".[152] Since 2002, CNKI has been brought to courts by several copyright holders challenging its digital copyright infringement, and the court decisions have been inconsistent. For instance, with regard to CNKI's acts of publishing copyright works without consent, they were confirmed to be copyright infringement in *22 scholars from Chengdu, Wuhan, and Chongqing v CNKI* (2002) and CNKI was ordered to pay copyright owners both remuneration and compensation; infringement was also established in *Senior Fan Yuanwu v CNKI* (2005), but with very little remuneration and no compensation; the same acts were deemed to be fair in *32 authors from Hebei Province v CNKI* (2005), in *Fan Shaohua v CNKI* (2006), and in *32 Masters and PhDs v CNKI* (2008), the last of which suggests that CNKL publish notices to masters and PhD students in all involved universities. Amongst these, the case below is of particular interest.

3.4.2 *Jiang Xingyu v CNKI*[153]

Professor Jiang Xingyu, born in 1920 and still active in research and writing, is a historian of Chinese drama and local opera. In October 2005 he found out that CNKI had digitised 132 pieces of his works, over 1 million words, without his authorisation. All the infringing works were sold on the Internet by downloading as well as in bookshops on a CD called "China Periodical Academy". On 14 November 2005 Professor Jiang litigated CNKI's infringement in Shanghai Second Intermediate People's Court. The plaintiff demanded total damages of RMB 120 000 yuan as the CNKI had digitised his 132 works for commercial purposes and breached his rights of copying, publishing, public communication on the Internet and remuneration.

CNKI claimed that China Periodical Academy is a project authorised by the relevant state department, the General Administration of Press and Publication, and that its digitisations were legal for (1) the plaintiff did not prove that he was the author and owner of the copyright of all the mentioned works; (2) the act of digitisation was lawful because it was

---

[152]   See http://www.global.cnki.net/grid20/index.htm, retrieved on 20 March 2011.
[153]   See 上海第二中级人民法院判决书 (2005) 沪二中民五 (知) 初字第326号, Shanghai Second Intermediate People's Court Judgment Number (2005) 326.

reprinting a published work by periodicals; (3) after receiving notice of the litigation, the defendant posted remuneration to the plaintiff but was rejected; this, however, showed that the defendant had no intention to breach any copyright.

On 25 March 2006 the case was concluded. The court stated: (1) the plaintiff is the author of the 132 works and holds copyright over the works. (2) Reprinting published works by periodicals, including public communication of the works on the Internet, is one of the permitted acts authorised by the 2001 CCL, unless the author has declared that such reprinting is not permitted; as the plaintiff did not do so, the defendant's uses of the 132 works did not breach the plaintiff's copyright, or his public communication right on the Internet; however, the 2001 CCL grants copyright owners right of remuneration, with which the defendant did not comply and thus infringed the plaintiff's right to such. (3) As currently there is no criterion available regarding remuneration for digitising works, following Articles 11,[154] 32(2),[155] 47(1) and 48 of the law, the court took into account the nature of the digitisation and communication in a digital library where people can benefit from it, and ordered the defendant to pay the plaintiff economic damages of RMB 38 000 yuan. In addition, the litigation expenses of RMB 3910 yuan were to be shared by both parties.

It should be noted that, firstly, the fact that the defendant's project was supported by a state organ was emphasised by both the defendant and the court throughout; and the court thus deemed such a commercial project to be in the "public interest". This mistaken interpretation overpowered the interest of state organs and violated the rights of individuals, in the name of the "public interest", which reflects the rule of man tradition and its influence on Chinese jurisdiction today. And secondly, the court employed almost the same clauses as in *Zheng Chengsi v Shusheng Digital Library* but drew completely different conclusions. Despite the flawed analysis on whether the defendant's act infringed the plaintiff's copyright in his 132 works – Article 22(4) grants certain acts of reprinting or republishing of published *articles on current events* only as permitted act – the court confounded the uses of copyright works in business sectors and in public libraries, and incorrectly approved the defendant's digitising copyright

---

[154] The copyright in a work shall belong to its author.

[155] Except where the copyright owner has declared that reprinting or excerpting is not permitted, other newspaper or periodical publishers may, after the publication of the work by a newspaper or periodical, reprint the work or print an abstract of it or print it as reference material, but such other publishers shall pay remuneration to the copyright owner as prescribed in regulations.

works without authorisation as lawful acts. Certainly, the court abused the access public interest in this case.

In addition, whilst copyright law provides statutory compulsory licensing for reprinting, republishing or excerpting published works, this has not been imposed by the courts, which also shows the underdevelopment of such in China. Currently, copyright permissions are obtained largely via authorisation from individual copyright holders and the most common procedures for that are twofold, "one-to-one agreement" and "notice to remove", of which the latter is empowered by the Communication Right Regulations 2006 and adopted by the majority of digital libraries, and the former is used particularly by one.

3.4.3 Super-Star Digital Library

超星数字图书馆, Super-Star Digital Library is famous in China for its unique approach of obtaining copyright authorisation through "one-to-one agreements", called 超星版权模式, "Super-Star Copyright Mode" (SSCM). To date, Super-Star Digital Library has signed agreements with 300 000 authors or right owners for using their copyright works, that is, digitising and keeping their works in its digital library and offering the works to its digital library readers via the Internet.[156] The SSCM is encouraged by Chinese lawmakers as well as IP experts including Professor Zheng Chengsi, who was a founder and promoter of the SSCM contract.[157] Mr Xu Chao also commented in June 2004 that in "lawfully solving the communication right in the Network environment", "the efforts in the SSCM are great and positive"; "it seems that providing specific regulations for digital libraries may be necessary".[158]

Nonetheless, Super-Star Digital Library has also been sued by several authors for its digitisation of their copyright works. For instance, Beijing Haidian District Court concluded six lawsuits in 2007 and five of the judgments were given to the plaintiffs.[159] The only winning case for Super-Star is as follows. In June 2007 Super-Star Digital Library was sued in

---

[156] See http://www.ssreader.com/zhuanti/15/sc.htm, retrieved on 20 March 2011.

[157] Ibid. See also 祝朝安, 借鉴超星经验、建设我国数字图书馆 《内蒙古图书馆工作》 2003年第1期11–14页; Chaoan Zhu, 'Use Super-Star Experience for Reference to Develop Digital Libraries in China', *Inner Mongolia Library Science* (2003), **1**, 11–14.

[158] See http://www.ssreader.com/zhuanti/15/ms_zong.htm, retrieved on 20 March 2011.

[159] See http://news.xinhuanet.com/book/2007-09/29/content_6811565.htm, retrieved on 20 March 2011.

Haidian Court by Wu Rui, a research fellow of the CASS.[160] The plaintiff claimed to be the author and copyright owner of "The Origin of Chinese Thoughts", which consists of three volumes and 990 000 words, and was published in September 2003. Two volumes and 644 000 words were digitised by the defendant without authorisation and sold on the Internet at a rather high price. Moreover, the plaintiff contacted the defendant asking for the infringement to stop but was rejected. The plaintiff wanted Super-Star (1) to stop the infringing act – to stop use and sale of the digital copy of the work in the digital library; (2) to publish a written apology in three named newspapers; (3) to publish a written apology on the digital library website; (4) to pay an economic damage of RMB 128 600 yuan (based on 200 yuan per thousand words); (5) to pay relevant fees of litigation, notarisation, investigation and transportation of RMB 16 865 yuan; and (6) to compensate emotional damage put at RMB 10 000 yuan.

The defendant opposed that, as a sought-after digital library that pays close attention to copyright and right of the public communication on the Internet, it had already signed an agreement with the plaintiff, on 14 January 2003, regarding the communication of his works in the network environment. Therefore, it did not breach the plaintiff's rights and should not make any apologies or pay any damages.

In court, debate was focused on whether the plaintiff had signed an agreement and whether the agreement had legal effect. The plaintiff insisted that he was once asked to sign an intention to authorise but not an authorisation agreement. However, the defendant presented a one-page signed document entitled "agreement on authorising copyright work to be collected".

On 21 December 2007 the judgment was issued in favour of the defendant. The court confirmed that the plaintiff was the legitimate owner of the copyright in the mentioned works but also signed an agreement on 14 January 2003 to authorise the defendant to use his work in the digital library. Thus, the defendant's act did not constitute an infringement. The court further pointed out that it had noticed that the book in issue was published after the agreement and the defendant's use of the work appeared to be profit-driven. However, on the one hand, the agreement was unclear about what works to use, and the extent, scale and method of such use; and, on the other hand, the development of digital libraries in China was in great demand and was thus supported by the court in defending the public interest in general. The plaintiff's petition was therefore dismissed.

---

160 See 北京海淀区人民法院判决书 (2007)海民初字第7610号, Beijing Haidian District People's Court Judgment Number (2007) 7610.

Alongside the continuous growth in Internet users all over the country, including in the massive rural areas and poor regions, the demand for and use of digital library services are increasing. Indeed, digital libraries in China, like the actual libraries, are of significance to the public's access to information and learning. The court decision obviously reflects this topical Chinese phenomenon and confirms the defence of the access public interest in the Chinese copyright regime. The outcome would probably be different in the UK or the US.

Wu Rui v Super-Star Digital Library accepts that SSCM followed a proper procedure for use of copyright works in the digital environment, and the legitimate effect of a signed copyright authorisation agreement. It also reminds interested parties to be thorough before signing an agreement for copyright authorisation. Indeed, the agreement is the key in copyright authorisation with SSCM, to which the plaintiff obviously did not pay enough attention to foresee the consequences back in January 2003. Hence, it is urged to regulate copyright authorisation agreements, which ought to be in line with Chinese contract law, to make certain contents compulsory and clear, such as what works are authorised for use, the period of time for which the licence lasts, the remuneration, nature, extent, scale and method of such use, and the liability for breach of contract, together with methods to settle disputes.

3.4.4 *Shusheng Digital Library v Apabi Digital Library (Shusheng v Apabi)*[161]

Recently, Shusheng Digital Library has been involved in copyright infringement disputes frequently, not as a defendant but as the plaintiff. On 15 July 2008 Haidian Court granted Shusheng another judgment regarding its appeal against Apabi's infringing acts over a copyright novel of 127000 words – *zhi li po sui*.

zhi li po sui is a popular novel written by Shi Kang and published in 2002. In October 2005, Shi Kang authorised Shusheng to digitise his novel and at the same time assigned his right of the public commutation on the Internet to Shusheng for ten years with an agreed annual remuneration. In June 2007 the plaintiff noted Apabi's infringing act, which consisted in uploading the novel online and selling digital copies of it. Shusheng requested the court to order Apadi (1) to cease the infringement, (2) to pay damages of RMB 6350 yuan, and (3) to pay the notarisation fee of RMB 283 yuan.

---

161   See 北京海淀区人民法院判决书(2008)海民初字第11424号, Beijing Haidian People's Court Judgment Number (2008) 11424.

The defendant refused to pay any damages and argued that, firstly, Apabi had deleted the mentioned novel from its collection, which satisfied the requirement of "notice to remove"; and, secondly, that Apabi had signed an agreement with the publisher of *zhi li po sui*, which included the right to communicate works on the Internet.

The court verified that Shusheng currently owned the network communication rights over *zhi li po sui*, as authorised by Shi Kang, for the author owns copyright of the work unless otherwise stated. The agreement the defendant signed with the publisher would not change the fact of the infringement since the publisher held no copyright over the author's works. However, for the following two reasons, the plaintiff's request of economic compensation was not fully granted: the defendant had deleted the work in issue after receiving the court notice of the appeal, which met the "notice to remove" procedure; and the defendant was a digital library that benefited the public and therefore should be supported in the light of the "public interest". Relying on Articles 47(1) and 48 of the 2001 CCL, the court ruled that the defendant (1) cease the infringement, (2) pay the plaintiff RMB 3175 yuan, and (3) pay the notarisation fee of RMB 283 yuan.

In *Shusheng v Apabi*, the court confirmed the "notice to remove" procedure that was granted by the Communication Right Regulations 2006, in conjunction with the access public interest in digital libraries, which was converted into the deduction of the penalty regardless of the defendant's for-profit orientation, and again demonstrated the Chinese characteristics in copyright enforcement.

In addition, it should be noted that, although the Regulations on Copyright Collective Management were enacted, the development of collective societies and licensing schemes in China is rather slow-moving. Hence, defending copyright has commonly been done by individual rights owners in the past. Shusheng, the digital library that holds the assigned network communication rights, acted in the role of a collective society not only in this case but also in others, which may reveal the future trend of copyright disputes.

4. DISCUSSION

Public libraries are information holders and transmitters, which have performed and are performing a very important role in society. Under the access public interest concept, copyright laws in all countries provide certain exceptions to enable some libraries' uses of works without being liable for infringement of copyright. The expansion of public libraries has been strongly influenced by economy and the culture, which has led to differentiation between the traditional public libraries in the West and those in China, not only in number, size, or facility, but also in conception and legalisation. Whilst diversities exist, the recent growth of digital libraries appears to be alike.

With a great contribution from the charity sector, public libraries in the West are well developed. On the one hand, the copyright laws present mature provisions regarding the use of copyright materials in the context of traditional libraries; and, on the other hand, the copyright managerial systems to deal with the matter have been suitably established. For example the collective licensing system, the PLR scheme, implemented in UK law in 1979 and under consideration in the US, which offers copyright owners compensation for the potential economic loss by allowing public libraries to lend their books. Nonetheless, the PLR ought to be extended to digital libraries on the Internet via licensing the uses of works in digital format.

However, the economic benefits have brought about court cases in the library sector regarding its use of copyright works. Courts, mainly in the US, have drawn a clear line between for-profit and non-commercial libraries, which has a direct effect on whether fair use can apply. The development of technology has stimulated the growth of public libraries as well as the development of copyright law. The Internet has become an important tool in information transfer and it has presented new challenges to fundamental copyright doctrines that are legal cornerstones for library services. It is of concern whether libraries may allow public access to digital works online, albeit not for profit, and whether the copyright exceptions would remain unaffected, since clearly this will affect the right holders' remuneration rights. However, it is admitted that this right would be consistent with library use. Copyright legislation has provided certain exceptions to public libraries that ensure they keep their roles in maintaining the balance between the two interest groups. Violation of the balance, regardless of the means and targets, implies breach of the public interest underlined by copyright.

To ensure the copyright laws are kept up to date, most national laws have implemented the WCT 1996, to improve the protection for copyright owners in relation to the use of their material on the Internet and through other new communications technologies, which include the EU Directive, the UK Gowers Report, the US DMCA 1998, and the Chinese Copyright Law 2001. In order to meet the rapid progress of IT, the former three copyright laws oblige the rulemaking to be kept under review every three years. Corresponding to library exemptions, they all define a qualified library as a non-profit library and constrain the fair dealing self-service copying and library privileges by whether the user's purpose is directly or indirectly commercial (no definition is provided though). The exemptions have been also revised to accommodate digital technologies and evolving preservation practices. Libraries' making of multiple digital copies is allowed in the US but not in the UK. However, the non-stop legal disputes on Google Library have shown that the copyright provisions for libraries are far behind the technological development and innovation of libraries, especially digital libraries. It should be made clear whether the library privileges may be applied in the digital environment and by digital libraries, together with the rights for digital reading and lending. In addition, Google Library has adopted a "notice to remove" procedure, which is practical for digital libraries and is currently a safe harbour provision in Chinese regulations. The "notice to remove" procedure restricts the uses of copyright works in the digital public library sector, supports the right owners' normal exploitation of their works for remuneration and commercialisation, and upholds their legitimate interests including moral rights; it thus meets the Berne three-step test. Nevertheless, the latest development in the long-running battle over Google Library has indicated that such procedure may be unauthorised by the Western courts. Will it affect the decisions of the Chinese courts in the long run? It will be interesting to find out in the future.

Reflecting the access public interest, to copy collections of any kinds for library preservation and archival purposes is allowed by current Chinese copyright law. The 2011 CCL sets forth the standard of the WCT 1996 and extends the exclusive right to the Internet. Moreover, the Communication Right Regulations 2006 give specific guidance for libraries communicating copyright works in the network environment and address safe harbours for ISPs, which provide information storage space and search or link services including digitisation in traditional libraries, although it is uncertain to which new network intermediaries the regulations extend. While the library privileges in the digital environment have been approved, questions remain for those new digital libraries: do new digital libraries' uses of copyright works of all kinds fall into this category? What are the justifications and provisions? It should also be noted that the Chinese authority went for administrative regulations instead of legislation to police the communication right on the Internet and to provide exceptions to the right, which continues to empower administrative organs.

Public libraries in China have been of particular importance to people's reading, learning and self-development. Akin to the education privileges, the library privileges are confirmed not only by Chinese copyright law but also by the general public, which explains why there have been no lawsuits regarding uses of copyright works against any traditional public libraries to date. On the contrary, numerous court cases have occurred in the digital library sector, a sector consisting of digitisation of collections of traditional libraries and new digital libraries, the latter usually offering no physical premises for their readers and accessible only online.

Since almost all actual open-to-public libraries are state-funded and managed, there is a confusion regarding the definition of public libraries in China: many, including lawmakers and IP experts, see that a public library must be large in size, and funded and owned by the state. Yet, these should not be the criteria; but rather whether the library collections are open to the public and are free or for no-profit, which can also apply to digital libraries. It should be noted that, although Chinese public libraries have adopted the membership system and some of them have set up different service projects for profit owing to the insignificance of their funding, their primary aim and function are providing the general public free access to information, which is the essential divergence between a public library and a for-profit library.

With the rapid expansion of the Internet, the potential market for digital reading and learning is massive. Thus, the establishment of digital libraries is supported by governments at all levels, carried out by traditional public libraries, as well as actively undertaken by profit-making private bodies, which has driven the growth of digital libraries over the country. The cases above have demonstrated that the courts and the digital library sector are both making progress in the past few years. It should be noted that, in the past, Chinese publishers did not own copyright over published works; the authors did. This is changing however: e-publishers have gradually grown up in China and normally hold copyright works' Internet communication rights, as in the case with CNKI and 中文在线 (http://www.chineseall. com). Moreover, with some digital libraries starting to sign contracts with authors not only for permission to digitise published work but also to publish new works online and authorising monopoly rights in the network environment, they no longer act in the single role of library but also as a publisher and a collective society at the same time. It is thus vital to have the relevant legal provisions made clear. In addition, whilst upholding the access public interest in the sector, Chinese law has made clear that the library privileges are for non-profit uses only. It, however, appears that currently the Chinese judges do not distinguish a non-profit digital library and a digital library for profit, which obviously results from the conceptions gained in those profit-orientated projects carried out by traditional public libraries owing to the sector lacking funding, which in a way has damaged the authorship public interest. Nevertheless, to be determined as public libraries, in both the traditional and digital context, they must be free for the public to use and the law ought to be enforced by Chinese courts.

Regarding copyright authorisation in public libraries online, both "one-to-one agreements" and "notice to remove" are granted and have obvious limitations. Whilst the time- and human-resource-consuming SSCM is another Chinese product and may be possible only in China at its early developing stage, the "notice to remove" procedure may suit the Chinese public libraries more. However, collective society and licensing schemes may be a mature answer, which are currently under development in China.

Chinese public libraries are obviously not able to meet the public demand, and essentially huge gaps exist just like the divergence between the country's rich and poor. China may learn from the Western experience and legally encourage charity and private sectors to contribute to the improvement of public library provision. If a number of Chinese Carnegies would use their wealth to establish free libraries for the poor, public libraries would definitely flourish in China. Moreover, the digital materials of the traditional public libraries are accessible only within the libraries' premises under the current library provisions. While use of copyright works for distance learning is authorised by Chinese copyright law and has facilitated constructive progress in the educational sectors, should distance reading also be granted, in the name of the access public interest? This, of course, must be kept in line with the Berne three-step test; it may be provided for certain purposes such as private study and non-commercial research and education.

The Chinese copyright provisions for public libraries are still under construction and therefore rather inadequate, although the lawmakers recognise the importance of setting up an effective legal system to meet international standards, and to ensure a balance between the increased rights of copyright owners and access to information. The library provisions in Chinese copyright law are somewhat sketchy and lack clarification of (1) the definition and limitations of qualified libraries, (2) the types of use covered, and (3) the types of fair reproduction permitted in both hard and digital format. Moreover, as a statute law country, the imprecise clauses certainly make the implementation of the laws more challenging. Moreover, Chinese courts ought to thoroughly take into account both the authorship and access public interest, and implement the rule of law throughout. As a country in favour of using litigation to promote law, yet which does not admit precedent as a source of law, how to keep the laws up to date may be worthy of the Chinese lawmakers' consideration.

China has no library law hitherto,[162] which is also one of the reasons for

---

162   Although it has been in drafting for years, see http://www.iolaw.org.cn/showNews.asp?id=20471, retrieved on 29 March 2011.

unnecessary confusion and disputes in the digital environment. A national law for libraries, concerning both traditional and digital environments, is therefore strongly recommended, which should clarify issues including:

- the definition of public libraries (including digital public libraries, which should be determined by whether they act as the general public's access points to knowledge and for learning, and also whether their main objective is non-profit);
- legal deposit (a legal deposit system is vital as it secures a comprehensive preservation of the nation's publications in all formats, makes access to intellectual and cultural heritage possible in the long term and benefits the public; China currently has no such provisions whatsoever);
- the public lending right (not provided by any law);
- inter-library loan (not provided by any law);
- types of fair reproduction in both hard and electronic formats (to be improved, 2010 CCL);
- the collective society and licensing schemes (to be improved, 2010 CCL);
- contracts regarding rights authorisation (to be improved, 2010 CCL);
- ISPs' safe harbour and "red flag" test (to be improved, 2006 Communication Right Regulations).

Besides, although it is unnecessary to place any notices for lawful protection in accordance with the Berne Convention, copyright notices should be promoted to increase the notion of copyright among the general public in China, as the nation's awareness of rights protection is in need of improvement. Public libraries do not have to police self-service copying, especially when it is not done on their premises, but they should be responsible for making users aware of the law, for which purpose the UK model may be adopted: putting up copyright notices in the library, next to photocopy machines and in computer labs, including Internet cafes in China's case. For better copyright understanding and protection in the future, the law ought to be widely known.

6. Public archives, public copyright and the public interest

Today's current records are tomorrow's archives.[1]

1. INTRODUCTION

The forms and definitions may be various, and the types may be diverse; archives, however, are the foundation of historical understanding and the main contributors to explaining and preserving the structures of the societies in which people live as well as giving meaning to people's own lives. By providing first-hand materials, archives are of critical importance for anyone who wants to know about people, places and events in the past, and for conducting research in many fields.[2]

Copyright law thus provides exceptions for reproduction and communication of a copyright work in records collected by archives analogous to the library privileges. Most public archives nowadays offer users access to their records as well as other relevant services including self-service facilities, which has resulted in certain discussions with regard to copyright. Challenge and further consideration of copyright have also come along with the development of IT and the spread of digitisation in the sector. However, issues that occur in the archives sector that are similar to those in public libraries shall not be reviewed in this chapter to avoid repetition.

Building and preserving records in the digital environment have become vital for public archives to fulfil their mission of providing long-term access to and use of records, and to meet the public's demand for a global open information system – online access specifically. For instance, the Scottish Archive Network (SCAN), founded in 1999, has set up and put

---

[1] See H. MacQueen, Scottish Executive Consultation on a Public Records Strategy (2005), 13.

[2] See J. Schwartz & T. Cook, 'Archives, Records, and Power: The Making of Modern Memory', *Archival Science* (2002), **2**, 1–19.

online "a single electronic catalogue to more than 20,000 collections of historical records held by 52 Scottish archives".[3]

Public archives, that is, state-owned archives, were once upon a time in China at all levels the means of control for the rulers and were inaccessible to the general public. The development of modern archives has been strongly influenced by the West and various laws and regulations have been enacted since the opening up to the world community; Chinese archives have been subject to dramatic changes in the last two decades. Today, while long-term preservation is of concern to archives together with collecting and archiving the cultural heritage in the digital environment and making it available for access on an ongoing basis, the opening and use of archival records are the topical focus of discussions in China and have produced enormous problems and challenges to its progressing system, particularly the balance between the rights of individuals and the state.

As regards public records, the Berne Convention requires member states to determine the protection to be given to official texts of a legislative, administrative and legal nature, and to official translations of such texts.[4] In China, copyright is not applicable to certain works, including laws, regulations, resolutions, decisions and orders of state organs, other documents of a legislative, administrative or judicial nature and their official translations.[5] Thus, Chinese government departments and the state entities do not claim copyright in most of their works done in the scope of their duties, and archival records of government documents are not protected by Chinese copyright, which is similar to the US legislation and different from the UK approach. In addition, whilst having been less discussed in China, the management of orphan works is distinctive and problematic.

These issues will be discussed with reference to the UK and US experiences in order to draw out perspectives that may help Chinese law and regulations in the sector and beyond to be improved.

2. PUBLIC ARCHIVES AND THE RELEVANT RULES

The Chinese have created a significant culture, which is also reflected in public archives' holding of 240 425 372 records, including records on tortoise shells and bones, ancient bronze articles, wood and bamboo slips,

---

[3] See http://www.scan.org.uk, retrieved on 20 March 2011.
[4] See Article 2(4).
[5] See Article 5, 2010 CCL.

stone engravings, silk and paper, amongst which the former three record-ing forms have represented three major stages of archival development in China.[6] Archival records illustrate vividly every historical step made by the Chinese people.

2.1   Prior to the Reform and Opening-up Policy

The development of archives in ancient China was extensively influenced by the complete and patriarchal clan system as the formation of archives and the system of archival vector, content and storage were closely related to the ancestral successive aristocratic systems.[7] Meanwhile, the advance of land and residence registration and the autocratic rule-of-man system made the ancient Chinese archives more comprehensive yet restricted.[8] In the Western Zhou Dynasty, a regulation on organising archives was adopted, emphasising archives' functions of collecting and preserving records, and was the earliest archival legislation in Chinese history.[9] The great philosopher Confucius considered archives a vital part of the cul-tural heritage and spent much time and effort to research and compile archival records. *Shang Shu*, "the Classic of History", one of his renowned works, was a compilation of documentary records related to events in the early Zhou Dynasty and before.[10]

While the Chinese written language was unified during the Qin Dynasty, it also imparted a political significance to archives; archives became more organised, centralised, and gradually turned out to be the emperor's 鞘中剑, "sword in the sheath", a tool of the ruling class.[11] Hence, on the one hand, the collection of archival records was paid even greater attention

---

6   See Shipping Xu, 'China's Recent Achievements in the Protection of Paper Archives, International Conference of the Round Table on Archives' (1999); retrieved on 8 March 2011 at http://old.ica.org/citra/citra.budapest.1999.eng/shuipping.pdf.
7   See 李伟山, 古代中国档案事业发展的政治探源 «贵州社会科学» 2006年3期 137–42页; Weishan Li, 'Development of Archives in Ancient China and Its Political Origin', *Guizhou Social Science* (2006), **3**, 137–42.
8   See 王英玮, 档案文化论 «档案学通讯» 2003年2期48–52页; Yingwei Wang, 'Archival Culture', *Archives Science Bulletin* (2003), **2**, 48–52.
9   Ibid.
10   See 刘耿生, 孔子编纂档案的历史贡献 «档案学通讯» 2001年6期71–80页; GengSheng Liu, 'Confucius' Historical Contribution on Archives Compilation', *Archives Science Bulletin* (2001), **6**, 71–80.
11   See 蒋卫荣 & 王铭, 关于中国档案事业史的若干问题断想 «档案学通讯» 2001年6期71–3页; Weirong Jiang & Min Wang, 'Some Thoughts on the Chinese Archival Development', *Archives Science Bulletin* (2001), **6**, 71–3. See also http://www.da.hz.gov.cn/daxh/xslw/t20060906_9619.htm, retrieved on 2 March 2011.

by the government, and, on the other hand, the early Chinese archival records consisted of exclusively administrative documents of the state and records of monitoring officers' behaviours.[12] The basic guiding principles of archival institutions throughout ancient China were the essential, imperial orders of the feudal society.[13] In addition, the mass production and extensive use of paper stimulated the advance of archives, including the forms of records and the managerial methods.[14]

Western archival management and methods of records keeping were introduced to China in the nineteenth century. After 1949, public archives were widely established over the country.[15] On 6 April 1956 the State Council issued the "Decisions on Strengthening the Nation's Archives" (Decisions). With acknowledgments of adopting the Soviet Union's experience of management and training in the archives sector, the Decisions affirmed the term "government archives" and the principle of centralised and unified management.[16] The collections of current records such as telegraphy texts, internal documents, minutes of meetings, memos of telephone conversations, and audio and video files were stressed, together with preservations of "records of revolution and old regime".[17] Furthermore, archives were described as institutions holding confidentiality or secrecy and were of a high priority for the interest of the state, and no one, including individual researchers, might access archives without official authorisation.[18]

Following the Decisions, archives were set up within almost all organisations at all levels,[19] where they were usually marked 机要重地、闲人勿

---

[12]　See 任汉中, 中国档案文化概论 (2000); Hanzhong Ren, *The Chinese Archival Culture* (2000).

[13]　See above, n. 7.

[14]　For instance, an original copy of Lu Ji's (AD 261–303, writer and literary critic in the Western Jin Dynasty) letter, titled, 'A Letter to a Friend Inquiring after His Health', has been reserved for more than 1700 years in Beijing Palace and the handwriting remains clear on a smooth paper. See Shipping Xu, 'China's Recent Achievements in the Protection of Paper Archives', International Conference of the Round Table on Archives (1999); retrieved at http://old.ica.org/citra/citra.budapest.1999.eng/shuipping.pdf.

[15]　See W.W. Moss, 'Dang'an: Contemporary Chinese Archives', *China Quarterly* (1996), 145, 112–29.

[16]　See Para 2.

[17]　Articles 1 and 4.

[18]　See Article 7(2). Also J.E. Nalen, 'Private Archives in China', *Libri* (2002), 52, 245, available at http://www.librijournal.org/pdf/2002-4pp241-262.pdf, retrieved on 10 March 2011.

[19]　It should be noted that all organisations were state-owned under the then planned economy.

进, "vital confidentiality, and authorised persons only";[20] even the information of archives' addresses was not open to the public. Continuing the old tradition, archives in New China were seen by the public as secret, stern and disciplinary places.[21]

The Decisions were the only regulation related to archives for over two decades. In accordance with the then planned economy, the Decisions generated huge numbers of archives at all levels as a political means for controlling the country and its people; the operations and records of public archives were under secrecy and too far for the general public to reach, in the name of the interests of the state.

2.2 An Opening-Up China Reflected in Public Archives

The economic reform since 1978 has brought China and its society a tremendous transformation that has also resulted in innovations in the archival sector. The Western modern concept of establishing archives for the benefit of the general public and not just for government has thus been introduced to the country.

2.2.1 The experiences in the West

In the West the concept of public archives for public use was instituted by the French Revolution, and in 1794 the French Archives Nationales were launched with jurisdiction over the records of the national government, provinces, communes, churches, hospitals and universities, and the archives were open to all citizens.[22]

The first US National Archives was established in 1926, a century and half after its Declaration of Independence.[23] In 1934 the National Archives Act was passed with the primary goal of providing the public with access to as much information as possible while preserving these records for future generations; the Act granted the National Archivist responsibility for and powers over legislative, executive and judicial records.[24] The huge growth of records during World War II necessitated the passage of

---

[20] See 马素萍，影响档案开放的因素分析《档案学通讯》2003年2期20-24页; Suping Ma, 'Analysis on the Factors Affecting Open Records', *Archives Science Bulletin* (2003), **2**, 20–24.

[21] See above, n. 8.

[22] See http://www.archivesnationales.culture.gouv.fr, retrieved on 11 March 2011.

[23] See R.A. Ross, 'Creating the National Archives' (2004), **36**(2), retrieved on 11 March 2011 at http://www.archives.gov/publications/prologue/2004/summer/nat-archives-70.html.

[24] Ibid.

a Federal Records Act in 1950, which authorised the National Archives to survey government records, investigate their management and disposal practices, and establish federal records centres for the intermediate storage of government records. The role given to the US National Archives in the disposal and secondary storage of relatively recent records also influenced the development of archives worldwide. The US National Archives declares that "records belong to the people".[25]

In 1966 the landmark legislation, the Freedom of Information Act (FOIA), was enacted and confirmed the public's legal right of access to government information.[26] As claimed in President Clinton's statement upon signing the 1996 FOIA amendments into law, it was "the first law to establish an effective legal right of access to government information, underscoring the crucial need in a democracy for open access to government information by citizens".[27] The FOIA was amended in 1996, 2002 and 2007 respectively to meet the rapid advance of IT, and requires all federal records, excluding those held by Congress, the courts, state or local government agencies, to be made available to the public either proactively or in response to a request within 20 working days, subject to certain conditions and exceptions.[28] The FOIA also sets out nine exceptions to the disclosure of records and three exclusions that permit an agency to withhold a record in part or in full in limited circumstances together with the appeal process.[29]

---

[25] See http://www.archives.gov/publications/general-info-leaflets/1.html, retrieved on 11 March 2011.

[26] See http://www.usdoj.gov/oip/foia_updates/Vol_XVII_4/page2.htm, retrieved on 12 March 2011.

[27] See http://www.usdoj.gov/oip/foia_updates/Vol_XVII_4/page2.htm. It should be noted that Sweden enacted the world's first FOIA on 2 December 1766, and the principle of "Offentlighetsgrundsatsen", openness, has ever since been enshrined in the Swedish legal system, in which the current FOIA was adopted in 1949 and amended in 1976; see Juha Mustonen, 'The World's First Freedom of Information Act' (2006), 9, retrieved on 2 March 2011 at http://www.chydenius.net/pdf/worlds_first_foia.pdf.

[28] See Section 552 of Title 5 of the USC.

[29] The exceptions are (1)(A) specifically authorized under criteria established by an Executive order to be kept secret in the interest of national defense or foreign policy and (B) are in fact properly classified pursuant to such Executive order; (2) related solely to the internal personnel rules and practices of an agency; (3) specifically exempted from disclosure by statute (other than section 552b of this title), provided that such statute (A) requires that the matters be withheld from the public in such a manner as to leave no discretion on the issue, or (B) establishes particular criteria for withholding or refers to particular types of matters to be withheld; (4) trade secrets and commercial or financial information obtained from a person and privileged or confidential; (5) inter-agency or intra-

In the UK, the Public Record Office (PRO) was brought in following the PRO Act in 1838 to reform the keeping of government and court records.[30] The Scottish Records Office (SRO) in Edinburgh, now the National Archive of Scotland (NAS), is the keeper for all Scottish public records.[31] In both the PRO and the SRO there was a long tradition of public access but the growing size of and demand for the public archives led to the Public Records Act 1958, which confirmed the public's statutory right of access to public records in the UK 50 years after the records being transferred to the PRO. On 1 January 1968 the Act was amended and public access was granted after 30 years of records transferring to the PRO.[32] Today, archives are defined as "original documents in any medium created and/or accumulated by an individual, a family, a corporate body or institution in the course of its daily life and work, which have been

---

agency memorandums or letters which would not be available by law to a party other than an agency in litigation with the agency; (6) personnel and medical files and similar files the disclosure of which would constitute a clearly unwarranted invasion of personal privacy; (7) records or information compiled for law enforcement purposes, but only to the extent that the production of such law enforcement records or information (A) could reasonably be expected to interfere with enforcement proceedings, (B) would deprive a person of a right to a fair trial or an impartial adjudication, (C) could reasonably be expected to constitute an unwarranted invasion of personal privacy, (D) could reasonably be expected to disclose the identity of a confidential source, including a State, local, or foreign agency or authority or any private institution which furnished information on a confidential basis, and, in the case of a record or information compiled by criminal law enforcement authority in the course of a criminal investigation or by an agency conducting a lawful national security intelligence investigation, information furnished by a confidential source, (E) would disclose techniques and procedures for law enforcement investigations or prosecutions, or would disclose guidelines for law enforcement investigations or prosecutions if such disclosure could reasonably be expected to risk circumvention of the law, or (F) could reasonably be expected to endanger the life or physical safety of any individual; (8) contained in or related to examination, operating, or condition reports prepared by, on behalf of, or for the use of an agency responsible for the regulation or supervision of financial institutions; or (9) geological and geophysical information and data, including maps, concerning wells.

[30] The PRO in Chancery Lane was opened in 1855 and gradually also became a repository for the administrative records of government, although there was no right of public access to them. See http://www.pro.gov.uk, retrieved on 20 March 2011.

[31] See H. MacQueen, 'Reform of Archival Legislation: A Scots Perspective', *Journal of the Society of Archivists* (2006), 26, http://www.era.lib.ed.ac.uk/bit stream/1842/2213/1/ReformOfArchivalLegislation.pdf, retrieved on 20 March 2011.

[32] See http://www.nationalarchives.gov.uk/policy/act/history.htm, retrieved on 20 March 2011.

selected for permanent preservation as evidence of purpose, function, organisation and operation".[33] In 2000 the FOIA was adopted in the UK and in 2002 the FOIA (Scotland) was enacted, which empowers the public with the "right to know" – government departments, including publicly-owned companies, are obliged to make their information available to the public on a national level. Articles 21–44 of the FOIA and Articles 25–41 of the FOIA (Scotland) list all types of information excepted from the disclosure.

In April 2003 the PRO and the Historical Manuscripts Commission joined together to form a new institution, The National Archives (TNA), which makes archival records available both onsite and online, and covers documents of England and Wales, whilst the National Archives of Scotland[34] and the Public Record Office of Northern Ireland remain separate. A further merger has taken effect; in October 2006 the Office of Public Sector Information (OPSI), a department of the Cabinet Office, joined TNA for stronger national archives to facilitate "a more responsive approach to the challenges of new technology" on the one hand, and "to realise the true value of information – as well as capturing the records of today for tomorrow's researchers" on the other.[35]

Implementing Directive 2003/98/EC,[36] the UK Re-use of Public Sector Information (PSI) Regulations 2005 came into force, in July 2005, to promote re-use of PSI. The regulations define "re-use" as using the records for a purpose other than the purpose for which the document was originally produced,[37] including a commercial one, and set out a time frame for a public sector body to respond to a request for re-use, which is 20 working days. The public sector body has the right to refuse the request provided

---

33   See http://www.archivesandmuseums.org.uk/scam/code.pdf, retrieved on 20 March 2011.

34   Which was known as SRO before 1999, see http://www.nas.gov.uk/about/history.asp, retrieved on 20 March 2011.

35   Retrieved on 20 March 2011 at http://www.nationalarchives.gov.uk/news/stories/133.htm and http://www.cabinetoffice.gov.uk/newsroom/news_releases/2006/statements/press_office/060621_opsi.aspx.

36   Which aims to stimulate knowledge-based economy in the EU with transparency and fair competition; it also sets out a harmonised framework in which PSI including digital content can be accessed as PSI is "an important primary material for digital content products and services and will become an even more important content resource with the development of wireless content services. Broad cross-border geographical coverage will also be essential in this context".

37   See Article 4.

the documents fall outside the scope of the Regulations.[38] A tribunal procedure is also laid down.[39]

The FOIA has set out a model for a practical system to enhance transparency, fairness and efficiency in public administration with the public's participation, and to contribute to establishing democratic government; whilst the re-use of the PSI regulations intends to stimulate information-based economic opportunities in the information era. Obviously, the role of public archives is of significance in this mechanism as they are holders and providers who make such information accessible for the general public as well as business, and challenges are continuously presented in their preservation and service of such information. Those challenges, as pointed out by TNA, include how the archives should act to secure (1) better information management to strengthen accountability, treat information with appropriate security, and release the potential of their assets; (2) readability of preserving digital information for future generations; and (3) availability and accessibility of information online.[40]

2.2.2 Chinese archives and public records

Aiming at "strengthening the management, collection and arrangement of archives and effectively protecting and using archives in the service of socialist modernisation",[41] the Archives Law came into force in China on 1 January 1988.[42] The law defines archives subject to "historical records in various forms, including writings in different languages, pictures, diagrams, audio-visual, etc., whose preservation is of value to the State and society and which have been or are being directly formed by State organs, public organizations and individuals in their political, military, economic, scientific, technological, cultural, religious and other activities".[43] But the law does not clarify "value to the State and society".

Most importantly, the Archives Law authorises the utmost use of public archives of all types and at all levels in divisions of state organs, public organisations, enterprises and other institutions.[44] Article 19 requires that:

---

[38] Articles 8 and 9.
[39] Articles 18–21.
[40] See the UK National Archives Annual Report published on 14 July 2008; retrieved on 20 March 2011 at http://www.nationalarchives.gov.uk/documents/annualreport07-08.pdf.
[41] See Article 1.
[42] And the Implementing Measures of the Archives Law was approved by the State Council on 24 October 1990.
[43] See Article 2.
[44] See Article 13.

Archives ... shall in general be open to the public upon the expiration of 30 years from the date of their formation. Archives in economic, scientific, technological and cultural fields may be open to the public in less than 30 years; archives involving the security or vital interests of the State and other archives which remain unsuitable for accessibility to the public upon the expiration of 30 years may be open to the public after more than 30 years. The specific time limits shall be defined by the national archives administration department and submitted to the State Council for approval before they become effective.

For the first time in Chinese history, public records are obliged to be open to the public.[45] The law further compels that catalogues of open records shall be published regularly for the public's convenience in use of archives.[46] Additionally, the State Archives Administration of China (SAAC) issued 17 more articles in December 1991 to detail the opening of state-owned archives.[47] The law also allows the general public to use the un-open archival records according to their needs in "economic construction, national defense construction, education, scientific research and other work".[48]

Nonetheless, Article 10 claims that "it is prohibited to archive any materials that should not be kept as archives pursuant to State regulations without due authorisation". The SAAC issued the Scopes of Archive and Non-Archive Materials in December 1987, which listed 16 categories of materials that should not be kept as archives,[49] including documents that had not been approved by *ling dao*, "the leadership",[50] or that had bypassed the immediate leadership,[51] and letters holding ordinary suggestions or criticism from the general public.[52] In December 2006 the SAAC issued the Regulations on the Scope of Archive Materials and the Termination of Archives, which reduced materials that should not be kept to four categories:[53]

---

45   See 李哲, 简述档案利用权与公布权的矛盾 《湖北档案》 2010年第8期15-17 页; Zhe Li, 'The Outline of Right of Using Archives and Right of Opening Archives', *Hubei Archives* (2010), **8**, 15–17.
46   See Article 20.
47   See Regulations on Opening of the State-owned Archives of the People's Republic of China, which came into force on 1 July 1992.
48   See Article 20.
49   Articles 2.1.1–2.4.3.
50   See Article 2.2.3.
51   See Article 2.4.2.
52   See Article 2.2.5.
53   See Article 4.

- copies of documents issued by higher authorities or copies made for fulfilling duty purpose, human-resource related documents of other departments;
- multi-copy of the documents issued by the department, un-finalised copies of any ordinary documents, letters and notes of telephone calls that need no transaction, and internal documents;
- documents issued by other authorities at the same level that need no transaction; and
- documents issued by lower authorities that have been copied to the department for reference or information purposes.

Other time, other manner; the SAAC issue in 1987 represented restricted sanctions in the central-controlled mechanism, where people's voices were not valued. The Regulations 2006 demonstrate an opening up in China and its progress in transparency and democracy,[54] although the term "internal documents" should be clarified.

Moreover, exchange of any public archives to foreigners was prohibited.[55] In all circumstances of the use of archives, "lawful identifications" must be possessed by the user,[56] which are defined as introductory letters or employee's cards from a Chinese organisation, or the Chinese national ID cards.[57] "Materials that should not be kept as archives" are not clarified; and open archives were then strictly for Chinese citizens only in gradually opening up China. While archives may be open to the public, the state wishes and in fact retains its absolute power of control.

The law also provides brief guidance to archives in different divisions. First, for the state-owned archival records, only the state-owned archives or state organs authorised by the state may make them public. Secondly, with regard to the archival records donated by or transferred from organisations or individuals, the priority in the use of such records is given to the organisations or individuals and restrictions on the use may apply in accordance with their desire. And thirdly, concerning collective or individually owned archives, the owners are eligible to make them public, without endangering the security and interests of the state or infringing the lawful

---

54 易嘉宁 李碧瑜, 政府信息公开背景下的档案开放与利用《云南档案》2010年第9期39–40页; Jianing Yi & Biyu Li, 'The Use and Open Archives Under the Open Government Information', *Yunan Archives* (2010), **9**, 39–40.

55 "Exchange" is the original text, which may be understood as "to make available". See Article 16.

56 See Article 19.

57 See Article 22, Implementing Measures of the Archives Law (Implementing Measures) 1990.

rights and interests of others.[58] Moreover, the law states that all the uses and exploitations of archives must be under the condition of defending the lawful rights and interests of archives and the rights owners.[59] These provisions have become the legal basis of defending private rights (including copyright) in the sector.

The Archives Law and the Implementing Measures were revised in 1996 and 1999 respectively, primarily to adopt the ongoing economic reform and social changes, that is, the increasing transformation of ownership of state-owned companies, and the rapid development of IT. The revised law encourages any use of public archives, and extends making archives available to the public to the network environment.[60] Public archives have ever since gone online lawfully.

Instead of totally prohibiting exchange of public archives to foreigners, the law states that "owners may deposit archives with or sell them to State archives repositories; selling of such archives to any units or individuals other than State archives repositories shall, according to relevant State regulations, be subject to approval of the archives administration departments of the people's governments at county level or above".[61] However, to sell archives to foreigners for profit is strictly forbidden.[62] Further, the law insists that

> collectively-owned or individually-owned archives whose preservation is of value to the State and society or which should be kept confidential shall be properly taken care of by the owners. If the archives are considered liable to serious damage or unsafe because of the adverse conditions under which they are kept or because of any other reason, the national archives administration department shall have the right to take such measures as may ensure the integrity and safety of the archives, such as by keeping the archives on the owner's behalf or, when necessary, by purchasing such archives or requisitioning them by purchase. [63]

Foreigners or foreign organisations may access and use open records in public archives provided that permission, either from relevant administrative departments or from the archives, has been obtained prior to the visit.[64] Whilst the confidentiality of archives is stressed in the name of the interest of the state and society, to sell archives to foreigners or foreign

---

58 Articles 21 and 22.
59 Ibid.
60 See Article 23(3), Archives Law 1996.
61 See Article 16, Implementing Measures 1999.
62 Ibid.
63 Ibid.
64 See Article 22.

organisations for profit or to give them archives as gifts may lead to criminal penalties.[65]

Still, the amended law gives no explanation about what is "of value to the State and society" and shows very limited flexibility to foreigners' or foreign organisations' access to archives. Yet one message is somewhat clear behind the clauses: while the opening up is unavoidable, the law strives to control the information as much as possible, and copyright may become a tool in this process.

The law gives the SAAC responsibilities for the administration, arbitration, and litigation of all archives,[66] which reflects the centralisation of power and the administrative enforcement in the sector. The law also clarifies that public archives at county level or above are responsible for the preservation and opening of records to the general public.[67] Permanent records are classified into three grades, which must be kept in archives at county level or above accordingly. The detailed implementation will be issued and explained by the SAAC; the law demands that public archives at lower level transfer their classified records to archives at county level or above in 10 or 20 years, consistent with the grades.[68] Nevertheless, the criteria of the classification are not explained.

Also the law declares that "state-owned archives shall be made public by archives repositories or State organs authorised by the State; no organisation or individual shall have the right to make public such archives without permission from such archives repositories or State organs"; as regards collectively owned or individually owned archives, "the owners have the right to make them public but they must abide by the relevant State regulations, and may not endanger the security and interests of the State or encroach upon the lawful rights and interests of others."[69] With no clarification of the "interests of the State", these provisions, on the one hand, demonstrate the overriding power of the interests of the State, and, on the other hand, are in conflict with copyright law. Chinese copyright, in line with international standards, has granted copyright owners exclusive rights over their creations, including the rights of publication and public communication on the Internet. By claiming records may be made public only by public archives, or if kept in non-public archives the publication must abide by the interests of the state, the archives law has obviously violated copyright owners' legitimate rights in their works.

---

[65] See Article 24.
[66] See Article 7 and also Articles 2, 3, 4, 11, 12, 13, 18, 19 and 22.
[67] See Article 6, Archives Law 1996.
[68] Articles 3 and 13(2), Implementing Measures 1999.
[69] See Article 22.

Notwithstanding, most government documents were maintained in secrecy and very few of the vast number of public records in different level archives have been accessible to the public until more recently. In 2000 Shenzhen Municipality Archives opened their once confidential "red-heading documents"[70] for public reference, which made the general public able to access all the documents in the archives either in person or make inquiries by phone or through the Internet. And many archives followed the lead thereafter. To 2006, 80 per cent of the Chinese archives have opened their "red-heading documents" to the general public.[71] By the end of 2007, 67.87 million documents were made accessible to the public in 3952 public archives at county level or above.[72]

Furthermore, all the 31 provinces/autonomous regions/municipalities and 36 departments of the State Council in China have formulated rules for making government affairs public, of which 28 provinces/municipalities have enacted local laws or regulations to make government information public and to pledge the general public the right of knowing and consulting all the policies regarding finance, personnel exchange, foreign affairs, trade and other key industries before coming into effect.[73]

2.2.3   China's regulations on open government information

The movement to opening government information in provinces and municipalities required legislation at national level. On 5 April 2007, modelling it upon the US FOIA, the Chinese State Council adopted the Regulations on Open Government Information (CROGI), which came into effect on 1 May 2008 to "ensure that citizens, legal persons and other organisations can obtain government information by lawful means, enhance transparency of the work of government, promote administration in accordance with the law, and bring into full play the role of government information in serving the people's production and livelihood and their economic and social activities".[74]

---

[70]   That is, 红头文件, which is a popular Chinese term for documents of all-level governments and organisations of the CCP as they are usually printed on red-colour-headed paper.

[71]   See http://www.people.com.cn/GB/paper464/17079/1498397.html, retrieved on 20 March 2011.

[72]   See http://www.stats.gov.cn/tjgb/ndtjgb/qgndtjgb/t20080228_402464933.htm, retrieved on 20 March 2011.

[73]   See 晓理, 我国档案立法现状及其发展 《中国档案》 2002年9期17-18页; Li Xiao, 'The Current Archival Legislation in China and the Prospect', *Chinese Archives* (2002), **9**, 17–18.

[74]   See also 何欢欢, 政府信息公开与档案开放 《档案管理》 2009年第4期16–18

The regulations define "government information" as "information made or obtained by administrative agencies in the course of exercising their responsibilities and recorded and stored in a given form".[75] They also confirm the state-owned archives' liability of making government information available to the general public and providing "reading places" and appropriate facilities for access to the information.[76]

Different scopes of disclosure are set out for administrative agencies at different level. In general the information should satisfy one of the following basic criteria:

- it involves the vital interests of citizens, legal persons or other organisations;
- it needs to be extensively known or participated in by the general public;
- it shows the structure, function and working procedures of and other matters relating to the administrative agency; and
- it should be disclosed on the administrative agency's own initiative according to laws, regulations and relevant state provisions.[77]

CROGI obliges the applicable government information to be made public within 20 days of its promulgation or revision.[78] State secrets, commercial secrets or individual privacy are excluded from the disclosure; although government information involving commercial secrets or individual privacy may be disclosed by administrative agencies with the consent of the right holder(s) or if administrative agencies believe that non-disclosure might give rise to a major impact on the public interest.[79] CROGI further states that it would be at the agencies' risk of personal criminal responsibility for the act of "disclosing government information that should not be disclosed".[80] Nonetheless, what is the "information that should not be disclosed"? CROGI does not provide a clear definition of the scope and conditions of the exemptions to the disclosure, which may halt the openness in practice.

The general public can require government agencies to provide

---

页; Huanhuan He, 'On Open Government Information and Open Archives', *Archives Management* (2009), **4**, 16–18.

[75]   Articles 1 and 2.
[76]   See Article 16.
[77]   See Article 9.
[78]   See Article 18.
[79]   See Article 14.
[80]   See Article 35(5).

information that has yet to be made public and a FOIA-similar request procedure has been set out.[81] The regulations encourage an on-the-spot reply with regard to any request for open government information; where an on-the-spot reply is impossible, agencies must provide a reply within 15 working days; if an extension of the time limit for replying to a request is needed, the agreement of the responsible person in charge of the office for open government information work should be obtained and the requester notified, and the maximum extension may not exceed 15 working days.[82]

CROGI intends to establish the first ever mechanism of government information disclosure in mainland China and is generally seen as a landmark effort to build an open and transparent government. The regulations not only provide for public access to government information but also authorise the public's right to know; moreover, the regulations emphasise the transparency of the government, promote the rule of law in government administration and confirm that public information ought to serve the public. Additionally, as pointed out by Mr Zhang Qiong, the regulations are expected to ensure that government departments are effectively monitored by the general public and thus reduce corruption,[83] which is widely acknowledged as the biggest problem that may cause the system to collapse.[84] With much to improve, CROGI has made a step forward for the publicly demanded democracy, which may be a considerably long process and to which public archives' contribution will be invaluable.

3. RECORDS IN PUBLIC ARCHIVES

While the public's rightful access to archives has struggled a long way before being finally established in China, the use of records has brought out a great diversity of challenges for the sector.[85] Copyright over records

---

81 See 陈忠海 刘东斌, 从政府信息公开看 《档案法》 的修改 《档案学研究》 2010年第3期30-32页; Zhonghai Chen & Dongbin Liu, 'On Modification of the Archives Law from Government Information Disclosure', *Archives Science Study* (2010), **3**, 30–32.

82 See Article 24.

83 Mr Zhang is the deputy director of the Legislative Affairs Office of the State Council. See report on the CROGI Press Conference at http://www.gov.cn/wszb/ zhibo47/content_593777.htm, retrieved on 20 March 2011.

84 See Michael Johnston, 'Corruption in China: Old Ways, New Realities and a Troubled Future', http://people.colgate.edu/mjohnston/MJ%20papers%2001/ currhist.pdf, retrieved on 20 March 2011.

85 See 蒋锦萍, 《档案法》 修改中有关档案开放利用需要明确的几个问题 《中

in both traditional and digital contexts has been intensely discussed by scholars over the last 10 years but the guidance to archives remains un-clarified, as Chinese archives law and regulations do not offer any provisions in this regard.[86] Such lack of clarification on copyright over archival records has resulted in numerous court cases since the creation of open archives law. For instance, an early judgment in 李淑贤 & 王庆祥v贾英华, *Li Shuxian & Wang Qingxiang v Jia Yinghua*, confirms that the defendant's "fair use", without rational and specific explanation of the term "fair use", of archival records including the plaintiff's letters and diaries is lawful and does not breach the plaintiff's copyright;[87] and a later court decision in 隋有禄 v 王文波 & 同心出版社, *Sui Youlu v Wang Wenbo & Tongxin Publisher*, upholds that the plaintiff should enjoy the copyright over his photographic records, and that any publication of copyright records conducted by archives ought to be authorised by the copyright owner even if the publication is for a non-profit purpose; while the defendants' access public interest defence failed, the court approved that to sign a legitimate contract in advance would be of help in copyright disputes – on that basis the publisher was found blameless even if the act of infringement representative of archives was confirmed.[88] The latter case demonstrates a fair interpretation of copyright law and the public interest; defending the authorship public interest, it confirms copyright in unpublished works, the owners' rights to make such records public, and government departments' obligation to obey the law and to respect the legitimate rights of individuals.

In addition, another severe question arises in the sector. Where should

---

国档案» 2009年5期 58-59页; Jingping Jiang, 'Issues Re Use and Open Archives in Modification of the Archives Law', *China Archives* (2009), **5**, 58–59.

86   See for example王少辉, 档案网站管理中的版权保护 «上海档案» 2007年 第5期20–22页, Shaohui Wang, 'Copyright Protection in Internet Archives', *Shanghai Archives* (2007), **5**, 20–22; 徐拥军, 西方档案学对中国档案学的借鉴意义 «档案学通讯» 2005年2期 19–22页; Yonhjun Xu, 'What Should Chinese Archives Learn from the Western Archives?' *Archives Science Bulletin* (2005), **2**, 19–22; 张东华, 对档案馆藏数字化的法律思考 «档案学通讯» 2004年2期13–16页, Donghua Zhang, 'Discussions on the Digitisation of Archives', *Archives Science Bulletin* (2004), **2**, 13–16; 连志英, 档案著作权保护与档案信息资源利用 «档案与建设» 1999年 9期 19–21页; Zhiying Lian, 'Protection of Archival Works and the Use of Archival Information', *Archives & Construction* (1999), **9**, 19–21; 任伟, 档案工作与保护著作权之研究 «档案学通讯» 1997年 5期26–8 页; see Wei Ren, 'A Study on Archives and Copyright Protection', *Archives Science Bulletin* (1997), **5**, 26–8.

87   See 北京西城区人民法院判决书 (1990) 西民字第2213号, Beijing Xicheng District People's Court Judgment Number (1990) 2213.

88   See 北京朝阳区人民法院判决书(2006) 朝民初字第13937, Beijing Chaoyang District People's Court Judgment Number (2006) 13937.

the line be drawn between access to and use of archives, and the right of privacy? Privacy, the emerging right that may be understood as the ability of people to control the flow of information about them and thereby to reveal it selectively, has been established in the West as one of the fundamental human rights.[89] Yet, China currently has adopted no privacy law; the justification of privacy is derived from the Constitution, on which the courts and law practitioners also heavily rely. The Chinese Constitution asserts that the personal dignity of citizens is inviolable, and therefore that libel, false accusation or false incrimination directed against citizens by any means is prohibited,[90] and both civil and criminal liabilities are granted for the breach of privacy that constitutes a crime.[91] Nevertheless, in the absence of specific law and regulations, the enforcement is feeble and confusing, as shown in the lawsuit below, which is the first court case in China dealing with the opening and use of archival records and privacy.[92]

3.1   Right of Access v Right of Privacy? *Lu Jiandong* Case[93]

In December 1995 the SDX Joint Publishing Company (SDX), one of the best-known publishers in China, published "The Last 20 Years of Chen Yinke",[94] a biographical book portraying Mr Chen Yinke, a famous Chinese scholar and his life in 1949–1969, and showing the plight of his academic and spiritual world, and his adherence to academic freedom. Lu Jiandong, the author, had spent several years to research the relevant first-hand information in archival records. More than 200 out of the total 524 footnotes in the book quoted the records from Guangdong Provincial Archives, Sun Yat-Sen University Archives, Beijing University Archives, Fudan University Archives and the Archives of Guangzhou Municipal Bureau of Culture. The book sold out very quickly and was reprinted three

---

[89]   See S.D. Warren & L.D. Brandeis, 'The Right to Privacy', *Harvard Law Review* (1890), **4**(5), 193–220.

[90]   See Article 38.

[91]   Articles 252 and 254, General Principles of Criminal Law in the People's Republic of China.

[92]   See also 冯伯群，引用档案惹出的一场官司—— 《陈寅恪的最后二十年》出版以后 《档案春秋》2006年3期10–14页, Boqun Feng, 'A Lawsuit Provoked by Use of Archives – After Publishing "The Last 20 Years of Chen Yinke"', *Spring & Autumn Archives* (2006), **3**, 10–14; 冯伯群，引用档案惹出的一场官司—— 《陈寅恪的最后二十年》 出版以后 《北京档案》 2003年1期22–6页, Boqun Feng, 'A Lawsuit Provoked by Use of Archives – After Publishing "The Last 20 Years of Chen Yinke"', *Beijing Archives* (2003), **1**, 22–6.

[93]   See (2000) 二中执字第1522号; the Second Intermediate People's Court Judgment Number (2000) 1522.

[94]   That is, 陆键东，陈寅恪的最后二十年 (1995).

times in half a year; one of the main reasons for the surprising success was the huge amount of archival references used in that book, through which readers learnt some unexplored truths.

However, in March 1997 Lu Jiandong together with the SDX were sued in the Beijing Dongcheng District People's Court, for the misuse of the archival records in referring to one of the not-so-positive characters in the story, Long Qian. The plaintiffs were Long's two daughters and they claimed that the description accompanied by the quotation of archival records on pages 144 to 152 had breached their father's rights of privacy and publicity. In support of the claim, the plaintiff presented memorial speeches given by several leaders of the then central government at their father's funeral, which were published in newspapers in January 1979.

The first judgment was given in favour of the defendants. It affirmed that Lu's opening the archival records of Long to the public had violated Article 22 of the Archives Law and should be censured, but that the use of the relevant archival records was faithful and fair, and that it had no intention to and as a matter of fact did not infringe Long's right of privacy and publicity.

On 20 September 1998 Long's daughters appealed to the Beijing Second Intermediate People's Court on the grounds of (1) the defendant's breach of the Archives Law to open the state-owned archival records, (2) Beijing Dongcheng District People's Court's authorisation of the defendant's misuse of the archival records, and (3) the defendant's infringement of Long's rights of privacy and publicity.

On 29 September 1999 the Intermediate court overturned the first judgment. The final judgment ruled that Lu Jiandong had used the archival records for embellishing the facts with critical comments of his own, which was unlawful and had consequently breached Long's right of privacy and publicity. The two defendants were ordered (1) to publish an admission of guilt in a nationwide newspaper, (2) to cease any reprint or publishing of the book before amending the relevant chapters and (3) to compensate the plaintiff RMB 4000 and 1000 yuan respectively.[95]

The Lu Jiandong case has had a great impact not only on the Chinese archives but also on Chinese authors, academics and the general public. For the archivists, debate was focused on learning and seeking the fine line between fair and unfair open use of archives; for authors and academics, this case and the later similar *Wu Si* case[96] led to discussions on academic

---

[95]   See (2000) 二中执字第1522号; the Second Intermediate People's Court Judgment Number (2000) 1522.

[96]   In which the author Wu Si, an established Chinese historiographer, together with the publisher lost the litigation in both Beijing Xicheng District People's

autonomy and intellectual integrity; for the general public, the right to write and the right to know are of their concern and demand.

The rulings given by the two courts in this case were controversial since they were basically poles apart. Firstly, the judgment of the district court was given to the defendant although in conjunction with an affirmation of Lu's breach of the openness of state-owned archives, which later in the intermediate court was dismissed. The intermediate court explained that most records Lu quoted in his book were 30 years old and Lu used but did not publish the original records. Secondly, the district court declared that Lu's use of the relevant archival records was faithful and fair while the intermediate court found that the use was unjust and unfair as, on the one hand, Lu had shown his strong personal opinion on Long, which was obviously negative, and, on the other hand, those archival records were related to Long's personal life and privacy and therefore should not be used on a large scale. Thirdly, the lower court deemed that Lu had no intention to and did not infringe Long's right of privacy and publicity, whereas the higher court held that Lu's misuse of the relevant records had damaged Long's image and reputation in public, therefore infringement of Long's right of privacy and publicity was confirmed.

Interestingly, the lower court decision in this case has, for the first time in a Chinese judgment, showed humanity among its usual monotonous lines by giving understanding of the author's enthusiasm and endeavour and thus pardoned his opening the records to the public. The final judgment failed to explain the distinctions between the open and unlawfully opened archival records, the use and misuse of archives, and the distinction between unlawfully open and fair use of archival records.

The Chinese law and regulations encourage the public to use archives including the non-opened records for private study or research purpose, and the public is entitled to use state-owned archival records such as quoting the records in their research or literature;[97] nevertheless, to open the records in any format is restricted. To open archival records is described as to publish the original archival records partially or

---

Court and Beijing First Intermediate People's Court for the infringement of right of privacy and publicity in his book *Mao Zedong's peasant – Chen Yonggui*, which used a large number of archival materials as well. See the Beijing First Intermediate People's Court Final Judgment Number (2003) 8949.

[97]   See 何欢欢，政府信息公开与档案开放《档案管理》2009年第4期16-18页; He Huanhuan, 'On Open Government Information and Open Archives', *Archives Management* (2009), **4**, 16–18.

completely, or the specific content of the records, to the public, for the first time, via seven named practices.[98]

Lu's visit to archives as well as his obtaining and access to the records were apparently legitimate, and the quotations of the records in his book were legal. The court also clarified that he did not improperly open the records to the public. Then, only one question remains: what was the ground to justify that Lu's use of the records was unlawful? Privacy? Where is the law then?

Nevertheless, in accordance with Article 22 of the copyright law, the author's act of using the records was within the exceptions and fair as it was conducted for private study and research purposes, and also the resources used were clearly indicated in his book.

3.2 Records in Public Archives

The legitimate use of records is crucial in archives, and so to understand and regulate the copyright over the records is of importance.[99] Records, published or unpublished, held by public archives may be classified, in accordance with current copyright law and based upon the status or ownership of copyright, into the following categories:

- copyright is owned by individual(s);
- copyright is owned by a legal entity or organisation;
- copyright is owned by the state;
- orphan works; and
- copyright-free works.

The first two categories are comparatively straightforward. First, amongst records that are under copyright protection, created by authors or other citizens, when the copyright is owned by the author or other rightful private individuals. These records, according to the Chinese copyright law include works done in employment except where otherwise stated,

---

98   Namely (1) through newspapers, publications, books, audio-visual and electronic publication; (2) through radio and television; (3) through public dissemination such as computer information network; (4) through reading or broadcasting in public; (5) through publishing original records or compiling abstracts; (6) through sale, distribution or display copies of records; (7) through exhibiting or displaying records or the copies. See Article 23, Implementing Measures of the Archives Law of the People's Republic of China.

99   See 理明, 政府信息公开 ≠ 档案信息公开 《浙江档案》 2008年第1期26–28 页; Ming Li, 'Open Government Information ≠ Open Archival Information', *Zhejiang Archives* (2008), **1**, 26–28.

the records of celebrities' works, and letters written by private individuals to the government. This is different from the UK and US provisions: any copyright over works under employment for fulfilling duties should be owned by the employers, unless otherwise stated. Second, many of the records' copyrights are held by the archives or other institutions rather than individuals. Chinese copyright law makes a legal entity or organisation the author of a work if the work is created according to the intention and under the supervision and responsibility of such legal entity or organisation.[100] These include any works of catalogue, compilation, or research published by archives or other institutes for different purposes. However, while records are works of compilation, it must be agreed in advance for the archives or other institutes to claim copyright over such works, as Chinese law provides that "the copyright in a work of compilation shall be enjoyed by the compiler".[101] In the case of transferring a record, unless otherwise stated in a legitimate contract, the copyright remains with the original holder, which applies to all records under copyright protection that are transferred to, sold to, deposited with, or donated to archives. Archives can give no permission to reproduce any records of which they are not the copyright owners.

The last three categories are complex and diverse, and so are detailed below.

3.2.1   Orphan works

An "orphan work" in the 2010 CCL is 作者身份不明的作品, a "work of unknown authors" – the official translation – the original text literally means a "work that the status of the author(s) is unclear"; and the term for copyright protection of orphan works is "fifty years ending on December 31 of the fiftieth year after the first publication of the work".[102] The law asserts that "in the case of a work of an unknown author, the copyright, except the right of authorship, shall be exercised by the lawful holder of the original copy of the work. Where the author has been identified, the copyright shall be exercised by the author or his heir in title."[103] Thus, copyright over orphan works that are kept in Chinese public archives, by law, are owned by the state prior to the author being identified.

Orphan works in China are more an archive than a library issue mainly because, on the one hand, public libraries are lately introduced to the

---

[100]   See Article 11, 2010 CCL.
[101]   See Article 14.
[102]   See Article 18, Implementing Regulations 2002.
[103]   See Article 14.

country, most of them established after the Cultural Revolution and thus holding new collections, and, on the other hand, for the reasons stated earlier, namely that archival collections in China have always been valued and are comprehensive.

But orphan works are a problem of complexity currently deliberated intensively by lawmakers, rights groups and others in the West. In the US, the "Shawn Bentley Orphan Works Act 2008" struggled to be officially introduced to Congress on 24 April 2008,[104] as for the EU, the Memorandum of Understanding on Diligent Search Guidelines for Orphan Works was signed on 4 June 2008, in the framework of the European Digital Libraries Initiative.[105]

The latter is rather well received as it clearly (1) respects copyright in the use of orphan works; (2) appreciates the necessity for cultural institutions to digitise orphan works and to make them available online; (3) promotes the collaboration between the two interest groups; and (4) defines interest balanced by "due diligence" guidelines for identifying and locating right holders for the lawful use of orphan works.[106]

The guidelines provide a particular definition, which states that "a work is 'orphan' with respect to rightholders whose permission is required to use it and who can either not be identified, or located based on diligent search on the basis of due diligence guidelines" and demands that such search "must be both in good faith (subjectively) and reasonable in light of the type of rightholder (objectively)".[107] Detailed criteria of "due diligence" are given, which include the main principles: (1) the search is done prior to the use of the work, (2) the search is done title by title or work by work, and (3) the relevant resources would usually be those of the country of the work's origin; also archives are required to establish procedure and methodology of the search and further matters of orphan works according to the guidelines.[108] Moreover, the guidelines seek to prevent future orphan works and offer relevant measures that could help, and urge further development of databases with information on orphan works.[109]

---

[104]   See http://thomas.loc.gov/cgi-bin/query/C?c110:./temp/~c110Id209a, retrieved on 4 March 2011.

[105]   See respectively http://www.thomas.gov/cgi-bin/query/F?c110:1:./temp/~c1 10MJrTJW:e299: and http://www.eblida.org/uploads/eblida/2/1213704515.pdf, retrieved on 4 March 2011.

[106]   See p.2.

[107]   See Article 1.2, Sector-specific Guidelines on Due Diligence Criteria for Orphan Works, http://ec.europa.eu/information_society/activities/digital_librar ies/doc/hleg/orphan/guidelines.pdf.

[108]   See Article 2.1, ibid.

[109]   Articles 3.1 and 3.2.

The US Orphan Works Act 2008 adds Section 514 to the Copyright Law, which provides for limitation on remedies in cases involving orphan works, the satisfaction of which must include "performing and documenting a qualifying search in good faith", registering a "notice of use", providing attribution to the owner of the infringed copyright and indicating such use.[110] While a diligent search is sketchily explained as "reasonable and appropriate",[111] the act intends to establish a "database for pictorial, graphic, and sculptural works", which requires relevant copyright owners to register with the Register of Copyrights.[112]

The Act results in immense arguments. It is welcomed by the libraries and archives sector as the Act provides a safe harbour from statutory damages for them and their users while a reasonable search is conducted.[113] Moreover, the Public Knowledge group remarks that the act represents "the first pro-user change to U.S. copyright law in almost two decades".[114] However, it is also criticised by many[115] and described as "unfair and unwise" primarily because "it excuses copyright infringers from significant damages if they can prove that they made a 'diligent effort' to find the copyright owner" and "makes no distinction between old and new works, or between foreign and domestic works".[116] Instead, Professor Lessig proposed a patent-like system for solving the problem:

> Congress should require a copyright owner to register a work after an initial and generous term of automatic and full protection. For 14 years, a copyright owner would need to do nothing to receive the full protection of copyright law. But after 14 years, to receive full protection, the owner would have to take the minimal step of registering the work with an approved, privately managed and competitive registry.[117]

---

[110]   See Section 2(b)(1)(A).

[111]   See Section 2(b)(2).

[112]   See Section 3(a).

[113]   See Library Copyright Alliance Re the Orphan Works Act 2008, retrieved on 5 March 2011 at http://www.arl.org/bm~doc/lca-senate-orphan-works-s-2913-17june2008final.pdf.

[114]   http://www.publicknowledge.org/alertfax/save-orphan-works.

[115]   For instance, "representing over 250,000 creators worldwide", licensing organisations have joined together as "Artists United Against the U.S. Orphan Works Acts", retrieved on 5 March 2011 at http://www.illustratorspartnership.org/01_topics/article.php?searchterm=00273.

[116]   See L. Lessig, 'Little Orphan Artworks', *New York Times* (20 May 2008), http://www.nytimes.com/2008/05/20/opinion/20lessig.html, retrieved on 5 March 2011.

[117]   Ibid.

Obviously, Professor Lessig's proposal provides a convenient means for managing and controlling copyright works and may be effective in preventing future orphan works. Nonetheless, it would, on the one hand, violate the Berne Convention, which authorises copyright as an automatic right, and, on the other hand, breach freedom of expression, which is recognised as a human right under the UDHR. On the contrary, the EU approach demonstrates superior comprehensions of the international treaties, as well as the existent circumstances and problems, and offers feasible solutions and guidelines that may meet the challenges of orphan works in today's setting.

So far, only one case with regard to orphan works has occurred in China, yet it has been debated intensively over the country. For instance, a collective academic conference on the topic of "Copyright Issue Regarding 'The First Half of My Life'" was held in Beijing by the Copyright Society, the General Administration of Press and Publication, China Publishing, and the IP Teaching and Research Centre of Renmin University in November 2007.[118] The dispute under discussion was about the ownership of copyright over a book – *The First Half of My Life*, which is a biography of 爱新觉罗 溥仪 (Pu Yi), the last emperor in China. The book, published in 1964 by Qunzhong, a state-owned publisher that is a part of the Ministry of Public Security, with the assistance of one of its editors Li Wenda, explores the life of the last emperor with a profusion of historical stories[119] – from a child emperor of the Qing Dynasty, to the puppet emperor during the Japanese invasion, to a prisoner then an ordinary citizen in New China – and has been very well received throughout the country. By 1987 over 170 million copies had been sold in China.[120]

After Pu Yi's death on 17 October 1967, the copyright over the book was eventually granted to his wife, Li Shuxian, by the Beijing Intermediate People's Court in January 1995 and confirmed by the Beijing High People's Court in June 1996,[121] as Chinese copyright law provided that

---

[118]   See http://data.chinaxwcb.com/zhuanti/wdqbs/Index.html, retrieved on 13 March 2011.

[119]   See http://gb1.chinabroadcast.cn/9223/2007/06/20/882@1642314.htm for one of the chapters.

[120]   See http://data.chinaxwcb.com/zhuanti/wdqbs/newshf/200711/1573.html, retrieved on 13 March 2011.

[121]   Li Shuxian was the plaintiff in that long-lasting court case, and Li Wenda and Qunzhong Publishing were the defendants as Li Wenda openly claimed joint authorship and copyright in the book and supported by Qunzhong with a series of promotional activities. See 北京中级人民法院判决书(1989) 中民字第1092号, Beijing Intermediate People's Court Judgment Number (1989) 1092; and 北京高级人民法院判决书 (1995) 高知终字第18号, Beijing High People's Court IP Final

after the copyright owner's death the copyright in a work should be transferred in accordance with the Inheritance Law.[122] Li Shuxian rejected Qunzhong's request to republish the book with some more private and darker information about her husband. Instead, she authorised another publisher, Dongfang, to publish a series of books on Pu Yi that included the original book. On 9 June 1997 Li Shuxian passed away.[123] Dongfang published the agreed six books, including the original book, in 1999. In 2006 Qunzhong republished the so-called "full-version" of the book anyway, which was criticised by Pu Yi's younger brother, Pu Ren, for the "full version" infringed the family's privacy. Pu Ren then gave his authorisation to Tongxin to publish the book together with Pu Yi's diary.[124]

In August 2007 Qunzhong sued at the Beijing Xicheng District Intermediate People's Court, claiming the book to be an orphan work as the only inheritor of the author had passed away and had left neither children nor other family.

Xie Xizhang, the Chief Editor of Tongxin, was contacted by Qunzhong informing him that it would be an act of copyright infringement to publish the book; also an official letter was received that was issued on 13 September by the NCAC requiring Tongxin to cease publication for Qunzhong had filed a lawsuit to claim the book as an orphan work. Tongxin promptly replied with its legal consultant's advice and explained that it had obtained Pu Ren's consent; and on 19 September a telephone call was received expressing the same demand, made by Mr Xu Chao.[125] In the same month, Tongxin published the book including Pu Yi's diary alongside Pu Ren's preamble and a renowned historian's comments.[126]

On 25 September 2007 the court issued a public announcement stating that, as such case was filed and the book was claimed as an orphan work after Li Shuxian's death, any lawful inheritor should come forward to claim the inheritance of the copyright; if no such claim was made in a year, the court would issue a judgment in accordance with the relevant

---

Decision Number (1989) 18.

[122]   See Article 19.

[123]   See http://case.ipr.gov.cn/ipr/case/info/Article.jsp?a_no=127364&col_no=1003&dir=200710, retrieved on 14 March 2011.

[124]   See http://www.chinanews.com.cn/cul/news/2007/10-13/1048087.shtml, retrieved on 14 March 2011.

[125]   See Xizhang Xie's bolg, http://blog.sina.com.cn/s/blog_475b6ef801000cho.html; retrieved on 14 March 2011.

[126]   See http://www.chinanews.com.cn/cul/news/2007/10-13/1048087.shtml, retrieved on 14 March 2011.

law.[127] Until very recently, no one has approached the court to make such a claim. Great discussions were carried out from the day of the court announcement, which primarily focused on two questions: Was the book an orphan work or not? If the book was an orphan work, who should own the copyright?

Whilst most believed that the book was certainly an orphan work because Li Shuxian was the current copyright holder and none of Pu Yi's family including Pu Ren was her lawful successor;[128] some argued that Pu Ren and other family members may be the "second-order" successor(s) according to the Inheritance Law, and so Qunzhong had no justification to claim the book as an orphan work; and a few thought that it was an inheritance rather than a copyright issue.[129] Holding that, under the circumstances, the book was an orphan work, the court explained that "if the book was confirmed as an orphan work, the copyright would be owned by the state".[130] Other scholars considered that the copyright could be owned by the collective organisation that Li Shuxian worked at,[131] as the law asserts that "an estate which is left with neither a successor nor a legatee shall belong to the state or, where the decedent was a member of an organisation under collective ownership before his or her death, to such an organisation".[132]

Nonetheless, on 22 August 2008 Mrs Jin, a niece of Pu Yi's, who looked after Li Shuxian in her last years, came forward to claim being the inheritor of the copyright over the book, with an authorisation from Li Shuxian that was written before her death requesting her to put the copyright into auction.[133] Mrs Jin said that the court's announcement reminded her about the authorisation, which had been forgotten for years.[134] The court thereafter acknowledged that the book did not fall into the category of orphan works.[135]

---

[127] See http://data.chinaxwcb.com/zhuanti/wdqbs/Index.html and http://law.cctv.com/20071126/100487_1.shtml, retrieved on 14 March 2011.

[128] See also http://news.sina.com.cn/c/2007-11-27/095814396480.shtml, retrieved on 14 March 2011.

[129] See for example http://data.chinaxwcb.com/zhuanti/wdqbs/ytgd/200711/1609.html, retrieved on 14 March 2011.

[130] In accordance with Article 19 of the 2001 CCL; see para 5, ibid.

[131] See http://article.chinalawinfo.com/article/user/article_display.asp?ArticleID=44212, retrieved on 14 March 2011.

[132] See Article 32, the Inheritance Law.

[133] See http://www.china.com.cn/book/txt/2008-08/30/content_16361238.htm, retrieved on 14 March 2011.

[134] Ibid.

[135] Ibid.

Essentially, the book was never an orphan work by any means. When the copyright was inherited by Li Shuxian, apparently it did not change the fact that Pu Yi was the author of the book: the author was known, his family was known as well, and there was no rationale whatsoever to see the book as subject to orphan work status after Li Shuxian's death. In the absence of any will or authorisation, the copyright should be transferred as provided in Article 19 of the 2001 CCL, in accordance with the provisions of the Inheritance Law, which provides that the order of inheritance is as follows:

> first in order: spouse, children, parents; and second in order: brothers and sisters, paternal grand parents, maternal grand-parents. When succession opens, the successor(s) first in order shall inherit to the exclusion of the successor(s) second in order. The successor(s) second in order shall inherit in default of any successor first in order.[136]

Pu Ren is obviously the "second in order".

This Chinese drama reveals the situation at present in respect of orphan works and beyond. Firstly, the definition of orphan works provided in current copyright law is inappropriate and the regulations are rather vague, which may result in confusion and future copyright violation especially in the digital environment; for example, Internet archives must have a clear guidance on distinct difficult-to-find owners' works and orphan works while archiving online contents, which are being mass produced hourly; also the understanding of orphan works generally speaking is very limited. Secondly, the announcement of the court is double-edged: it shows the court's effort to keep in line with the law and make information publicly accessible, but also reveals the immaturity of the interpretation of the law. Thirdly, the NCAC's interruption in this case was not of any assistance for appreciating laws and regulations, which again raises a couple of vital questions: What should be the main responsibilities for administrative authorities – to promote the law or to enforce the law? How should the administrative authorities fulfil their duties fairly? And thirdly, Qunzhong's acts efficiently illustrate those state-owned and formerly privileged organisations in China. They have strong ties to governmental

---

[136] See Article 10. Although adopted in 1985, the current Inheritance Law is strongly marked by the then planned, state-controlled economy; it offers an exceedingly limited successor list and no provision for intellectual property and no clarification for order of successor. For instance, it provides that "when succession opens, the successor(s) first in order shall inherit to the exclusion of the successor(s) second in order"; what about in the absence of "first in order"?

departments, they are not accustomed to rules that are not in their favour, and they are not ready for or, one should say, do not want to accept fair competition.

The Pu Ren book case reflects the influence of the traditional overriding power of state authority in contemporary China and the high risk of violating not only individual rights but also laws in upholding such power. This should be regarded as a severe reminder in China's adaptation of the rule of law.

3.2.2 Works that are unprotected by copyright

Records in this category consist of works in the public domain and of those not under the protection of copyright law. Copyright works, once they enter the public domain, should be available for free use for any purpose; while those not in the protection of copyright are somewhat diverse especially as regards government documents.

In China copyright protection does not apply to government documents for the benefits of the public. While "a work of the United States Government" is defined subject to a work prepared by an officer or employee of the United States Government as part of that person's official duties, the US copyright protection is not available for any work of the United States Government.[137] Use of such records is copyright-free as in China.

The UK takes a different approach concerning government documents. Government departments do not own copyright over any works but Crown copyright applies to any work "made by Her Majesty or by an officer or servant of the Crown in the course of his duties".[138] Most archival records originated by government departments are protected under Crown copyright.[139] Crown copyright is administered by the OPSI, which clarifies that any Crown copyright work "may be reproduced free of charge in any format or medium provided it is reproduced accurately and not used in a misleading context".[140] Where any of the Crown copyright works are being republished or copied to others, the source must be identified and the copyright status acknowledged. Furthermore, Crown copyright images may be reproduced only with a payment of a fee, and digital copies of Crown copyright documents may be used only for private

---

[137] See Section 101.
[138] See Article 163, CDPA 1988.
[139] See Article 164.
[140] Other than the Royal Arms and departmental or agency logos; retrieved on 15 March 2011 at the National Archives website, http://www.nationalarchives. gov.uk/legal/copyright.htm.

study or non-commercial research and instruction or examination for education purposes.[141]

In addition, the CDPA 1988 grants protection to works "made by or under the direction or control of the House of Commons or the House of Lords", which were within the scope of Crown copyright prior to the Act, under Parliamentary copyright, for 50 years, the same as Crown copyright.[142] The Parliament states that listed Parliamentary copyright materials "may be reproduced without formal permission for the purposes of non-commercial research, private study and for criticism, review and news reporting provided that the material is appropriately attributed".[143] The OPSI provides several licensing schemes including Click-Use Licensing, the online licences, for re-use of any public information, including Crown and Parliamentary copyright works.

Crown and Parliamentary copyright are criticised by many who believe that PSI should be for the public.[144] While certain government agencies certainly obtain huge profits from the distribution of PSI, some urge for more detailed rules regarding PSI re-use,[145] and others argue that public information should be available for all or used for the benefit of the national economy.[146] Guardian Technology has also campaigned for the government to stop charging individuals, businesses and other public bodies to access and re-use non-personal information collected by government organisations.[147] Further, the principle of encouraging public access to the law is far more important than securing the Crown or state-owned copyright in general.[148]

---

[141] Ibid.

[142] See Article 165.

[143] See http://www.parliament.uk/site_information/parliamentary_copyright. cfm, retrieved on 15 March 2011. It should be noted that the Parliamentary Licence does not cover use of images and broadcasts of the Proceedings of Parliament.

[144] See E. Derclaye, 'Of Maps, Crown Copyright, Research and the Environment', *EIPR* (2008), **30**(4), 162–4.

[145] See H. MacQueen, 'Appropriate for the Digital Age? Copyright and the Internet', in C. Waelde & L. Edwards (eds), *Law and the Internet* (2009), 183–225.

[146] See S. Saxby, 'Crown Copyright Regulation in the UK – Is the Debate Still Alive?' *International Journal of Law and Information Technology* (2005), **13**(3), 299–335. For instance, in 2001 Centrica and Ordnance Survey, the national mapping agency, reached a £20 million out of court settlement to resolve a copyright action against the Automobile Association (owned by Centrica) for the use of the maps. See http://www.ordnancesurvey.co.uk/oswebsite/media/news/2001/march/centrica.html, retrieved on 15 March 2011.

[147] See http://www.guardian.co.uk/technology/2006/jul/20/epublic.guardianweeklytechnologysection, retrieved on 15 March 2011.

[148] See N. Cox, 'Copyright in Statutes, Regulations, and Judicial Decisions

Certainly, there is the obvious need to provide wide access to government information in a democratic society where such right has been legitimately granted to the public; it is also challenging to remove any power of control from any government. China is an illustrative case in this regard but is not the only one that has more action to take.

3.2.3 State-owned copyright

China has no legislation with regard to state-owned copyright yet. Currently, the NCAC is drafting the Regulations on the Management of State-owned Copyright Works, which explain that state-owned works comprise the following:

- works given by citizens, legal entities and other organisations as gifts;
- works given by citizens as gifts according to their wills;
- works having no inheritor or lawful receivers after citizen's death;
- works having no lawful receivers after the transformation or termination of the legal entities or other organisation; and
- works received via other lawful means.[149]

At an official meeting of "experts' consultation" in February 2008, the book case was once again mentioned and discussed with regard to the state's ownership over orphan works. Three main opinions were voiced: (1) the copyright over orphan works should be maintained by the state provided that there is a prior formal judicial process of identification of the work as an orphan after which a public announcement must be made; (2) the copyright should be owned by the state "immediately" at the time when it is confirmed that no lawful rights owner or inheritor of a copyright work exists, so that copyright works would never be orphan; and (3) copyright over orphan works is an intellectual property right, which consists of both tangible and intangible rights but still a property right, thus both inheritance law and copyright law apply.[150] The three experts' opinions are diverse yet representative. Whilst opinion (1) appreciates the government's socialist policy while stressing the rule of law; opinion (2) reminds the author of the old dark days of the state overpowering all rights and laws; and opinion (3) follows Article 19 of the 2001 CCL and

---

in Common Law Jurisdictions: Public Ownership or Commercial Enterprise?' *Statute Law Review* (2006), **27**(3), 185–208.
[149] See http://www.gov.cn/gzdt/2008-02/18/content_892809.htm, retrieved on 15 March 2011.
[150] Ibid.

supports the approach of solving the problem of orphan works in accordance with the Inheritance Law. Nevertheless, if the dispute over a work may apply inheritance law, then is that work an orphan work?

It should be noted that two out of five types of state-owned copyright works in the draft regulations are in fact orphan works. To allocate the state as the copyright owner of orphan works is not a bad idea provided, firstly, that the information is known and available to the general public; secondly, that the procedure for the potential rights owner to regain the copyright is trouble-free and clear; and thirdly, that the relevant revenue is used for the public and in the public interest. However, as presented in the book case, it is rather risky to authorise such claim without a legitimate system of supervision, which ought to be established by relevant laws together with clarification of "other lawful means".

4.   DISCUSSION

While archives in the West have established their role as information provider for the public and the user-friendly pattern, and now focus on solving problems mainly in the digital environment, the use of public archives in China is topical and generating contentious questions. The change of social and economic policies and the evolution of the society have brought the public archives in China new functions as well as challenges. From serving the ruler to "serving the society and benefiting the people",[151] from only listening to the state and esteeming the interest of the state to answering the public's demand and respecting intellectual property rights, the development of Chinese archives has experienced and is experiencing great tests. For the purpose of state control yet in the name of the "public interest", China has made an attempt to emphasise the necessity and rationality of current archives at all levels, which in the past were maintained under strict confidentiality, and made public archives inaccessible for the public. The use of archives as a means of controlling people was the state's interest but not the public interest. Undeniably, keeping records under secrecy for the state's interest has hampered the progress of public archives to date, in particular the opening and use of archives.

The opening-up policy opened China's door to the world and brought in experiences from the developed countries of the West. First of all, the Archives Law made an initial effort to make public records accessible to

---

151   See the State Archives Administration of China website, http://www.saac.gov.cn.

the public; and second, CROGI authorises Chinese public archives to make government information available to the general public by providing reading places and other access facilities. "Today's current records are tomorrow's archives:" CROGI is of significance to the constructive development of public archives in China. Obviously, CROGI has taken a step further towards establishing a mechanism of "right to know" as well as an open government. However, CROGI needs certain clarifications. As has been demonstrated in the UK and the US laws, these include more precise provisions for the exceptions to disclosure, clarification of terms with regard to criminal responsibility, and definition of "information that should not be disclosed". Furthermore, CROGI ought to provide that all disclosure information must be detailed and complete in order to avoid giving the public insubstantial information, which would be likely to happen and would then allow those government departments "lawfully" to violate the public's "right to know". It should also be appreciated that, without an independent authority to supervise the performance of the government openness, the implementation of CROGI will be more demanding.

The current archives law should be amended to meet the requirement of the emergence of the social and technology developments, to make a more positive change to the old archival traditions and to make archives a part of the beneficial social resources for the general public like public libraries in China. The law may include the following prospects:

- to obliterate the state-owned monopoly right of opening 30 years records to the public in accordance with CROGI;
- to specify copyright, namely the rights of publication and communication, and the duration of the protection of the copyright records in public archives;[152]
- to stipulate copyright of the compilation or abstract of archival records;
- to clarify the concept of private archives and the rights and the state's exercise of appraisal authority towards private archives;
- to abolish the distinction between Chinese and non-Chinese citizens in the use of opened archives;
- to include statutes on digital archival records, the definition and force and effect;[153]

---

[152] The current Articles 20 and 22 are incompatible with the Copyright Law.

[153] With its 457 million Internet users, China is now the first country in the world to have made digitisation of its records not only a trend but also a need.

- to append new offences in digital environment;
- to require archives to place promotional notices of both copyright and archives laws; and
- to allow re-use of public sector information insofar as it otherwise is prevented by the existence of copyright.

Archival records are varied, and the rights involved in the opening and use of the records may be somewhat complicated in certain circumstances. To simplify the mentioned categories, records in public archives are of only two categories: non-copyright records and copyright records, of which the latter consist of two types of right, tangible and intangible rights of the records. The tangible right, ownership of the archival records entity, should belong to the archives repositories, with exceptions of those deposited or donated by, transferred from or consigned by any organisations or individuals. The intangible right, copyright of the archival records, must be reserved by the copyright owners.

These two rights should both be assured while opening or using archival records. In the case of opening non-copyright records to the public, the archives repositories should have the right to make decisions on those non-open records; for the open records, any party should have the right to do so unless legal extension has been granted beforehand. As to the copyright records, the same practice should be appropriately complied with as with the provisions of copyright law, in which case there must be official authorisation, or exception from the copyright owners must be obtained, before opening them to the public.

For the use of records, firstly, of the opened records, it is unnecessary to gain any permission from any party for non-copyright records; permission should be obtained by the copyright owners. Secondly, of the non-opened records, consent should be granted by archives repositories only for non-copyright records, and for copyright records approval should be attained from both the archives repositories and copyright owners. Certainly, royalties should be paid to the copyright owners if copyright applies.

In order to make public archives truly serve the society and benefit the people in China, a rule of law system must be established in the sector and provided to the public, of which certainly fair and wise laws are the foundation. Such system must safeguard private rights including copyright and privacy in the light of the public interest, and with the general public's participation and supervision; thus the state would have no basis to breach people's lawful rights, which is compelled by the public interest, a concept that was promoted as the state interest in the past and ought to be redefined and renewed. Only then will public records belong to the people.

With regard to orphan works, the 2010 CCL ought to be revised to offer it a correct definition and clear provisions. However, neither the US "database for works" nor a patent-like system should be imposed as a solution; Chinese copyright should learn from the EU experience to balance the two interest groups in line with the Berne Convention. China may adopt a database system, which should strive to provide comprehensive and up-to-date databases not only for orphan works but also for the problematic state-owned copyright, which ought to embrace the exhaustive information on records of orphan works and state-owned copyright works held in all public institutes. Meanwhile, the licensing system should be established with easy-to-follow schemes and be regulated.

While Crown and state-owned copyright enable governments to be the owners of public information, as a result of any copyright in their information government agencies may retain control of it through licensing policies. It should be admitted that the right to access and use public information ought to be owned by the general public; either Crown copyright or state-owned copyright should be the public's copyright. Hence, any policies on use or re-use of such should be made to safeguard the public's interest and on the basis of the public interest. Copyright should not become a tool of government control by any means.

Conclusion

Despite the country's long history, the establishment of a modern legal system in China began in 1978 along with the adaptation of its economic reform policy. While the rapid growth of the domestic economy has dramatically improved the standard of living for many Chinese, the rise of the Chinese economy has also changed the global economic landscape, especially after China's accession to the WTO. Conflicts thus occurred between tradition and innovation, and between Chinese culture and Western civilisation, which are also reflected in the development of copyright protection in China.

Like many other modern laws, copyright is certainly foreign to the Chinese legal system. On the one hand, its principle of safeguarding private property rights in created works contravenes the traditional Chinese value of sharing intellectual works with the community and benefiting the masses. On the other hand, its stress on prioritising individuals' interest over the state's interest on the basis of the authorship public interest challenges the ideology of China's socialist platform, on which the state's interest has been seen as the public interest in general, maintained beyond all individual interests and rights. Hence, copyright law was disregarded before and for over a decade after its introduction in 1990; it was seen as legislation to benefit foreigners and breach China's interest, and its formation and coming into effect were delayed in the name of the socialism public interest. Even if the law was enacted in 1990, Chinese authorities struggled to appreciate that the purpose of copyright was to encourage creativity and learning, and its protection aimed also to be in the public interest of a different dimension. The provisions were marked by such failure of insight; and it may be fair to say that the 1990 CCL was primarily initialled and exercised as an instrument to satisfy the international community and that its enforcement was thus problematic.

Adhering to the Berne Convention, the 1990 CCL authorised copyright owners certain rights to control their works, subject to a number of limitations, some of which were not within the Berne three-step test. In addition to the legitimate 12 exceptions, the law stated that copyright owners must not prejudice the public interest in exercising their copyright, although the law offered no clarification of what constituted "the public interest"; also without any further illumination of what was meant, the law did not provide protection for works the publication or distribution of which were prohibited by law. Such clauses revealed the then authorities' anxiety about an open information flow and their objective of sustaining a centrally controlled power within the newly established copyright system. That system originated in the West and backed individual gain and free expression, so representing the values of the Western world; it demanded a much more open context to make the law work.

China's motivation in joining the world economy demonstrates the demand of incessant economic growth. This state interest is shared by the general public along with the public authorities and is also stimulating the subsequent improvement in copyright protection. The 2001 CCL, which is comparatively more clearly and thoughtfully written, and shows a more comprehensive understanding of copyright, has strengthened the protection of copyright for both Chinese and foreign rights owners. Amongst other amendments, the 2001 CCL extends the scope of copyright and narrows down the limitations and exceptions of the rights, aiming to satisfy the requirements of the TRIPS and to uphold the authorship public interest in copyright regime. Nevertheless, Article 4(1) maintains that "works the publication or distribution of which is prohibited by law shall not be protected by this Law", which may also be understood as a provision enabling repression of free expression within the Chinese copyright regime. In 2010 Article 4(1) was removed from the revised copyright law as a result of a dispute between China and the US before the WTO. Article 4 of the 2010 CCL states that "the publication and dissemination of works shall be subject to the administration and supervision of the State", which preserves the Chinese government's power to control information in the name of copyright.

The tremendous expansion of the Internet in China has not only challenged the imperfect copyright law but has also instituted dynamic links to the rest of the world and has become a powerful vehicle for the Chinese public to advocate and defend their rights and needs for a democratic government and society, where free flow of information, free expression, right to privacy and right to know are lawfully ensured. Whilst the rights of public communication on the Internet have been granted in line with the WCT 1996, Chinese laws and regulations authorise legitimate access to copyright works and certain exceptions for educational institutes, libraries and archives.

Nonetheless, the extensive legal framework in China has a major impact on the amount of information available online, and the extent to which the Internet can be used as a means for free expression by the general public. While a guarded openness is accepted and welcomed by the Chinese public, China should carefully exercise the power of censorship; restrictions on the free flow of information ought to be based upon the protection of the public interest, including national security and public morals, and ought to be regulated by law. Any decision to censor must be justified and monitored, and must be exercised only when other measures are unavailable as alternatives to protect the public interest at issue, including the authorship public interest.

Currently, China's copyright administrative enforcement is justified by the authorship public interest clause in Article 48 of the 2010 CCL, which is still the favoured measure for settling infringement disputes. Whether China's dual-track system for the protection of copyright and its restriction of judicial power is effective is open to question. The enforcement of copyright law in China has been compellingly influenced by the traditional legal culture, in which the rule of man was essential. As a result, Chinese copyright, on the one hand, granted administrative authorities a quasi-judicial power to enforce the law; and, on the other hand, at all levels courts' interpretations of the law are shaped by various factors, including government at all levels. The lack of independence of the Chinese judiciary limits their ability to implement objective justice, the fundamental nature of the rule of law. In conjunction with its joining the world economy, China has begun to reform its legal system, and the state constitution has embraced the Western liberal approach of the rule of law. Such legal domination is stipulated by economic development and calls for a necessary precondition of democracy, which is the command of the Chinese public.

It is suggested that an independent court system should be established in the long run to secure the justice of the law, including copyright. The administrative authorities may persist with copyright protections: complaints may be filed at copyright administrative departments, while an initial inspection of the complaint may be carried out by the departments. However, administrative authorities should not be granted the power to take legal action against copyright infringers; at most, only insignificant copyright disputes should be settled via administrative means. Suspected copyright infringements with confirmed or uncertain significant damages, especially in the case of breaching the public interest, should be transferred to and dealt with in the courts. Certainly, regulations must be provided to give the public easy-to-follow guidance, and these should define the public interest in a Chinese context and state how the line is drawn between significant and insignificant infringements. Nevertheless, the main mission of the copyright administrative authorities should be to promote the conception of copyright in society generally and to provide public service, including management of copyright and assistance, to copyright communities.

In accordance with the Berne Convention and TRIPS, Chinese copyright law provides exceptions for certain uses of works in sectors such as education, libraries and archives. Such exceptions promise rights of access to and use of copyright works, including digitised works, and contribute to a well-informed citizenry and educated population in society. The 2010 CCL offers educational exceptions in Article 22(6) and Article 23, although they are rather vague and incomplete. The Chinese education privileges at present are based more upon the long-lasting practice of prioritising education than on the access public interest concept. These education provisions should be made more clear and rational to legalise the nationally accepted education privileges, including learning, teaching, study and assessment in both actual and virtual environments; this ought to be in accordance with the Berne three-step test. While the public interest often grants users rights to access and use works and overrides copyright owners' rights of profit in the education sector, Chinese copyright law should encourage the establishment and advance of collective societies and licensing to balance the two interest groups, the copyright owners and the users. In addition, education should be future-oriented and concerned with value. Copyright and other laws should be embraced within China's education curricula in schools and universities to promote creativity and the culture of the rule of law, together with its public interest-oriented tradition, thus providing the rule of law with a solid foundation in a Chinese setting amongst future generations.

Also, libraries have immense value in education for teachers, while students rely on their resources to accomplish learning and research. More than that, the public libraries in China act as second classrooms and are of great importance to Chinese people's learning and access to knowledge. Hence, library privileges are also commonly accepted in traditional public libraries and their digitisation of collections, where no copyright disputes have occurred to date. But it is otherwise with digital libraries. Arguments have essentially manifested the absence of relevant legal provisions, including a definition of public libraries. Article 22(8) permits libraries to reproduce their collection for the purposes of display or preservation without defining a qualifying library, which may be outlined as a library, actual or virtual, that is open to the general public for free or non-profit and also provides the public with access to its collections for free or not-for-profit. Digital public libraries ought to be entitled to library privileges as well as being for the purpose of promoting learning in the digital era. Besides the proposed national library law, legitimate collective management and licensing are vital to the development of public libraries, both offline and online, in China; they too are commanded by the public interest.

With regard to public archives, the situation in China is somewhat unique. As an instrument aiding the government's manipulation of the nation that was traditionally kept under conditions of secrecy, the opening of Chinese archives to the public is of significance. The maturity of modern archives and various matters arising with access to public archives are currently one of Chinese people's greatest concerns. For instance, the term "orphan works" is still unfamiliar not only to the general public but also to Chinese lawmakers. The current definition of orphan works in Chinese copyright law is deficient and misleading: it seems that when the author or right holder of a work is subjectively unknown or absent, then the work is orphan; this has been illustrated in the *Pu Ren* case. A more objective description should be given, which ought to state that a work is orphan when the copyright owner (and not only the author) of the work is currently anonymous or unable to be located after a duly diligent search; and that the work is protected within the term of copyright subject to exceptions if the right holder cannot be found; and give clear guidance on the extent of the search to be made before the exceptions apply.

Furthermore, the state currently claims copyright over orphan works. In effect, as illustrated by the *Pu Ren* book case, this may lead to the violation of individuals' rights, with the government-owned enterprise as well as the court publicly disregarding the author's successors' rights and dignity. Regulations on the state's claim to copyright are urged; these should embrace clear provisions for the requirements of such claims, including orphan works, rights of public access to and use of such works, licensing and management, release of such works to the rightful owners, settlement of disputes and the supervision of management.

Public archives will play a more and more important role in *seeking* truth through facts. The CROGI took effect in May 2008 and confirms not only public archives as the public's access points to information as Chinese libraries do, but also the public's right to know. Obviously, this links to a commitment to the transparency of government and the fight against corruption. Government departments are thereby obliged to disclose their information to the public promptly. Government information, in accordance with Chinese law, is excluded from copyright protection and is therefore free for the public to use and reuse. Ensuring the flow of information to the public, including individuals and the media, the CROGI may also boost the progress of free expression in China as expressed in Article 35 of the Constitution: "citizens of China enjoy freedom of speech and of the press". However, the CROGI needs to be perfected over time. The most concerning clause would be Article 35 (information that should not be disclosed), which ought to be clearly indicated.

Mostly the changes made within the Chinese archives sector are encouraging: all public archives are now lawfully open to the public. However, foreigners' access is still restrained as several levels of permission are required, which reflects China's long history of isolation from the rest of the world and also Confucianism's 内外有别, "inner and outer must be differentiated", which has been applied not only at a national level but has also had an intensive influence on all aspects of Chinese people's life until this day, such as dealing with family issues or handling affairs at work.

Indeed, the 2010 CCL continues to implement the unequal standard of protection for foreign and Chinese right owners, which shows China's intention of seeking a balance to satisfy international standards that individual rights are highlighted within China on the one hand, and simultaneously retain the values of socialism that emphasise collective benefit on the other. Collective or individual benefit: China seems to be in the midst of a struggle about choosing one over the other. Such a phenomenon exists within Chinese copyright law and beyond; it is one of the fundamental questions to which the answer is presently sought, and one must be given. While the metaphor of the invisible hand justifies the individualism in the West, China may establish its own principle of balance that would be supported by Confucianism and other major thoughts, and would possess a strong basis in Chinese society: harmony of individuals and collective benefits. This might be understood as follows. The collective is a collection of many individuals, which means: first, individual benefits including their rights ought to be lawfully secured, and restrictions on individual rights may be justified only for either the benefit of the individual or the benefit of the collective; second, sustaining collective benefit is certainly vital as it affects many individual benefits, and it is rational that, in circumstances where an individual's benefit is going to damage a collection of individual benefits, the latter may override the former. The two should be balanced together, not be chosen one over the other.

Civilisation belongs to and is enjoyed by human beings generally; more creations and diversity will obviously result in a richer cultural heritage internationally and a more civilised world. Moreover, copyright has been developed from an initial means of printing control to today's intellectual property law safeguarding private property right and stimulating creativity; it should be maintained as such rather than as a tool of political control in any format. For these reasons, the attempt to unite developing against developed countries in the copyright regime should not be advocated. As demonstrated in this project, the law and enforcement of copyright in developing countries such as China should be improved and such improvement is not only urged by developed countries such as the UK and the US but also demanded by the people of China; the establishment and development of Chinese copyright have been particularly benefiting from international pressure and experience. Hence, on the one hand, China should be more open towards any criticism and should perfect its copyright protection in accordance with international treaties as well as the demotic circumstances of China. On the other hand, the international community should respect the nation's history and culture, and appreciate China's effort and progress with regard to copyright. The promotion of a good understanding and a positive attitude are always more effective, in copyright and beyond. Nonetheless, copyright is never an isolated law; China's adaptation of the rule of law is of significance as it has provided a basis for copyright protection. Obviously, China's integration and interpretation to the Western liberal tradition will not succeed without the country's continuing determination and endeavour in the quest, as well as constructive advice and assistance from the West. Nevertheless, a harmonious world is the real balance in the public interest, which as the ancient wise man, Confucius, said "大道之行也，天下为公",[1] "when the great harmony prevails, the world community will be equally shared by all".

---

[1]　See «礼记», Classic of Rites.

Appendix: Timeline of Chinese history[1]

Ancient China	Xia c.2100–1800 BC
	Shang 1700–1027 BC
	Zhou 1027–221 BC
Early Imperial China	Qin 221–207 BC
	Han 206 BC–AD 220
	Three Kingdoms AD 220–265
	Jin 265–420
	Sixteen Kingdoms 304–439
	Southern and Northern Dynasties 420–588
Classical Imperial China	Sui 580–618
	Tang 618–907
	Five Dynasties and Ten Kingdoms 907–960
	Song 960–1279
	Yuan 1279–1368
	Ming 1368–1644
	Qing 1644–1911

Contemporary China	Republic of China 1911–1949	Warlordism 1912–1928
		Japanese Invasion 1937–1945
		Civil War 1945–1949
China Now	People's Republic of China (in mainland China) 1949– Republic of China (in Taiwan Island China) 1949–	

---

[1] The origins of the Neolithic in China can be traced back to about 12 000 BC along the Yellow River. The Chinese began farming from about 5000 BC, with rice cultivated in the south and millet grown in the north. The earliest Chinese writing was believed to be invented between 3000 and 4000 BC, while ancient Chinese literature attributed the origin of the Chinese script to a man named Cang Jie, who is believed to be the official historian of the legendary Yellow Emperor. The wheel was invented around 2500 BC and provided more effective means of transport for the rulers.

Bibliography

Afori, O.F. (2008), 'An Open Standard "Fair Use" Doctrine: A Welcome Israeli Initiative', *EIPR*, **30**(3), 85–86.

Aitken, W.R. (1971), *A History of the Public Libraries Movement in Scotland to 1955*, School Library Association.

Alford, William P. (1995), *To Steal a Book Is an Elegant Offense: Intellectual Property Law in Chinese Civilization*, Stanford University Press.

Browne, Delia (2009), 'Educational Use and the Internet – Does Australian Copyright Law Work in the Web Environment?', *SCRIPTed*, **6**(2), 449–66.

Brownsword, Roger (ed.) (1993), *Law and the Public Interest*, Franz Steiner Verlag Stuttgart.

Burrell, Robert & Coleman, Allison (2005), *Copyright Exceptions: The Digital Impact*, Cambridge University Press.

Butler, Eamonn (2007), *Adam Smith: A Primer*, Institute of Economic Affairs.

Chen Chuanfu (2003), 'Intellectual Property Law in the Information Age', *Journal of Academic Libraries*, **2**, 9–14.

Chen Chuanfu (2002), 'Prevent Intellectual Property's Damage to the Public Interest', *Information Management*, **6**, 5.

Chen Lihui (1998), 'The Internet and the Reform of the Social Organisational Model: An Ongoing Deep Social Transformation', *Social Science Research*, **6**, 11–28.

Chen Liying (1999), 'Free Internet: "The Chinese and the Western Set Menu"', *Chinese Internet Times*, **4**, 86.

Chen Zhihong (2003), 'IP Questions Raised by New Services in Public Libraries', *Information Research*, **3**, 14–17.

Chen Zhihong (2002), 'Reflect the IP Problem of the New Services in Public Libraries', *Library Forum*, **2**.

Chen Zhonghai & Liu Dongbin (2010), 'On Modification of the Archives Law from Government Information Dislosure', *Archive Science Study*, **3**, 30–32.

Chen Zhongli (2010), 'Seminar on *san shen he yi* IPR Judicial Protection', National Intellectual Property Strategy Office.

Cornish, Graham P. (1998), 'Libraries and the Harmonisation of Copyright', *EIPR*, 241.

Cornish, William & Llewelyn, David (2007), *Intellectual Property: Patents, Copyright, Trade Marks and Allied Rights*, Sweet & Maxwell.

Cox, Noel (2006), 'Copyright in Statutes, Regulations, and Judicial Decisions in Common Law Jurisdictions: Public Ownership or Commercial Enterprise?' *Statute Law Review*, **27**(3), 185–208.

Cui Yongdong & Long Wenmao (2002), 'Analysis on Traditional Chinese Legal and Administration Culture', *Journal of Renmin University of China*, **6**, 97–103.

Davies, Gillian (2002), *Copyright and the Public Interest*, Sweet & Maxwell.

Deng Shengli (2000), 'A Survey on the Development of Digital Libraries in China', *Information and Documentation Services*, **6**, 14–17.

Deng Shengliang, Townsend, Pam et al. (1996), 'A Guide to Intellectual Property Rights in Southeast Asia and China', *Business Horizons*, 43–51.

Deng Zhenglai (2005), 'Tribune of Political Science and Law', *Journal of China University of Political Science and Law*, **23**(1), 3–23.

Derclaye, Estella (2008), 'Of Maps, Crown Copyright, Research and the Environment', *EIPR*, **30**(4), 162–4.

Derclaye, Estella (2008), *The Legal Protection of Databases: A Comparative Analysis*, Edward Elgar.

Dong Naiqiang (2002), *The History of Libraries in Chinese Higher Education*, People Education Press.

Edwards, Lilian (2006), 'From Child Porn to China, in One Cleanfeed', *SCRIPTed*, **3**(3).

Edwards, Lilian & Charlotte Waelde (eds) (2000), *Law and the Internet*, Hart Publishing.

Fan Bingsi (2000), 'On Emphasizing the Research of Public Libraries', *Library*, **6**, 1–4.

Feng Boqun (2003), 'A Lawsuit Provoked by Use of Archives – After Publishing "The Last 20 Years of Chen Yinke"', *Beijing Archives*, **1**, 22–6.

Feng Boqun (2006), 'A Lawsuit Provoked by Use of Archives – After Publishing "The Last 20 Years of Chen Yinke"', *Spring & Autumn Archives*, **3**, 10–14.

Feng Xiaoqing (2003), 'Balance, the Theoretical Foundation of Intellectual Property Law', *Intellectual Property*, **6**, 16–19.

Feng Xiaoqing (2004), 'Studies on Intellectual Property Law', *Jiangsu Social Science*, **1**, 210–216.

Feng Xiaoqing (2007), 'Value of the Intellectual Property Law: Studies on its Balance Mechanism', *China Law*, **1**, 67–77.

Fitzgerald, Brian (2008), 'Copyright 2010: The Future of Copyright', *EIPR*, **30**(2), 43–49.

Gadd, Elizabeth (2001), 'An Examination of the Copyright Clearance Activities in UK Higher Education', *Journal of Librarianship and Information Science*, **33**(3), 112–125.

Gao Zhiming & Zhang Demiao (2009), 'The Development and Governance of Internet in the Context of Social Harmony', *Journal of the Postgraduate of Zhongnan University of Economics and Law*, **5**, 9–15.

Ginsburg, J.C. (1990), 'A Tale of Two Copyrights: Literary Property in Revolutionary France and America', *Tulane Law Review*, **64**(5), 991–1031.

Goldstein, Paul (2001), *International Protection of Intellectual Property*, West Group.

Goldstein, Paul (2001), *International Intellectual Property Law: Cases and Materials*, Foundation.

Griffiths, V. (1997), 'Copyright and Public Lending in the United Kingdom', *EIPR*, 499.

Grosheide, F.W. (2001), 'Copyright Law From a User's Perspective', *EIPR*, 321–5.

Guo Xingye (2005), 'The Difference between Online Copyright Infringers and Digital Libraries', *Research on China Administration for Industry & Commerce*, **9**, 62–3.

Gurnsey, John (1995), *Copyright Theft*, Aslib Gower.

Hayhurst, William (1984), 'Copyright and the Copying Machine', *Canadian Business Law Review*, **9**(2), 129.

He Baohong (2005), 'Governance of the Internet: From the Technical Prospect', *Telecommunications Network Technology*, **10**, 1–3.

He Huanhuan (2009), 'On Open Government Information and Open Archives', *Archives Management*, **4**, 16–18.

He Huo (2009), 'Boycott Vulgarity and Promote the Healthy Development of the Internet', *China Internet*, **3**, 5.

He Rui (1999), *From Linen's Late Years' Blueprint to Socialism with Chinese Characteristics*, Chinese Academy Social Science Press.

Ho Kenneth (1995), *A Study into the Problem of Software Piracy in Hong Kong & China*, IPD.

Hughes, Lorna (2004), *Digitizing Collections – Strategic Issues for the Information Manager*, Facet Publishing.

Hu Xinping, Shen H.M. & Zhang Zh.M. (2011), 'Research on the Construction of the Regional Cloud Digital Library', *Information Studies: Theory & Application*, **2**, 77–80, 84.

Jefferson, George (2000), *Libraries and Society*, James Clarke Lutterworth.

Jiang Jingping (2009), 'Issues Re Use and Open Archives in Modification of the Archives Law', *China Archives*, **5**, 58–59.

Jiang WR & Wang Min (2001), 'Some Thoughts on the Chinese Archival Development', *Archives Science Bulletin*, **6**, 71–3.

Johnston, Michael (2001), *Corruption in China: Old Ways, New Realities and a Troubled Future*, Colgate University.

Krass, Peter (2002), *Carnegie*, John Wiley & Sons.

Lazar, J.C. (1996), 'Protecting Ideas and Ideals: Copyright Law in the People's Republic of China', *Law and Policy in International Business*, 27.

Lessig, Lawrence (2008), 'Little Orphan Artworks', *New York Times,* 20 May.

Li Guohai (2003), 'Analysis on the Concept of Public Interest in Intellectual Property Law', *Social Science*, **4**, 472–5.

Li Ming (2008), 'Open Government Information – Open Archival Information', *Zhejiang Archives*, **1**, 26–28.

Li Qiang (2006), 'Earnestly Treat the Abuse of Intellectual Property Rights', *E-IP*, **7**, 60–61.

Li Weishan (2006), 'Development of Archives in Ancient China and Its Political Origin', *Guizhou Social Science*, **3**, 137–42.

Li Xiaolin (1996), 'Shenzhen Library Promoting Self-Development through Serving the Society', *Chinese Culture*, **5**(1), 1.

Li Yuxiang (2004), 'The Perfection of Legal Limitation on Intellectual Property Rights', *People Justice*, **6**, 52–6.

Li Zhe (2010), 'The Outline of Right of Using Archives and Right of Opening Archives', *Hubei Archives*, **8**, 15–17.

Lian Zhiying (1999), 'Protection of Archival Works and the Use of Archival Information', *Archives & Construction*, 919–21.

Liu Chucai (1997), 'Modern Concept & Library: Ten Years Reform & Practice of Shenzhen Library', *Journal of the Library Science in China*, **22**(3), 54–57, 71.

Liu GengSheng (2001), 'Confucius' Historical Contribution on Archives Compilation', *Archives Science Bulletin*, **6**, 71–79.

Liu Jingming & Yang Jianghua (2007), 'Attention to Equal Education for Children in Poverty', *Journal of HuaZhong Normal University*, **2**, 120–28.

Liu Wenhua (ed.) (2001), *Circumvention of the Conflict between the WTO & IP System of China*, China City Press.

Liu Wenjing (2006), 'Why Is It Difficult to Define the Public Interest?' *Procuratorial Daily*, 25 August.

Liu Zhong (2009), 'On the Differentiated Tribunals in China's Court', *Law and Social Development*, **5**, 124–35.

Ma Suping (2003), 'Analysis on the Factors Affecting Open Records', *Archives Science Bulletin*, **2**, 20–24.

MacQueen, Hector (2009), 'Appropriate for the Digital Age? Copyright and the Internet', in Charlotte Waelde & Lilian Edwards (eds) *Law and the Internet*, Hart, pp.183–225.

MacQueen, Hector (2005), 'Copyright Law Reform: Some Achievable Goals?' *AHRC Copyright Research Network Conference*.

MacQueen, Hector (2006), 'Reform of Archival Legislation: A Scots Perspective', *Journal of the Society of Archivists*, 26.

MacQueen, Hector (2005), Scottish Executive Consultation on a Public Records Strategy, p.13.

MacQueen, Hector (2010), 'The Scrolls and the Legal Definition of Authorship', in Timothy H. Lim & John J. Collins (eds), *The Oxford Handbook of the Dead Sea Scrolls*, Oxford University Press, pp. 723–748.

MacQueen, Hector & Waelde, Charlotte (2006), 'UK Copyright Law in the Digital Environment', *Electronic Journal of Comparative Law*, **10**(3).

MacQueen, Hector, Waelde, Charlotte & Laurie, Graeme (2007), *Contemporary Intellectual Property: Law and Policy*, Oxford University Press.

Maine, Henry J. Sumner (1861), *Ancient Law*, Oxford University Press.

Mao Wei, Qian Tianbai & CNNIC (2004), 'To Commemorate Mr Qian Tianbai', CNNIC.

Matsuura Koïchiro (2002), 'Education for All: The Unfulfilled Promise', 21st Century Talks Session on Education for All: Always Tomorrow's Concern?, UNESCO.

Mazzone, Jason (2009), 'Administering Fair Use', *William and Mary Law Review*, **51**, 395–415.

Mertha, Andrew (2005), *The Politics of Piracy: IP in Contemporary China*, Cornell University Press.

Minto, John (1932), *A History of the Public Libraries Movement in Great Britain and Ireland*, Allen & Unwin and Library Association.

Mitchell, Paul & Bourn, Simon (2006), 'HRH The Prince of Wales v Associated Newspapers Limited: Copyright versus the Public Interest', *Entertainment Law Review*, **17**(7), 210–13.

Moss, W. (1996), 'Dang'an: Contemporary Chinese Archives', *China Quarterly*, **145**, 112–29.

Nair, A.S. & Stafford, E.R. (1998), 'Strategic Alliances in China: Negotiating the Barriers', *Long Range Planning*, **31**(8), 139–46.

Nalen, James E. (2002), 'Private Archives in China', *Libri*, **52**, 245.

Norman, Sandy (1999), *Copyright in Public Libraries*, 4th edn, LA Publishing.

Picciotto, Sol (2002), 'Copyright Licensing: The Case of Higher Education Photocopying in the United Kingdom', *EIPR*, 446.

Picciotto, Sol (2003), 'Defending the Public Interest in TRIPS and the WTO', *EIPR*, 229.

Post, J.B. & Foster, M.R. (1992), *Copyright: A Handbook for Archivists*, Society of Archives.

Potter, Pitman B. (2001), *The Chinese Legal System: Globalization and Local Legal Culture*, Routledge.

Public Law Project & JUSTICE/Public Law Project (1996), 'A Matter of Public Interest: Reforming the Law and Practice on Interventions in Public Interest Cases', Public Law Project.

Qian Tianbai (1996), *Development of the Internet in China*, CNNIC.

Ren Hanzhong (2000), *The Chinese Archival Culture*, China Archives Press.

Ren Wei (1997), 'A Study on Archives and Copyright Protection', *Archives Science Bulletin*, **5**, 26–8.

Rodney, Ross (2004), 'Creating the National Archives', *TNA*, **36**, 2.

Rose, Ernestine (1954), *The Public Library in American Life*, Columbia University Press.

Rose, Mark (1993), *Authors and Owners: The Invention of Copyright*, Harvard University Press.

Rose, Mark (1998), 'The Author as Proprietor: *Donaldson v Becket* and the Genealogy of Modern Authorship', *Representations*, **23**, 51–85.

Saxby, Stephen (2005), 'Crown Copyright Regulation in the UK – Is the Debate Still Alive?' *International Journal of Law & Information Technology*, **13**(3), 299–335.

Schlesinger, Michael (1997), 'Intellectual Property Law in China: Part I – Complying with TRIPs Requirements', *East Asian Executive Reports*.

Schwartz, Joan & Cook, Terry (2002), 'Archives, Records, and Power: The Making of Modern Memory', *Archival Science*, **2**, 1–19.

Sha Zhilong (2009), 'Problems and Measures of the Intellectual Property Rights in the Construction of Digital Libraries', *Journal of Academic Library and Information Science*, **2**, 3–5.

Shen Rengan (1998), *Combat Piracy and Protect Copyright*, Hai Tian Press.

Shen Rengan (2001), *Discussions On Copyright*, Hai Tian Press.

Sherman, B. & Strowel, A. (eds) (1994), *Of Authors and Origins: Essays on Copyright Law*, Oxford University Press.

Shi Zhengliang (2007), 'The Modernisation of Traditional Moral Education', *Journal of China Education*, **12**, 17–19.

Shouzhen Zhong (1992), 'A Comparative Study of the Origin of Libraries in the West and East', *Library Theory & Practice*, **4**, 41.

Simon, D.A. (2010), 'Teaching without Infringement: A New Model for Educational Fair Use', *Fordham Intellectual Property, Media & Entertainment Law Journal*, **20**, 528.

Simone, J.T. (2006), 'Silk Market Fakes: Light at the End of the Tunnel?' *China Business Review*, **33**(1), 15–45.

Song Xuechao (2006), 'Hold Your Horses CC – Thoughts After Attending the CC China Launch Conference', *Journal of Law Application*, **10**, 85–94.

Stone, Elizabeth (1967), *Historical Approach to American Library Development*, University of Illinois.

Su Tania & Li Cheng (2008), 'Copyright Protection of Haute Cuisine: Recipe for Disaster', *EIPR*, **30**(3), 93–101.

Sun Jinqing (2010), 'Developing a Healthy Internet: The Only Right Way to Go', *China Telecommunications Trade*, **7**, 34–6.

Sun Liping & Lu Hiayan (2001), 'The Retrospection on Library Legislation in Taiwan Region', *Journal of Academic Libraries*, **6**, 25–33.

Sun Y (2005), 'Women's Position in Family & Society', *Modern China Research*, 4.

Tan Lingling (2002), 'The Enlightenment of the First Digital Library Case in China', *Law Journal of Shanghai Administrative Cadre Institute of Politics & Law*, **6**, 76–9.

Tang Dehua (ed.) (2003), *The Amendments of Copyright Law*, People's Court Press.

Tang Guanhong (2004), 'A Comparative Study of Copyright and the Public Interest in the United Kingdom and China', *SCRIPTed*, **1**(2), 272.

Tang GH (2010), 'Is Administrative Enforcement the Answer? Copyright Protection in the Digital Era', *Computer Law and Security Review*, **26**(4), 406–17.

Taplin, Ruth (2005), 'Managing Intellectual Property in the Far East – The Case of China', Thomson Reuters.

Taylor, L.J. (1980), *Copyright for Librarians*, Tamarisk Books.

Terras, Melissa (2007), 'Review of Lorna M. Hughes' "Digitizing Collections – Strategic Issues for the Information Manager"', *Literary and Linguistic Computing*, **22**(1), 105–6.

Wall, R.A. (1998), *Copyright Made Easier*, Aslib.

Wang Bingzhao et al. (2006), *The Compendious History of Education in China*, Beijing Normal University Press.

Wang J. (1983), 'Two Historical Materials of Library History', *Library Science*, **2**, 88.

Wang Qian (2009), 'Direct Copyright Infringement in the Network Environment', *Oriental Law*, **2**, 12–21.

Wang Qian (2006), 'Discussion on Indirect Infringement of the Information Allocation Service Providers', *Intellectual Property*, **1**, 11–18.

Wang Qian (2010), 'Further Studies on Video Sharing Websites' Copyright Infringement', *Studies in Law and Business*, **1**, 85–94.

Wang Qian (2010), 'Studies on Copyright Infringement in Search Engine's Snapshot Service', *Oriental Law*, **3**, 126–39.

Wang Qian (2008), 'Studies on Video Sharing Websites' Copyright Infringement', *Studies in Law and Busines*s, **4**, 42–53.

Wang Qian (2010), 'The Effect of the Safe Harbour Provision under the Regulations on the Protection of the Right to Network Dissemination of Information', *Legal Science*, **6**, 128–40.

Wang Qian (2009), 'Third Discussion on Indirect Infringement of the Information Allocation Service Providers', *Intellectual Property*, **2**, 3–12.

Wang SH (2001), 'Copyright Protection in Internet Archives', *Shanghai Archives*, **5**, 20–22.

Wang Xianlin (2004), 'Intellectual Property Rights: The Abuse', *Law*, **3**, 107–112.

Wang Y (2007), 'Children's Health on the Internet', *School IT Education*, **6**, 11–13.

Wang Yingwei (2003), 'Archival Culture', *Archives Science Bulletin*, **2**, 48–52.

Warren, S. & Brandeis, L. (1890), 'The Right to Privacy', *Harvard Law Review*, **4**(5), 193–220.

Waters, Donald J. (1998), 'What are Digital Libraries?' *CLIR*, 4.

Wei Zhi (2004), 'The Sacrosanct Intellectual Property Rights', *E-IP*, **3**, 52–3.

Weng Guomin (ed.) (2001), *WTO and Intellectual Property Protection*, Shanghai World Publishing Corporation.

Wingrove, N. (1995), 'China Traditions Oppose War on IP Piracy', *Research Technology Management*, **38**(6).

Woodmansee, M. & Jaszi, P. (1993), *The Construction of Authorship: Textual Appropriation in Law and Literature*, Duke University Press.

Wu Yongzhen (2001), 'Copyright Problems in Digital Library Construction', *Information Science*, **8**, 801–803, 808.

Xiao Li (2002), 'The Current Archival Legislation in China and the Prospect', *Chinese Archives*, **9**, 17–18.

Xu Chao (2004), 'Some Issues Regarding Copyright Administrative Protection', *China Copyright*, **1**, 8–12.

Xu Chao (2007), *Three Progress on Protection of Internet Copyright*, Sina.

Xu Shipping (1999), 'China's Recent Achievements in the Protection of Paper Archives', *International Conference of the Round Table on Archives*, International Council on Archives.

Xu Ying (2002), 'The Internet, Public Domain and Living Politics – Discussion on the Number Digit Democracy', *The Journal of Humanities*, **3**, 141–6.

Xu Yonhjun (2005), 'What Should Chinese Archives Learn from the Western Archives?' *Archives Science Bulletin*, **2**, 19–22.

Xue Hong (2008), 'Copyright Exceptions for Online Distance Education', *IPQ*, 213–29.

Yang Yushi & Dong Lusi (2002), 'Analysis on IBM Digital Library Projects', *Researches in Library Science*, **10**, 27–28.

Yao Chunjie (2007), 'The IPR Issues and in Digital Library', *Library Tribune*, **2**, 97–99.

Yi Jianing & Li Biyu (2010), 'The Use and Open Archives Under the Open Government Information', *Yunan Archives*, **9**, 39–40.

Yu Dan (1996), *Yu Dan's Understanding of the Analects*, Zhonghua Book Company.

Yu Peter K. (ed.) (2007), *Intellectual Property and Information Wealth: Issue and Practice in the Digital Age*, Praeger Perspectives.

Yu, Priscilla & Donald Davis (1998), 'Arthur E. Bostwick and Chinese Library Development: A Chapter in International Cooperation', *Libraries & Culture*, **33**(4), 389–406.

Zeng Xianyi & Ma Xiaohong (2006), 'A Dialectic Study of the Structure and Basic Concepts of Traditional Chinese Law and an Analysis of the Relationship Between li (ceremony) and fa (law)', *Front Law China*, **1**, 34–52.

Zhang Donghua (2004), 'Discussions on the Digitisation of Archives', *Archives Science Bulletin*, **2**, 13–16.

Zhang, Marina Y. & Stening, Bruce W. (2009), *China 2.0: The Transformation of an Emerging Superpower and the New Opportunities*, John Wiley & Sons.

Zhang Ping (2000), 'Copyright on the Internet: Review Six Writers v Shiji Ltd', *Law and Technology*, **1**, 84–89.

Zhang Qianfan (2005), 'What Consist of the Public Interest? Aims of Administrative Law and the Balance', *Comparative Law Study*, **5**, 1–14.

Zhang Xiumin (2006), *The History of Printing in China*, Zhejiang Guji Press.

Zhang Yanbo, Luo YCh & Wang FL (2011), 'Interpretation of A Guide to Intellectual Property Protection Policy in Digital Library Resources Development and Services', *Journal of Library Science in China*, **1**, 59–63.

Zhao Erxi, Ke Shaomin et al. (1928), *The Draft History of Qing – The Bibliography of Zhou Yongnian*, Tianya Books.

Zheng Chengsi (1997), *Copyright Law*, Renmin University of China Press.

Zheng Chengsi (ed.) (1999), *Essays on Intellectual Property Law*, CUPL Press.

Zheng Chengsi (2002), 'Looking into the Revision of the Trade Mark and Copyright Laws from the Perspective of China's Accession to WTO', *EIPR*, **24**, 313.

Zheng Chengsi (1984), 'The Future Chinese Copyright System and Its Context', *International Review of Industrial Property and Copyright Law*, 141–52.

Zheng Chengsi & Pendleton, Michael (1987), *Chinese Intellectual Property & Technology Transfer Law*, Sweet and Maxwell.

Zhu Chaoan (2003), 'Use Super-Star Experience for Reference to Develop Digital Libraries in China', *Inner Mongolia Library Science*, **1**, 11–14.

Zhu Kun, Kong M. & An Y.H. (2006), 'The Functions of Small- and Medium-Size Public Libraries', *Library and Information*, **4**, 85–87.

Zhu Suli (2000), 'Professionalisation of Judges in China: Its Historical Cause, Current Situation & Future Solution', *Journal of Comparative Law*, **14**(3), 233–65.

Zorn, Werner (2006), *A Review on the Early Works of China Connecting to the Internet*, Xinhua Net.

Online Resources

http://202.84.17.11/english/htm/20010221/376092.htm

http://202.99.23.245/zdxw/18/19990813/19990813181.html

http://ap.google.com/article/ALeqM5jy9NYSibUWEKVrY8BYF2rVn3WbqgD930L4H00

http://article.chinalawinfo.com/article/user/article_display.asp?ArticleID=44212

http://bbs.hacker.cn/redirect.php?fid=217&tid=25972&goto=nextoldset

http://bbs.soxj.com/dispbbs.asp?boardID=53&ID=63606&page=1

http://blog.sina.com.cn/s/blog_448b7469010089po.html

http://blog.sina.com.cn/s/blog_475b6ef801000cho.html

http://blogs.msdn.com/livesearch/archive/2008/05/23/book-search-winding-down.aspx

http://books.google.com/googlebooks/library.html

http://case.ipr.gov.cn/ipr/case/info/Article.jsp?a_no=127364&col_no=1003&dir=200710

http://chinanews.sina.com/tech/2004/0917/0339118411.html

http://club.163.com/viewArticleByWWW.m?boardId=v-tdkj&articleId=
  v-tdkj_114f9d74b242a40_0&boardOffset=0
http://cn.creativecommons.org/en/abouten/development-of-ccchina
http://creativecommons.org
http://data.chinaxwcb.com/zhuanti/wdqbs/Index.html
http://data.chinaxwcb.com/zhuanti/wdqbs/newshf/200711/1573.html
http://data.chinaxwcb.com/zhuanti/wdqbs/ytgd/200711/1609.html
http://ec.europa.eu/information_society/activities/digital_libraries/doc/hle
  g/orphan/guidelines.pdf
http://english.ipr.gov.cn/ipr/en/info/Article.jsp?a_no=45342&col_no=118
  &dir=200701
http://english.peopledaily.com.cn/200111/08/eng20011108_84101.html
http://english.peopledaily.com.cn/200601/10/eng20060110_234314.html
http://english.peopledaily.com.cn/english/200004/20/eng20000420_39348.
  html
http://finance.people.com.cn/BIG5/1037/5282438.html
http://gb1.chinabroadcast.cn/9223/2007/06/20/882@1642314.htm
http://googleblog.blogspot.com/2005/08/making-books-easier-to-find.html
http://googleblog.blogspot.com/2005/09/google-print-and-authors-guild.
  html
http://googleblog.blogspot.com/2006/06/germany-and-google-books-
  library.html
http://hul.harvard.edu
http://it.sohu.com/20060516/n243251957.shtml
http://law.cctv.com/20071126/100487_1.shtml
http://love.club.sohu.com/search_wedding.php
http://luoyonghao.blog.sohu.com/10904378.html
http://map.opennet.net//index2.html
http://myy.cass.cn/file/1999050111627.html
http://news.bbc.co.uk/1/hi/business/4358768.stm
http://news.bbc.co.uk/1/hi/entertainment/5052912.stm
http://news.bbc.co.uk/1/hi/technology/4377984.stm
http://news.bbc.co.uk/1/hi/technology/4512831.stm
http://news.phoenixtv.com/mainland/200705/0523_17_122895.shtml
http://news.sina.com.cn/c/2007-11-27/095814396480.shtml
http://news.sina.com.cn/china/1999-9-19/15748.html
http://news.sina.com.cn/comment/1999-10-21/24207.html
http://news.sina.com.cn/comment/1999-12-14/41971.html
http://news.sohu.com/20080421/n256429133.shtml
http://news.xinhuanet.com/book/2007-09-29/content_6811565.htm
http://news.xinhuanet.com/edu/2007-01-04/content_5562872.htm
http://news.xinhuanet.com/edu/2007-07-24/content_6420220.htm

http://news.xinhuanet.com/edu/2007-12/28/content_7330848.htm

http://news.xinhuanet.com/english/2006-05/23/content_4585984.htm

http://news.xinhuanet.com/it/2002-05/27/content_411044.htm

http://news.xinhuanet.com/newmedia/2008-05/29/content_8274247.htm

http://old.ica.org/citra/citra.budapest.1999.eng/shuipping.pdf

http://opennet.net/about

http://opinion.people.com.cn/GB/7232788.html

http://patent.gov.uk/copy/tribunal/uukdecision.pdf

http://query.nytimes.com/gst/fullpage.html?res=990CE4DE153EF934A1
 5751C0A963958260

http://scientific.thomsonreuters.com/media/newsletterpdfs/2005-04/chine
 se-ip.pdf

http://society.people.com.cn/GB/8217/122500/index.html

http://sx.sooxue.com/gaokao/gkkd/gkzc/200711/63865.html

http://tech.qq.com/a/20080520/000269.htm

http://thomas.loc.gov/cgi-bin/query/C?c110:./temp/~c110Id209a

http://topic.csdn.net/t/20041002/15/3424047.html

http://unpan1.un.org/intradoc/groups/public/documents/APCITY/UNP
 AN002120.pdf

http://w2.eff.org/Censorship/Internet_censorship_bills/barlow_0296

http://web.simmons.edu/~schwartz/462-defs.htm

http://zhidao.baidu.com/question/27599061.html?fr=idrm

www.21dmedia.com

www.ala.org

www.archives.gov/publications/general-info-leaflets/1.html

www.archivesandmuseums.org.uk/scam/code.pdf

www.archivesnationales.culture.gouv.fr

www.arl.org/bm~doc/lca-senate-orphan-works-s-2913-17june2008final.pdf

www.authorsguild.org/advocacy/articles/authorsguildsuesgooglecitingma
 ssivecopyrightinfringement.html

www.berlin8.org

www.beyondthebookcast.com/wp-images/ALPR_IB0208 Academic_Lic
 ense_Press_Release.pdf

www.bj.cyberpolice.cn/index.htm, retrieved 28 May 2008

www.bjreview.com.cn/quotes/txt/2007-07/24/content_69996.htm

www.bl.uk/news/2008/pressrelease20080109a.html

www.bodley.ox.ac.uk

www.cabinetoffice.gov.uk/newsroom/news_releases/2006/statements/press
 _office/060621_opsi.aspx

www.cadal.zju.edu.cn/Index.action

www.carnegieuktrust.org.uk

www.cctv.com/news/china/20010816/450.html

www.chethams.org.uk andhttp://innerpeffraylibrary.co.uk
www.china.com.cn/book/txt/2008-08/30/content_16361238.htm
www.china.com.cn/news/txt/2007-01/09/content_7628071.htm
www.chinacourt.org/public/detail.php?id=13920&k_title=张新民&k_con
   tent=张新民&k_author=
www.chinacourt.org/public/detail.php?id=244434
www.chinadaily.com.cn/china/2007-08/29/content_6066310.htm
www.chinadaily.com.cn/china/2008-02/28/content_6494029_3.htm
www.chinadaily.com.cn/chinagate/com.html
www.chinadaily.com.cn/english/doc/2005-05/31/content_446995.htm
www.china-judge.com
www.chinanews.com.cn/cul/news/2007/10-13/1048087.shtml
www.cla.co.uk
www.cnki.net/gycnki/gycnki.htm
www.cnnic.net.cn/download/2007/20thCNNICreport-en.pdf
www.cnnic.net.cn/download/manual/en-reports/1.pdf
www.cnnic.net.cn/html/Dir/2003/10/22/1001.htm
www.cnnic.net.cn/html/Dir/2003/10/22/1003.htm
www.cnnic.net.cn/resource/daily/2002-11/15.pdf
www.copiepresse.be/13-02-07-jugement-en.pdf
www.copyright.com/ccc
www.copyright.com/ccc/viewPage.do?pageCode=ac1-n
www.copyright.gov/1201/anticirc.html
www.copyright.gov/1201/docs/2006_statement.html
www.copyright.gov/1201/docs/librarian_statement_01.html
www.copyright.gov/legislation/pl107-273.pdf
www.cqcourt.gov.cn
www.da.hz.gov.cn/daxh/xslw/t20060906_9619.htm
www.digitalpreservation.gov/library
www.eblida.org/uploads/eblida/2/1213704515.pdf
www.edu.cn/cernet_jian_jie_1327/20060323/t20060323_91159.shtml
www.edu.cn/introduction_1378/20060323/t20060323_4285.shtml
www.educause.edu/issues/dmca.html
www.ets.org
www.gapp.gov.cn/GalaxyPortal/inner/zsww/zongsu3.jsp?articleid=9922&
   boardpid=715&boardid1=11501010111515
www.gd.gov.cn/govpub/gdyw/200704/t20070425_15503.htm
www.gdwto.org.cn/dynamic/img/030416/002.doc
www.global.cnki.net/grid20/index.htm
www.google.co.uk/search?q=Internet+China&hl=en&start=0&sa=N
www.google.com/press/pressrel/print_library.html
www.gov.cn/gzdt/2008-02/18/content_892809.htm

www.gov.cn/wszb/zhibo47/content_593777.htm
www.gov.cn/zwhd/2006-05/29/content_294127.htm
www.guardian.co.uk/technology/2006/jul/20/epublic.guardianweeklytech
    nologysection
www.guardian.co.uk/technology/2006/jun/29/news.google
www.guoxue.com/wk/000243.htm
www.hm-treasury.gov.uk/independent_reviews/gowers_review_intellectu
    al_property/
www.huarong.gov.cn/xwzx/ShowArticle.asp?ArticleID=1045
www.huarong.gov.cn/xwzx/ShowArticle.asp?ArticleID=1457
www.ideals.uiuc.edu/bitstream/2142/3995/2/gslisoccasionalpv00000i00083
    _ocr.txt
www.illustratorspartnership.org/01_topics/article.php?searchterm=00273
www.iolaw.org.cn/showNews.asp?id=12406
www.iolaw.org.cn/showNews.asp?id=20471
www.isc.org.cn/ShowArticle.php?id=8005
www.isoc.org
www.iwf.org.uk/police/page.22.htm
www.la-hq.or.uk
www.lala.org
www.law.ed.ac.uk/ahrc/script-ed/vol3-3/editorial.doc
www.lboro.ac.uk/departments/dils/lisu/list03/list03.html
www.loc.gov
www.marketingservicestalk.com/news/web/web103.html
www.mcsc.com.cn/index.do
www.met.police.uk/computercrime
www.mii.gov.cn/art/2006/05/22/art_21_13930.html
www.moe.edu.cn/edoas/website18/09/info4009.htm
www.moe.edu.cn/edoas/website18/87/info33487.htm
www.moe.edu.cn/edoas/website18/level3.jsp?tablename=2038&infoid=12
    12720810243182
www.moe.edu.cn/edoas/website18/level3.jsp?tablename=2225&infoid=33
    368
www.moe.edu.cn/english/laws_e.htm
www.nas.gov.uk/about/history.asp
www.nationalarchives.gov.uk/documents/annualreport07-08.pdf
www.nationalarchives.gov.uk/legal/copyright.htm
www.nationalarchives.gov.uk/news/stories/133.htm
www.nationalarchives.gov.uk/policy/act/history.htm
www.ncac.gov.cn
www.ncac.gov.cn/GalaxyPortal/inner/bqj/include/detail.jsp?articleid=143
    03&boardpid=168&boardid=1150101011160101

www.ncac.gov.cn/GalaxyPortal/inner/bqj/include/list_column_2.jsp?Boar
    dID=1913&boardid=1150101011161402

www.neea.edu.cn/buttom/english.htm

www.nlc.gov.cn/GB/channel1/index.html

www.nlc.gov.cn/old/old/dloff/scientific6/sci_7.htm

www.nlc.gov.cn/service/guanyuguotu/baogao.htm

www.opendemocracy.net/media-copyrightlaw/gowers_4160.jsp

www.openrightsgroup.org/2006/12/06/gowers-review

www.ordnancesurvey.co.uk/oswebsite/media/news/2001/march/centrica.
    html

www.parliament.uk/parliamentary_committees/lords_press_notices/pn10
    0807st.cfm

www.parliament.uk/site_information/parliamentary_copyright.cfm

www.people.com.cn/GB/it/51/20030209/919987.html

www.people.com.cn/GB/paper464/17079/1498397.html

www.plr.uk.com

www.pro.gov.uk

www.publications.parliament.uk/pa/ld200102/ldjudgmt/jd010712/news-1.
    htm

www.publicknowledge.org/alertfax/save-orphan-works

www.rsf.org/article.php3?id_article=19603

www.rsf.org/article.php3?id_article=24126

www.saac.gov.cn

www.scan.org.uk

www.scio.gov.cn/glfw/dt/200806/t186902.htm

www.scio.gov.cn/syyw/tbtt/200806/t187012.htm

www.sipo.gov.cn/sipo/xwdt/ywdt/2008/200802/t20080218_233414.htm

www.sipo.gov.cn/sipo2008/mtjj/2008/200805/t20080523_403811.html

www.sipo.gov.cn/sipo2008/yl/2007/200804/t20080402_365958.html

www.smth.edu.cn/frames.php

www.southcn.com/law/fzzt/200304290184.htm

www.spp.gov.cn/site2006/2006-02-23/00016-324.html

www.ssreader.com/zhuanti/15/ms_zong.htm

www.ssreader.com/zhuanti/15/sc.htm

www.stats.gov.cn/tjgb/ndtjgb/qgndtjgb/t20080228_402464933.htm

www.stats.gov.cn/tjsj/ndsj/shehui/2006/html/0307.htm

www.stats.gov.cn/was40/gjtjj_en_detail.jsp?searchword=1979&channelid
    =9528&record=1

www.stats.gov.cn/was40/gjtjj_en_detail.jsp?searchword=GDP&channelid
    =9528&record=7

www.szlib.gov.cn/cgi-bin/OPAC/TopicLibrary.cgi?id=VODSYS

www.szlib.gov.cn/english/serv/feaserv.html

www.szlib.gov.cn/newsshow.jsp?itemid=204
www.thegreatwall.com.cn/phpbbs/index.php?id=80341&forumid=4
www.thomas.gov/cgi-bin/query/F?c110:1:./temp/~c110MJrTJW:e299
www.ucsusa.org/global_security/china/chinese-perspectives-on-transpare
   ncy-and-security.html
www.unsco.org
www.usdoj.gov/oip/foia_updates/Vol_XVII_4/page2.htm
www.wipo.int/about-ip/en/ipworldwide/pdf/cn.pdf
www.wipo.int/treaties/en
www.wrightslaw.com/idea/idea.2004.all.pdf
www.wto.org/english/news_e/pres01_e/pr243_e.htm
www.wwm.cn/Research/guo_liang_2005_toc.htm
www.xwcbj.gd.gov.cn/news/html/zxdt/article/1216216895529.html
www.ycwb.com/gb/content/2003-02/14/content_490267.htm
www.zdnet.fr/actualites/imprimer/0,50000200,39355239,00.htm
www2.chinadaily.com.cn/china/2007-09/02/content_6073626.htm
www3.beidabiz.com/bbs/viewthread.php?tid=4567

Index